About the author

Margaret Daymond is a Professor Emeritus in the English Department at the University of KwaZulu-Natal and a Fellow of the University. Most of her research has been on women's writing. She has edited fiction by writers such as Bessie Head, Lauretta Ngcobo, Frances Colenso and Goretti Kyomuhendo as well as major anthologies of women's writing (*Women Writing Africa: The Southern Region*, New York 2003) and feminist criticism (*South African Feminisms*, New York 1996). Her numerous articles on fiction and other writing by Zoë Wicomb, Buchi Emecheta, Doris Lessing, Ellen Kuzwayo, Sindiwe Magona, Yvonne Vera, Nadine Gordimer, Hilda Bernstein, Agnes Lottering, Ellen MacLeod and Eliza Fielden also cover genres such as autobiography, letters, travel writing and short stories.

Everyday Matters

Selected letters of Dora Taylor,
Bessie Head & Lilian Ngoyi

Edited by MJ Daymond

First published by Jacana Media (Pty) Ltd in 2015

10 Orange Street
Sunnyside
Auckland Park 2092
South Africa
+2711 628 3200
www.jacana.co.za

© M J Daymond, 2015

Front cover:
Photo of Bessie Head and Lilian Ngoyi © Drum Social Histories / Baileys African History Archive / Africa Media Online
Photo of Dora Taylor © Sheila Belshaw (private collection)
Letters in the background © A2251, Historical Papers Research Archive, University of the Witwatersrand

All rights reserved.

ISBN 978-1-4314-0948-8

Cover design by Shawn Paikin
Set in Adobe Garamond Pro 12/15pt
Printed and bound by Creda Communications
Job no. 002403

Also available as an e-book:
d-PDF 978-1-4314-0949-5
ePUB 978-1-4314-0950-1
mobi file 978-1-4314-0951-8

See a complete list of Jacana titles at www.jacana.co.za

Contents

Preface vii
Introduction xi

Dora Taylor's life and writing 1
Dora's 1963 letters to Sheila Belshaw 18
Dora Taylor's life and letters after 1963 71

Bessie Head's life and writing 81
Bessie's letters to Paddy Kitchen 101

Lilian Ngoyi's life and writing 247
Lilian's letters to Belinda Allan 262

Afterword 347
Bibliography 355
Index of names 359

Preface

Editorial decisions about reproducing private, personal letters as accurately as possible but also making them easy to read in the public form of print can be complicated. Each set of letters is presented here in a form that is as close to the original as modern conventions designed for print will allow. Each set has been arranged in date order and all of the letters have been numbered sequentially for ease of reference.

In order to acknowledge the intimate nature of these personal letters, the writers and recipients have been referred to by their first names – Lilian, Dora and Bessie – but occasionally, for example in connection with Bessie Head and Dora Taylor as writers of fiction, the literary convention of using the writer's surname has been followed.

The lightest possible hand on the text has been used; most spelling has been silently regularised as has some of the punctuation where ease of comprehension seemed to require it. The style of dating the letters and the format of the sender's address has been made as uniform as possible. From January 1981, Bessie Head began putting her name in the first line of her address; it is a practice she may have taken from Paddy Kitchen. Some other stylistic individuality has also been regularised. For example, Bessie Head used block capitals for book titles and Dora Taylor used underlining but for this book these have been changed to italics. Where underlining does appear in other connections, it is the writer's own. As all three writers occasionally used the 'ize' ending as well as 'ise', these variations have not been changed and nor has their use of full stops after abbreviations.

Lilian Ngoyi always wrote on prepaid blue air letters which had to be folded and sealed for posting; Dora Taylor occasionally used them and so did Bessie Head, especially when she wanted to reply urgently to a letter she had just collected and so wrote her missive in the post office itself. Some of these air letter forms had pictures on the back or inside.

Lilian and Dora always wrote by hand, but Bessie typed most of her letters when she wrote at home. (Her handwritten letters have been marked as such.) All three sets of letters often show the signs of compression made necessary by the size of the paper the writers were using, with ideas and messages crammed in at the end of the page or added in the margins or at the top of the letter. Letter 17 is the most graphic example of Dora cramming her thoughts into as small a space as possible. It is written on lined notepaper and in it her copperplate handwriting gets smaller and smaller until three lines of writing are squeezed into one ruled space. On the last page, added messages to her family are crushed into every available spot and her signature, 'Mummy' is almost invisible.

When using air letters, Dora Taylor did not always begin a new paragraph on a new line but, so as to economise on space, used marks such as //. In these cases, a line break has been introduced. Lilian Ngoyi did not use paragraphing at all; it has, however, been introduced in the long, autobiographical letter (letter 93) for ease of reading. She also had a propensity for capital letters which has been followed here, but some silent adjustments to her spelling have been made in the same spirit in which she asked her correspondents to 'piece it up' if her autobiographical letter were published. Her always eloquent idiosyncrasies of language are untouched. Dora Taylor often referred to her friends and neighbours by an initial only and, as they were all private figures, this practice has been followed throughout. Obviously missing words have been editorially supplied in square brackets and the occasional brief editorial cut has been indicated in the same way, but there has been no rewriting. Because the writers' original presentation has been followed as nearly as possible, the three sets of letters are not uniform in their printed style.

The letters are now to be found in various places: Dora Taylor's are in private possession at present but will be deposited in the

Preface

University of Cape Town Libraries' Special Collections. Permission to publish them has kindly been given by Sheila Belshaw. Lilian Ngoyi's letters are in the Manuscript Collections of the William Cullen Library, University of the Witwatersrand, and permission to publish them has kindly been given by Memory Mphahlele. Bessie Head's letters are in the BH Papers in the Khama III Memorial Museum in Serowe, Botswana. Permission to publish them has been given by the Bessie Head Heritage Trust, c/o Johnson & Alcock Ltd. In each case, the permission is gratefully acknowledged.

In my compiling, editing and introducing these letters, friends and colleagues have been unfailingly generous in their help and support and I would like to thank the following people in particular: Belinda Allan, Sheila Belshaw, Lindy Blignaut, Muriel Clutten, Anita Craig, Catherine Daymond, Gail Gerhard, Colleen Goldsworthy, Betty Govinden, Cathy Gregerson, Barbara Harrel-Bond, Aaron Head, Howard Head, Tom Holzinger, Heather Hughes, Eva Hunter, Bridget Impey, Lara Jacob, Gasenone Kediseng, Mary Lederer, Scobie Lekhutile, Ester Levinrad, Leloba Molema, Memory Mphahlele, Faresi Mukiwa, Doreen and Michael Muskett, Nqaba Ngoyi, Heather Parker, Michelle Pickover, Glenda Robson, Corinne Sandwith, Barbara Sproul, Gillian Stead-Eilersen and Ed Wilson.

Introduction

These personal, private letters from women belong together in as much as they record their joys and sorrows as they tried to live principled lives in adverse conditions in southern Africa. In her heyday, each woman had occupied an important position in public life. Dora Taylor was the unofficial secretary of the Non-European Unity Movement from the 1940–60s as well as a prolific writer, and at the same time she was a teacher, mother and housewife; Lilian Ngoyi was a leading trade unionist in the 1950s and '60s who served on the ANC's national executive, and at the same time she worked from home as a seamstress so that she could be an effective mother and housewife; Bessie Head became an internationally acclaimed African novelist in the 1960s and '70s, and she too worked at home as a market-gardener, mother and housewife. Thus all three inhabited, equally and simultaneously, both the domestic and the public spheres, and their letters show that everyday life allowed them no protective division between these spheres.

The letters published here were written after Lilian and Dora had been forced out of political activism but were still living out the consequences of their involvement. (The ways in which this happened in each woman's life are explained in the individual introductions to their letters.) Bessie had withdrawn more voluntarily from the political scene and once she was in Botswana she preferred to observe the machinations of exile and local politics from the side-lines. All three women were, at the time of their letter-writing, living much more secluded lives than they once did, but still felt directly affected by national and international power struggles.

Their letters' primary appeal is that we meet all three public figures in the intimacy of their personal, domestic lives. Contact through their writing allows us to understand in detail what the blend of public and private required of them in their daily lives: how they coped with the political or civic forces that intruded on their everyday worlds; what they thought and felt about more ordinary matters; and how they managed the particular crises and upheavals of their lives.

Each set of letters tells its own distinct story and each set comes from different decades of the twentieth century. The earliest set is from Dora Taylor who corresponded with her daughter Sheila for a little over four decades until her death in 1976. From this voluminous collection, the letters of 1963 have been chosen because they contain the moment at which, grief-stricken, Dora had to acquiesce to the loss of her cherished home in Cape Town. It was from this home that she had run her varied activities; it had been the centre of her family and intellectual life as well as a haven in which she, her husband and a close friend, I B Tabata, had produced books by which they hoped to be remembered. Her letters show that this physical and emotional loss affected Dora's sense of identity very deeply, for she felt that her life lost some of its meaning when she could no longer be useful to others who had not the resources to cope with political, economic and cultural oppression. She does not, however, simply lament her loss, for her letters also reach for the courage and determination to appreciate what could counterbalance it: her husband, her loving daughters and their families, and her intellectual life.

The other two sets of letters are similar in bulk to Dora's, but they cover a longer time-span, continuing over several years from their inception to each writer's death. Lilian Ngoyi's letters to Belinda Allan (a friend in Europe who gave her financial support) begin in the 1970s, at a time when she had been banned from political activity for almost a decade, and end with her death in 1981. As very few written copies of her political speeches survive, these letters offer unique access to her intuitive skill with language as well as a rare insight into her personal life. In them we meet a woman who has been stripped of her life's work in the ANC and the trade unions, and who has simultaneously been denied her means of earning an income. Her letters are not self-pitying, but the early ones reveal a woman who is summoning all her mental and emotional resources just to hold herself together and to keep going from day to day. The early letters show that she endured her poverty and loneliness with stoicism, never quite losing her hope that one day her country would come to its senses. Then, towards the end of her life came a brief, near-miraculous recovery when her home was materially refurbished and her spirits rose. As she was also given the means to move around Orlando and Johannesburg, she could meet again the friends and comrades from whom she had been separated for many years. Her delight in these changes had, however, to be offset by her concurrent witnessing of the continuing violence in Soweto after the uprising of 1976, and in letter 126 we see something of the old fire-brand Lilian in her harrowing account of police brutality against children.

Bessie Head's letters to Paddy Kitchen (a fellow-novelist who lived in England) began in the 1960s and continued, with one break, until her death in 1986. Bessie's lively mind shapes her correspondence with everyone, but the exuberance and range of subject matter in her letters to Paddy indicate that although the two women did not meet until late in their lives, they had found from the beginning of their correspondence a real affinity with each other (as Bessie says in letter 22) as well as being professional colleagues.

Bessie Head had felt compelled to look for refuge in Botswana in 1964, a few years before this correspondence began, because South Africa's racism had denied her a context in which she could write. In Serowe she was able to restore something of what she needed when she built a little house for herself and her son. But Bessie did not escape unscathed and although her letters tell of the joyous creation of a home, they also convey continuing personal crises. Her unstable mental health and her eventual hospitalisation loom large in the letters until the late 1970s. Accompanying this story is her courageous decision to forge a novel, which became *A Question of Power* (1974), in which she undertook, through an account of her experiences, to present her hard-won understanding of crucial moral and spiritual issues. Her narrative grapples with questions such as the co-existence of good and evil in individual people as well as societies, the obligations of individual persons in relation to their community, and the great responsibility of everyone, but particularly those who hold power, to eschew hierarchy and to think of themselves as merely ordinary, everyday people. Also present in the letters are her stormy relations with editors and publishers. At first her son, Howard, with his friends, toys and books, was a constant source of joy in her letters, but later problems arose between them and her last letters record her anguish as he became increasingly hostile and uncontrolled. A quiet counterbalance to her woes was her gardening, which, along with her writing, her lively questioning mind and her pleasure in ideas, kept her going.

Besides their individual life dramas, these letters show that the writers experienced much in common. They record both the familiar concerns of daily family life – matters of health, money, jobs, housing, children and schooling – even while they present the pressures imposed on them by the external, political forces of their day. Such forces were all-pervasive and did not impact only on those who chose to engage. In the second half of the twentieth century in South Africa, any and every ordinary person could find their domestic world disrupted by an invading state. Apartheid shaped, controlled and politicised the private lives of everyone. For three centuries (long before the Nationalist Party came to power in 1948) successive governments had believed it necessary to regulate every person's life in order to protect their covert or overt policies of racial separatism. Thus white governments drew up legislation that affected where people could live and work, where their children could go to school, what jobs they could hold and what they could be paid, where and how they could travel, with whom they could associate, what they could read.

Apartheid had an overweening ambition to control what the people of South Africa thought, especially about each other. Fortunately for posterity, courageous individuals such as Lilian, Bessie and Dora resisted its pressure, and as history shows, no state has in the long run succeeded in controlling the thoughts and feelings of its people. In South Africa too, as these letters promise, those in power would ultimately be proved wrong about what their measures could achieve. But the fact remains that for many decades laws were passed which permitted state intervention in every aspect of African, Indian and coloured peoples' personal and public lives, and which allowed the relentless intimidation of white opponents of racist policies. This was the atmosphere in which Lilian and Dora wrote and which continued to influence Bessie's writing although she no longer lived directly under apartheid conditions. All three women lived, thought and wrote towards the vital alternative of an equal and just society.

As well as the climate of fear which shaped much of the twentieth century, these letters reflect the ordinary pleasures and joys of daily life because, in opposing the state, all three writers gave particular value to the emotional anchorage that a home could give. This is another reason for the letters' appeal. Wide-spread oppression required caution in the expression of opinions (as Lilian frequently says), but these letters are often frank and courageously honest and could be so because they were written to a friend or family member with whom each writer enjoyed a relationship of intimate trust. Dora Taylor wrote to her daughter, Sheila, who lived in Zambia; Bessie wrote to a fellow novelist who lived in England, Paddy Kitchen; Lilian wrote to an English woman, Belinda Allan, who supported her financially, first as a member of Amnesty International and later in a private capacity.

Letters are one of the constituents of history, but as personal documents they also exist at a tangent to history. Thus it is that the major events that have entered the historical record are not necessarily what these letter-writers concentrated on. The impact of seemingly minor matters in personal, daily life could be felt equally strongly and in tandem with that of major public events, this meant that the expected balance between private and public could easily be upset. Dora Taylor, a widely published and perceptive literary critic herself, often read her own letters with a critical eye and so was acutely conscious of the sometimes odd juxtapositions and even ironic relations between public and private matters in them. Once, setting these relations straight, she remarked to Sheila after describing the new furnishings in her sitting room:

It may seem strange for us to be making a little modest beauty around us when the coming of the Republic may bring heaven knows what hazards to our peace and well-being. Perhaps I mentioned it before, that in the general atmosphere of danger around us, our few pleasures become more precious, more consciously felt: music, roses in the garden, gentleness towards others (10 October 1960).

So, as these letters mingle the realms of their subject matter, we come to appreciate why, when the writer is on home ground, the 'ordinary' and local is not felt or recorded as separate from the 'important' and national. As in great novels about daily life, what we might customarily think of as different realms are actually experienced as related parts of a whole.

Even at the height of their activism, making a home was crucial in the lives of Lilian, Bessie and Dora, but their claims to the homes that they created were not particularly based in rights derived from birth and nor could their claims be secure or permanent. All three experienced displacement and at some point felt alien to their setting. Dora immigrated to South Africa and after successfully making a home for herself and her family in Cape Town was forced to abandon it. Lilian's family were economic migrants to Johannesburg and then found themselves forced to live in a demarcated area, in a 'matchbox' house not of their choosing. For much of her childhood Bessie had no home and, as an adult, had to leave South Africa in order to create a home for herself. Their stories belie many of the dominant assumptions in South Africa today in which 'belonging' is tied only to 'origins' thus making it a right only by birth, and so denying it to those deemed mere immigrants or 'settlers'. But the stories of these three women, black and white, suggest the limitations of such assumptions. Their letters show that through her own enterprise each one was for a period able to anchor her life in a particular home, thereby creating for herself – in terms of newly emerging criteria that modify the sole criterion of origins – a 'history of presence' and, in relation to others, a life of 'economic and social value' (Brown 2013: 83).

For all three women the process of creating a home entailed

adaptation, which enabled them to develop a subjective sense of belonging, but the trajectory was different in each case. Broadly speaking, for Lilian Ngoyi and Dora Taylor 'home' came to entail loss, whereas for Bessie Head it came to mean creative achievement. Once Lilian Ngoyi was banned, her home in Orlando became a prison; it was also a dwelling which, because she could not work, she could not afford to maintain and so its disintegration came to mirror the attack on her as a person. And to begin with, her place of living, the 'matchbox' house in Orlando, had never been one of her own choice, and it is likely that it was only through her work for others that she created a sense of belonging in it. Dora Taylor had known the delights of an orderly, productive family and intellectual life that was centred on her home in Cape Town until the nationwide intimidation that followed the massacre at Sharpeville in 1960 forced her to take up a life of exile outside South Africa. Her letters reveal that, because she had not known a secure family home in childhood, the loss of the home she had created in adult life carried the flavour of death for her. Bessie Head's story reverses these two stories of loss. Like Dora, she had never known a family home of her own, had never felt that she belonged anywhere or to anyone, until she managed to build a tiny house for herself and her child. What she called 'the first brick thing I shall ever own' (Vigne 1991: 98) was on the outskirts of Serowe in Botswana. Because its existence was not threatened by the state, her home became a place where she believed she could establish the tranquil routines and proximity to an ancient culture that she needed for her writing. In this way, and despite the differences in the stories that they tell, these women's idealising expectations of 'home' make their letters comparable and mutually informative.

Each of these women was a pioneer. It was largely the unjust social system of apartheid that was responsible for them not finding a permanent, homely anchor for their identity and sense of belonging. But a measure of alienation also came about because each of these women had created for themselves a life that was considerably different from society's general expectations of women in their time. In the 1960s, very few black women in Africa could aspire to become writers, let alone writers who built an international reputation for themselves as did Bessie Head. Very few white women dared to stand up against the legislation and customs that enforced racial separation as did Dora Taylor. Very few women had the intuitive political skill and the courage to lead a unionised African labour force to resist apartheid as did Lilian Ngoyi. Without public resources for their work, these women had perforce to do it from home while maintaining a full domestic routine. And to their courageous actions, the tranquillity of each woman's home had, to some extent, to be forfeit.

Their letters position each woman at the centre of a web of connections. By the time of her 1963 letters, Dora's daughters had married, moved away from Cape Town and had children of their own, and so Dora's letters transmit messages and bits of family news to and fro. With Sheila, she shared an interest in writing, the theatre (ballet as well as plays) and reading. She also gave much thought to planning holidays for her extended family. Lilian's network was composed not of family, but of people in the United States and Europe who supported her both materially and spiritually, and her letters record her efforts to keep track of this circle. She counted some of her correspondents real friends, telling Belinda that her letters are 'soothing to my soul and comfort to my difficulties' (letter 120). Bessie's letters record her intellectual life as well as her domestic activities. Sometimes she liked to put her correspondents in touch with each other or to pass on news about mutual friends, but intellectual exchanges were of primary importance to her and so she created a web of ideas as much as of people. To this end she judged carefully which of her ideas would find acceptance with each of her correspondents. With Paddy Kitchen she found so much immediately in common that her letters show little of the selectivity that she practiced when writing to other people.

Other points of comparison emerge from these women's letters. For all three, cherished everyday objects, the presence of friends as well as family, and their gardens were vital constituents of 'home'. One of Bessie's most telling statements is that 'a house is someplace to put things you love intensely' (letter 21). For her, it was her books.

Like Dora, Bessie cared little for the material value of objects; her possession became numinous because they embodied memories of friends and family, making her 'home' a treasure house of memory. As she writes to Sheila, guiding her in packing up their home, it is evident that Dora sees her daughter as clearing out a treasure trove of memories. Lilian Ngoyi's letters, on the other hand, contain little mention of her dilapidated furniture and other possessions until she reports that many basic, now inadequate, items have been replaced following the intervention of friends abroad, and then her joy makes evident the extent to which, like Dora and Bessie, her selfhood was bound up with her household objects.

In saying that her home had to be a treasure house, Bessie added immediately that it must be 'more than that'. Although she worked in solitude, her home needed friends in it to make it complete. For Dora too, 'home' needed to be an open space in which people could come and go, enjoying a free exchange of ideas. In her case, police surveillance put an end to such pleasures, and she found herself having to turn her home into a retreat; by 1963, the time of the letters here, her home had become a place of secretive, even clandestine, life. Lilian's letters contain only occasional mention of how much she missed friendly interactions in her home, perhaps because she simply had to acquiesce to what the state had imposed on her. What dominates is her constant concern with how she could make ends meet and her gratitude to those who were helping her materially.

All three women took pleasure in their gardens. As she had been taught the techniques of growing vegetables in an arid climate, Bessie's was a technically well-informed interest. In her letters she treats her own garden as both a pleasurable source of food and of recreation. It was where she could experiment with seedlings (often grown from seeds sent by friends abroad) which would then be used in Boiteko, the communal garden where she worked with women of the village. Her methods helped alien plants to adapt to the local climate – plants and person became indigenised in a process that can be understood as a metaphor for her own life as well as a practical reality. Lilian's little garden was a barometer of her emotional well-being; when her spirits were good so were her flowers, carrying a colourful message of hope to all passers-by, but when she was struggling – with worry over her alcoholic daughter, for example – her flowers drooped in neglect and weeds were allowed to take over. For Dora, who loved the English Romantic poets, the beauty of flowers was mostly an aesthetic matter and, as she grew lonelier in later life, her letters convey her determination to take pleasure in the peace and solitude of the garden that she nurtured.

Their personal life-stories also share some points in common. Bessie Head and Dora Taylor were both illegitimate orphans who had known little happiness in their childhood. For a brief time after her mother's death, Dora was cared for by a loving grandmother, but following her death responsibility for Dora's upbringing was taken by a disciplinarian school teacher who told her sternly that she would carry the stigma of her origins all her life. Bessie's experience was similar but made even more cruel by the racial factor. As a child she believed that her coloured foster mother was her natural mother, only to be informed in her early teens that her mother was, as a teacher put it to Bessie, a 'mad' white woman who had been locked away and that Bessie would always have to bear the stigma of her mixed-race origins. (Their stories are told more fully in the introductions accompanying their letters.) In contrast, Lilian indicates in her autobiographical letter (letter 93) that her early family life was happy and that, although they were always poor, her parents were both caring and well-respected in their community. Her father died comparatively young, and her widowed mother came to live with Lilian and her husband in Orlando. News of her mother's death in 1971 begins Lilian's letters and she remarks on her gratification in being helped to give her mother a 'splendid' funeral (letter 84); this would have mattered to Lilian for personal reasons but also because she took pride in being descended through her mother from the distinguished Mphahlele family.

Because their letters express each writer's personality so clearly, allowing us to feel she is someone we know, or can imagine, it is tempting to speculate what these women, who never met, might have had to say to each other had they ever come face to face. Dora

Introduction

Taylor read and admired Bessie Head's fiction in the 1960s and, in the decade before, there is also a remote chance that their paths might have crossed in Cape Town when Bessie lived there, long before she had published anything. They both moved in left-wing political circles in the 1950s and they had places in common that might have brought them in contact. For instance, Bessie Head visited the Stakesby Lewis hostel frequently; it was there that she met her husband, Harold Head. One of the people who had lived there some years earlier was Dora Taylor's friend and colleague, I B Tabata. Even if the time difference makes it unlikely that they ever came face to face at the hostel, their interests gave them places and allegiances in common and there is an imaginable chance that they attended the same meetings elsewhere in the city.

Had they met, would these three women have recognised that the idea of 'home' was vital to their productive lives; that they had intellectual interests in common; that they shared a love of reading (Lilian's letters are filled with requests for books); and that their political ideals took the same form – a country of equality and justice for all, of freedom of choice and the right to fulfil their inborn talents? This is speculation of course, but such a fancy does bring forward what reading their letters can offer us. It suggests that besides the intrinsic appeal of each set of letters, their being brought together in this book offers us a rare chance to reflect on and compare these women's hopes and dreams and to recognise where, how and why their thoughts about themselves in their world intersect.

Margaret Daymond
Durban
November 2014

Dora Taylor
(1899–1976)

Dora Taylor's life and writing

Dora Taylor corresponded with her daughter, Sheila, for over four decades. The letters published here are all from 1963, the year in which events in South Africa forced Dora to realise that she could not continue to live in her home in Cape Town and that a rootless life of exile probably lay ahead. The crisis conveyed in these letters brings forward all the components of Dora Taylor's personality and identity; she was simultaneously wife and political activist, mother and writer of fiction, literary critic, friend, teacher and journalist. While her active engagement with the public world was vigorous, her domestic life was equally productive and dear to her heart. In fact, they were not separate realms in her mind or experience. All that she cared about found its place in her home. Because she was with her husband in America, who was on a sabbatical in 1963, her letters also confront us with the irony that Dora's most eloquent letters about 'home' were written from elsewhere, rather than from the place on which she placed such value. As with much that is crucial to daily existence, the meaning that 'home' had for her had not required articulation until its absence and its permanent loss was upon her.

The 1963 letters also illuminate the courage it took for Dora to live her life both in the service of others and according to her own talents. The particular demand this made of her had its origins in the pattern of loss, deprivation and denial that had been established in her childhood, a pattern which called into question her right to be, to do and to mean. Her great dismay when this pattern seems to be repeating itself in later life can be seen in the many reflections on death that come in her letters when she has to articulate her feelings about the loss of her home. When her household is dismantled and all about to be put up for auction, she writes: 'It saddens me to think of our home being made nice before it vanishes for ever. It is like a woman whose face in death somehow becomes touched with the beauty of the days of youth' (letter 14). And again, this time more personally: 'I'm tasting the sorrow of the break up of a home, which usually happens after one is dead, and then it doesn't matter' (letter 17). Dora's dwelling on death may seem extreme as she had agreed with the decision not to return to Cape Town, but it indicates the depth of the emotional crisis she faced. And to some extent she faced this crisis alone, for Jim, her husband, was not keen to return to Cape Town because conditions for research in North America and Europe were better for him. Dora's sense of death is understandable too in view of the speed with which everything came to an end, for once Sheila had offered to close down the house, it took her just a month to arrange matters in Cape Town, and within two months of their decision it was all over.

Family, politics, writing
The deprivations of Dora's early life were Dickensian. She was born in Aberdeen in 1899, an illegitimate child of working-class parents. Her mother died when she was six years old and both James Jack, her father, and her stepmother neglected and ill-treated the child. The family lived in a tenement where Dora, left alone at night, was often terrified. A year or two later she was sent to live with her paternal grandparents who were so poor that they had to go regularly to a soup-kitchen to be fed, but Dora remembered this period as happy because she loved her kindly grandmother. After her grandmother's death, responsibility for Dora was taken by a woman Dora always referred to as 'Miss Craig'. She was a school teacher named Mary-Anne Craig who cared for Dora, saw to her education and taught her obedience and belief in God, but, rather than showing her affection, told her that being illegitimate made her 'different' and that her father had been a criminal. As a result, Dora suffered from nightmares and a life-long anxiety that she would be rejected by those around her.

In adolescence, she turned for emotional succour to literature, particularly the poetry of Shakespeare and Shelley. Eager to please, she worked hard at school and was accepted at Aberdeen University where she studied English Literature, graduating in 1922. At university she met her future husband, James Garden Taylor ('Jim' to her, 'JG' to others). He was one of seven children, his childhood home was happy and stable, and his parents wanted him to enter the ministry. Born with a club foot, he walked with a limp all his life and, although he was active in his early years, he suffered disability and constant pain in later life. Dora described him as 'the gentlest, most thoughtful man who ever lived' but his presence in her life was deeply resented by Miss Craig who did all she could to break the relationship.[1] After graduating, Jim worked for an engineering company in Manchester and then took up a post in the Psychology Department at the University of Cape Town. A year later, he came back to Scotland to marry Dora and, in 1926, took her with him to South Africa. They named their house 'Kintayre' after Kinfort, the village north of Aberdeen where Jim's parents lived, and adding 'tay' for themselves.

Their shared desire for social justice and their sympathy for oppressed people drew Dora and Jim Taylor to the 'left-wing clubs, debating societies, discussion groups, dramatic societies and … salon culture' of Cape Town. There was a vigorous group of radical intellectuals at the University of Cape Town itself and their Saturday evening meetings 'offered a generous and passionate intellectual and social milieu in which the Taylors immediately became absorbed' (Sandwith 2002a: 7–8).[2] At the Lenin Club where an anti-Stalinist group met, Dora Taylor got to know some of the leading black intellectuals of the day, among them Isaac Bangani Tabata (referred to as 'T' in her letters) who would become one of the main influences on her political and intellectual development. He was a founder member of the All-Africa Convention which was formed after the

---

[1] Much of this information is taken from an unpublished, incomplete draft of Dora Taylor's early life by her daughter, Doreen, and is used with kind permission of Michael and Doreen Muskett.
[2] Dora Taylor and the early practices of Marxist criticism in South Africa also forms part of Sandwith's recent book published in 2014.

Lenin Club split, chiefly over the question of whether the peasants or the urban proletariat would lead the liberation struggle in South Africa. Like Tabata, Dora and Jim joined the newly formed Workers' Party of South Africa (WPSA) and participated in its offshoot, the Spartacus Club. The WPSA went underground in 1938. Five years later a number of like-minded organisations entered a federal alliance known as the Non-European Unity Movement (NEUM), which, as its name suggests, positioned itself as the united front of those opposing the increasingly racist and discriminatory practices of the Union of South Africa (as it then was). I B Tabata was a leading member of the NEUM and Dora, although she had to remain in the background because of the country's separatist policies and the party's 'Non-European' public identity, became his close colleague.

After she was asked by the WPSA to give administrative assistance to I B Tabata, their working partnership gradually expanded to include discussion of their own writing and probably extended into the framing of policy and public documents for the NEUM. She had found a cause which gave focus to her own ideals, but it was one to which her contribution could not be publicly acknowledged. Ciraj Rassool describes Dora's role at that time as a 'clandestine and anonymous facilitation of political strategy and written political expression' (Rassool 2004: 404).[3] During the production of I B Tabata's first book, *The All Africa Convention: The Awakening of a People* (1950), Dora Taylor worked closely with him and continued to do so on his subsequent publications. While her work was well known to the inner circles of the NEUM (affectionate greetings in letters, for example, were often sent to the 'amanuensis') her own letters of the time indicate that she sometimes found the lack of public recognition difficult. There is no indication that Dora Taylor sought popular acclaim, but it is likely that she had a strong need for confirmation of her right to bring her talents and her knowledge to bear on her immediate world.

Dora Taylor did not begin writing because of her experiences of racialised injustice in South Africa (as letter 9 reveals, she had

---

3 Indicating that the need for Dora Taylor's anonymity is now over, *APDUSA Views* published a lengthy tribute to her in 2008. It is written in the first-person, but anonymously.

written poetry in Scotland), but the social and political challenges of her new country gave her writing fresh impetus and direction. One outlet was afforded her by the Spartacus Club where she gave lectures and participated in play-readings. She also wrote several plays for this group, and it was her research for a play about the Gcaleka chief, Hintsa, which led to her producing a pioneering study, *The Role of the Missionaries in Conquest* (1952), which was published under the pseudonym Nosipho Majeke.[4] This was the only book of hers that was published during her lifetime, and it was republished by the African People's Democratic Union of South Africa (APDUSA) in 1986. Still widely admired, it was a pioneering account of imperial conquest in southern Africa from the point of view of the conquered peoples of the region. Majeke argues that the missionaries' function, while bringing Christianity to the indigenous peoples, was to teach them to accept the 'lowly position [assigned to them by empire ...] and to endure the injustices of this world with the hope of a rich reward in the next' (1986: 3–4). She also points out that the missionaries encouraged the conquered peoples to accept that they should provide the labour on which capitalist industrial development depended, but could not expect to enjoy the fruits of their labour.

NEUM policy emphasised political education, arguing that this long-range strategy was required rather than the short-term campaigns espoused by other opposition groups. Tabata foresaw that uneducated migrant workers would be vulnerable to exploitation as strike-breakers in the cities and therefore argued that rural people in particular needed political education. Dora too saw education as crucial in all spheres of life, and besides the lectures she gave to

---

4 Hintsa (1789–1835) was the paramount chief of the Gcaleka people of the Xhosa nation. Some months after the frontier war of 1834, he was taken by Sir Harry Smith and an escort to recover cattle that the British said had been stolen by his followers. He was shot and killed while allegedly attempting to escape as the party crossed the Rharhabe River in the Eastern Cape. Some historians report that Hintsa was beheaded and his skull taken back to Britain, while others say that his corpse was mutilated and left for his followers to recover.

The pseudonym that Dora Taylor used for her book on the missionaries is a Xhosa version of her maiden name, Dora Jack; Dora, like Nosipho, means a 'gift'. Her plays have not been published, but there is a stencilled, bound copy of 'Fontamara' (Bitter Waters), produced by Prometheus Press of Durban, in the UCT collections. The play is based on a novel of that title by the Italian writer Ignazio Silone whom she reports meeting in America (letter 4).

various adult audiences, she worked for many years for the Junior Literary Society, selecting the material that appeared in its annual publications, *Treasure Caskets*. She wrote the introductions to these volumes and she answered, sometimes with Jim's help, the questions that young readers were encouraged to submit.

The value Dora placed on education is also reflected in the constant advice she gave to Sheila about her children's schooling and the care with which she chose the books she sent to her grandchildren. When her novels were posthumously published recently, one grandson remembered 'Little Granny' teaching him 'the value of books, being given books for every birthday and Christmas' and he commented on 'Her passion for literature, her encyclopaedic knowledge of the subject, her outpourings of writing, mainly by hand in her miniature copperplate, her sense of outrage at injustice wherever she saw it – above all, her kindness and gentleness'. Another grandson remembered 'a fiery, energetic and passionate person with drive and determination, who read to me every night at bedtime'. And a granddaughter remembers Dora as imparting 'a life-long love of literature [...] She passionately abhorred anything ugly or violent and was often moved to tears at images or reports of cruelty and violence around the world; these things truly caused her pain'.[5]

During the 1940s Dora Taylor regularly contributed socio-political analysis and literary criticism to the radical fortnightly magazine, *Trek*, which had an adult readership. J G Taylor occasionally wrote for it too. Much of her writing about issues such as democracy, education, the role of women, health and civil rights appeared under her own name but she sometimes used a pseudonym, particularly when her comments were translated into Afrikaans.[6] Her literary criticism was historically oriented and gave careful attention to the material circumstances in which works were produced. Today it is her focus on South African writers (from Olive Schreiner and Roy Campbell to new black writers and Peter Abrahams) that is remembered but, as her letters indicate, she also had a life-long

---

5 These family recollections were quoted by Sheila Belshaw at the launch of Taylor's novels in 2009. See Belshaw (2009).
6 See Sandwith (2002b) for a comprehensive bibliography of Taylor's writing.

passion for nineteenth- and early twentieth-century Russian fiction and literary criticism. Among her unpublished papers is a near book-length essay on Maxim Gorky.

What became more important to Dora than any of this work was the fiction that she wrote. Alongside her plays are short stories written from the 1940s onwards and often circulated among NEUM members, as were draft chapters of her novels. But, as with her plays, none of her fiction was published during her life. Recently, however, Sheila Belshaw's editorial work has led to the publication of some of Dora's short stories, in a volume called *Don't Tread on My Dreams* (2008), and her novels, *Kathie* (2008) and *Rage of Life* (2009). The short stories, written from 1949 onwards, pursue themes that are still painful: as Dorothy Driver puts it, 'on the one hand white greed, selfishness and myopia, on the other black entrapment, enforced complicity and impotent fury'. Dora Taylor's tragic sense arises both from her socialism and from her vision 'of what Europeans can and should learn, or should have learned, from some Africans about what it is to be human. Not being open to the African is a white loss' (Driver 2008: 288).[7]

Taylor's belief in a common humanity allows her to enter fully into the consciousness of the black characters in her novels, a move which later white writers felt they could not undertake. In *Kathie*, written in the early 1950s and set in Cape Town, she tells of two mixed-race sisters, one of whom, Kathie, is dark-skinned while the other, Stella, is fair. When Stella grasps the chance of being accepted as a white person and of enjoying the privilege that she thinks such an identity would bring, Taylor dwells on the humanity that Stella loses in the process. This strand of the story is offset by Kathie's love for a young African lawyer who is eventually killed by the police in the Eastern Cape. To cover up their violence, they accuse him of being a political agitator. Taylor's second novel, *Rage of Life*, was also begun in the 1950s but not completed until 1963–64 when

---

7 Driver also points out that Taylor's judgement as a socialist gives the stories relevance to the present world, dominated by economic failure as it is: 'she is concerned with the last kicks of a moribund culture, white capitalism in crisis, and the possibilities of a growing consciousness among blacks of their exploitation and oppression, and the possibilities of power' (Driver 2008: 288–9).

she was in North America. It is set in Sophiatown and tells of the love between city-bred Linda Malindi and the country-man, Simon Manzana. They are ultimately destroyed in the unequal political struggle with the 'powerful forces … which he [Simon] was far from understanding' (2009: 160). But in the process Taylor is able to show graphically how the land that Africans farmed had been jeopardised by the country's racialised economic and legalised practices in which whites made African men 'a human sacrifice – to their god – the mines!' (2009: 148).

Family life in 'Kintayre' was busy, happy and fulfilling. But after her daughters had all moved away from home to live in other countries and a degree of loneliness was upon her, Dora sometimes expressed an anxiety that she had not been a good mother to them, as she does at the end of these reflections on parent–child relations in a letter to Sheila:

> Children don't know their parents. They see them 'through a glass darkly'. And then just when they are old enough to begin to understand them and perhaps share their thoughts as grown-ups looking at life together – off they go, and thus never know their parents. Of course it is all part of the inexorable law of one generation breaking away from the other to lead its own life. But I do say, Sheila, taste the companionship of your children here and now with all your heart. Build up a positive relationship with them. I speak like this because I feel I did not give you, as children, all I should. Oh, I know I looked after you devotedly and all the rest, but I had something over and above to give you, and somehow I wasn't able to. I guess these are the thoughts of a person who is too much alone (2 March 1961).

Such thoughts recur in the letters of 1963, but her daughters do not agree with Dora's self-judgement. Muriel, the youngest daughter, suggests that her mother set herself exceptionally high standards in her determination 'to give us all the things she had lacked and to be the best mother she could in every way'. She says:

> I have very early memories that were absolutely joyful, I was secure

and loved. For me as the youngest this determination of hers backfired in that I was being spoon fed at an age when she had been standing in line in a soup kitchen. She was so determined that I was going to be well fed that I didn't dare refuse a mouthful. I was afraid of her although she never raised her voice. She was quietly, passionately intense in her mothering as in everything she did. And then, as she also suffered emotionally because she was so totally rejected by her aunts, uncles and cousins, not surprisingly she read my fear of her as rejection. I think she suffered from feelings of rejection all her life. She did her best to encourage us artistically and intellectually, and yet I found it difficult to communicate with her, and was quite unable to say what I felt. I've always regretted this, and I think that's why she wondered in what way she could have failed me.

Yet she was the best mother in the world. She was an inspiration to us, and I'd rather she could have spent more time, not less, on her own writing. We were extraordinarily fortunate in our home environment. I never for one moment felt deprived or neglected, and any negatives were far outweighed by all that was positive. I wish I could have told her all this (Private email, 26 January 2011).

Sheila's comment on her mother's self-doubt is 'how wrong she was!' (Belshaw 2009). She says that while Dora did not:

> methodically teach me or my sisters her socio-political beliefs, we imbibed them by listening and watching. She did actively teach me the history of art. She had twice (at least) been to Rome and Florence, Paris, Amsterdam, on her own to study the masters and drink in the beauty of their work. When talking to me about art (and drama too) she would glow with excitement at the wonder of it all (Private email, 1 September 2010).

But much of Dora's work was, of necessity, solitary, so that Sheila also remembers that when she and her sisters came home from school their mother was often absorbed in her work, bent over her typewriter and seemingly unaware of their presence. She was, says Sheila, not a physically demonstrative person and could be abstracted, but was never cruel or dismissive. In her more public life too, Dora's nature was restrained, even diffident, but her convictions were strong and she did not hesitate to speak out wherever she saw injustice.

External, political forces probably also fed Dora's anxieties about motherhood. In the early years, 'Kintayre' was an intellectual meeting point for a wide range of people. It became an 'open house, the centre of a number of overlapping groups, to which a regular stream of visitors came to discuss politics and art, hold play-readings, and listen to music' (Sandwith 2002a: 19). By the 1950s such a gathering place would have attracted the attention of the secret police, and Dora and Jim would have observed among their colleagues how surveillance could jeopardise the security and privacy needed for ordinary family life.[8] Therefore, although the Taylor children knew their parents' black and white political comrades as good family friends, Dora and Jim might well have felt that the less their children knew about specific people, plans and discussions, the better. (As extracts from her letters below indicate, the story that cannot be told was something Dora felt obliged to observe again while she was helping to set up I B Tabata's 1965 lecture tour of America.)

Because of the changing climate of the 1950s when political repression intensified, and because Jim's physical disability was worsening, 'Kintayre' had to become more of a refuge than an active centre. For a while it functioned as a safe haven in which Dora, J G Taylor and I B Tabata could gather to write their major books. Their need for a retreat and their sense of the vulnerability of their home can be traced in her letters. On 8 March 1959 she says that the family had for years lived 'knowing that the present pressures on human endurance must one day burst'. Dora's fears were warranted and the violent eruption she fears occurred within a

---

[8] Legislation such as the Pass Laws gave the police power to intrude without restraint on black people's private lives. While most of those white people who were morally disturbed by the regime tended to protect themselves by inaction, some white families were active in their opposition to apartheid and a few women have written about the state's pressure on their domestic lives. For example, Hilda Bernstein writes as a parent in *The World That Was Ours* (1989) and Gillian Slovo brings forward a child's point of view in *Every Secret Thing* (1997).

year during protests against the carrying of the hated 'dompas'.[9] As is now well known, police in the township of Sharpeville opened fire on protesters as they turned to flee. Men, women and children were killed; most had been shot in the back.

In the months after this massacre the Nationalist Government responded to the local and international outcry by banning political organisations and detaining active opponents of apartheid in increasing numbers. Regular reports of colleagues being arrested and held without trial reached Dora and Jim who were, by the beginning of 1963, in Harvard on sabbatical leave. Therefore, on advice from their friends, they decided that 'Kintayre' was no longer safe, that it was too dangerous to return home and that they had no choice but to go into exile.

Although she accepted this decision at first, once Dora knew that she had irrevocably lost her home, and with it the focus of her life's work, her personal grief was profound. The country's repressive conditions had absorbed her thoughts, her imagination and her actions for over thirty years. She had identified so fully with the democratic cause in South Africa that it had indeed become her home and 'Kintayre' the locus of all her endeavours. Her grief surfaced again in a characteristically selfless lament to Sheila, written a year later:

> I guess I'm sad about 'Kintayre' because it could have been a 'historic' kind of house. There Daddy did his book on perception – original research on the mind. There T did his challenging writing for 2 years, and I played my part in that. Our way of life was a kind of dedication (20 February 1964).

---

[9] African men had been compelled to carry passes in one form or other since colonisation began. After the 1913 Land Act, taxation of rural African households was increased but, while men had to earn money to pay taxes, their seeking work in the cities was severely restricted by the Pass Laws. All travel without a pass was unlawful and being caught without one's pass meant arrest followed by a fine or jail. Many efforts were made by the government to impose passes on women too. In 1913 their plans were successfully resisted but in the 1950s the government tried again. The largest of the women's demonstrations was co-led in 1956 by Lilian Ngoyi but ultimately the nationwide protests were to no avail and women too were compelled to carry passes. In 1960, another anti-Pass Laws campaign was launched. It was accompanied by pass-burning and widespread demonstrations, one of which led to the notorious massacre at Sharpeville.

In Cape Town Dora had found a course of action in which she believed and which counteracted the early deprivations in her life. The specific threat of a lonely exile was that a meaningful life would be denied her, echoing the cruel circumstances of a childhood which had left her without an easy, happy confidence in herself.

Sheila, Dora's correspondent

Dora and Jim Taylor had three daughters whose own talented work grew from their parents' interests in literature, painting and music. Sheila was first born followed by Doreen and then Muriel. Doreen married a lecturer in Music at UCT, Michael Muskett, and soon after they moved to England where they had two daughters. Doreen died in January 2015. Both concert musicians, they travelled widely giving recitals on early musical instruments such as the spinet, the recorder and the clarinet. Muriel was briefly married in Cape Town where she had a son. Later she moved to Northern Rhodesia where she taught and was active in amateur dramatics. There she married John Clutten; they have a son and three daughters. Muriel is a painter and currently lives in the Turkish sector of Cyprus.

Sheila Mary Belshaw went to Rustenberg High School for Girls and then, while working as a secretary, enrolled as a part-time student at the UCT Ballet School. When her interest in modern dance grew, she applied to the Martha Graham School in New York but was not granted a visa to enter the United States. She tried for study in London only to find that modern dance was not, at that time, taught anywhere in Britain. At a students' party she met her future husband, Colin, who was studying mining engineering. While he completed an honours degree, Sheila returned to Cape Town and remembers the six months that she spent with her parents during 1953 as a particularly happy time. She and Dora went to plays, films and concerts together. Charlie Chaplin's *Limelight* made a powerful impression on them both and, to this day, the film music recalls for Sheila her mother's strong affinity with Chaplin's universal waif. Dora seems to have found in this figure an emblem of her own childhood, a childhood which became the basis of her strong political sympathy with black South Africans who were made to feel that they did not belong and had no right to be alive (Rassool 2004: 406).

When Colin took up an appointment on a copper mine in Zambia, he and Sheila were married in Kitwe in a civil ceremony. Her parents were not able to attend because the train journey from Cape Town took five days and was very expensive. When a mine was opened in Bancroft (now Chililabombwe) the Belshaws were posted there, and so began a series of moves with each of Colin's promotions. Over the next thirty years he ran mines of various kinds in Zambia, in Tanzania (about which Dora writes during 1963) and Ghana. Of their three sons, all born in Zambia, Colin and Peter feature in Dora's 1963 letters as grandchildren whom she loves and in whose education she takes a keen interest, while Andrew's impending birth occupies her thoughts even as she has to contemplate exile.

While on the mines, Sheila took up one of her mother's great interests when she joined an amateur dramatics society, thus calling forth from Dora copious advice on possible plays for the group to perform. In the last two decades Sheila Belshaw has written several novels: *The Nightingale Will Sing* (1995); *Diamonds of the Sun* (1996); *Savage Paradise* (1997) and *Shadow of the Flame* (2005). When her youngest son was stricken with a rare form of bone cancer, she put all her energies into his survival and to sustain herself in the darkest days she kept a diary. Once his recovery seemed secure she decided to base a book on her diary which has recently been revised and republished as *Count to Ten* (2012). Sheila has published a murder mystery, *Pinpoint* (2011), a novel called *Dance to a Tangled Web* (2012) which follows the action and themes of the ballet *Coppelia*, and most recently a romance, *Golden Sapphire: A Love Story Set in Stone* (2014). She and her husband now divide their time between England, Menorca and Cape Town.

Other subjects in Dora's pre-1963 letters

The connections with her scattered family and friends that Dora sustained through letters were her lifeline but she also felt that they were no substitute for living contact with her children and grandchildren, saying that she could achieve 'only a shadowy contact through the pen' (2 March 1961). Private family matters are intertwined with the more public themes and preoccupations of the 1963 letters, as is her ability to see from many angles what she believes in and what she does. For example, when she advocates an active life of the mind, warning Sheila that 'life becomes dead stale if you are not looking ahead to something to exercise your mental energies, to give you zest for life' (3 May 1958), she also acknowledges wryly that perhaps she and Jim have become too immersed in intellectual life: 'Aren't we a mad pair, always consuming our strength over ideas. Age makes no diminution of feeling and thought. If anything, they are intensified' (23 February 1959).

Although she often expresses her desire to devote her energies to writing fiction, Dora's references to her own writing are usually brief, as when she remarks that 'the ability to write never solved human relationships. If anything [it] … sharpens the problems' (23 March 1959), or that she was 'too damn highbrow' to reach the popular market (17 April 1963). The fullness of this account of writing – she is referring to her second novel, *Rage of Life* – is relatively rare:

> I have greatly enjoyed the increase in power over the pen that steady work brings. This showed itself when I had to prepare a lecture this week. There was a control over the presentation of the material and facility in language that I found exciting. So one can grow till one dies! Of course I've been damned late over the novel writing. It was incredibly stupid to stop because the first one was (rightly) rejected. But the actual writing goes fast. I'm not a laborious reviewer of my work, like Flaubert, for example, who weighed up every word and sentence in *Madame Bovary* many times. In fact I still regard writing as a curious process of inspiration, once thought and feeling have been warmed up sufficiently to let spontaneity take over. I just don't know where the images and the dialogue come from at the moment of writing. Best not look into it too closely […] I visualised the action of the novel scene by scene as if it were on the stage or, better still, in a film. I see the actors moving from place to place and give them dialogue as in a play […] [My novel] really has action. In fact, I think it is influenced by the modern film. But it is a tragedy. That I can never get away from. I do want to go on without stopping now, to make up for all the 'wasted' years. It's so late! (12 November 1961)

As it turned out, Dora did not complete *Rage of Life* until 1963–64 when she was in North America, and did not embark on another novel once her exile from South Africa had become permanent.

The letters carry many assessments of South African and world politics in which her judgements are permeated by her standards of justice and equality. Political issues do not occupy a separate compartment in her mind or in her letters, indeed the permitted meandering of letters may have encouraged her seamless mix of domestic life and politics. For example, her affectionate remarks on one of Sheila's sons – 'How early the qualities of an individual show themselves [...] I'm sure affection is precious to him, though he has been taught to be the tough little man' – lead her straight into this broader reflection on man as a political animal:

> As I grow older and in the present state of S.A. see such evidence of a ceaseless brutality meted out to the people, human values and true affection become the core of life to me. What amazes us is the patience and endurance of the African people all these years, subjected as they are to every conceivable form of hardship but above all police brutality intensified night and day since the Sharpeville crisis. We in the same position would either be utterly depraved or mad with violence. The rare incidents where they, too, have struck back with senseless violence have been un-understandably rare. That is the chief grievance we have against a system in S.A. that is daily creating dehumanized people on both sides of the line, so that when violence breaks out, it is mostly the innocent, White or Black, who suffer. Sheila, we realise that you must have received in [Northern] Rhodesia a most inadequate and distorted picture of events in S.A. recently. If you knew in all the grim details, authenticated by personal eye-witnesses, the cruelty that has been going on, you would open your mind to the grave problems we are faced with [...] I speak now, Sheila, [so that] in case anything should happen to us, you will know that Daddy and I know that we belong to the majority of mankind. Our stand is rooted first in <u>knowledge</u>, not ignorance, reason and common sense, not blind fanaticism, and above all humanity (27 May 1960, Taylor's emphasis).

The note of 'in case anything should happen to us' is her response to the ominous beginning of the state's post-Sharpeville clamp-down on dissidents, although the vague phrasing suggests Dora's probable wish not to alarm Sheila unduly. Nevertheless, her words indicate the vulnerability that she and many other activist opponents of apartheid felt at the time and why she and her husband had to begin contemplating a life away from South Africa.

Anxiety permeates Dora's account of the state's wrong-doing as she tries to prepare herself and her family for what she feared was inevitable. But this was not her only note. Sometimes the novelist is strong in her and the interactions of politics with personal life (or the effect of reporting on it) strike her as comic. She writes, for example, of a friend detained for political reasons who has found that, ironically, his conditions in jail (enforced rest, solitude and a meagre, bland diet) have, 'quaintly enough' as she puts it, led to his ulcer being cured. Her comment is wry: 'Sorry to mix up ulcers with local politics. It is, willy nilly, a part of daily life these days' (31 January 1961).

The 1963 letters

The first letter of 1963 was written immediately on Dora's arrival in Harvard where she had gone to join Jim. She had left Cape Town in September of the previous year to visit Sheila and Muriel in Northern Rhodesia. From there she went to England and stayed with Doreen in Hemel Hempstead, and then sailed at the end of December on the *Queen Mary* to New York. As she writes, she has been away from Cape Town for five months, hence her remark at the end of this letter that she wants to go home as soon as she can.

Indications that there might be problems about returning to Cape Town can be traced in the letters beginning with Dora's remark in May that she may spend time in England while Jim stays on in the U.S. for a conference, so that her arrival in Cape Town will coincide with his. Delay is necessary because 'I'm advised not to return alone now'. By August Dora is indeed in England and reports that the escape of Tabata, his partner Jane Gool, and a colleague from South Africa has made the Taylors decide to sell 'Kintayre'. Then matters move very quickly. In mid-September, Dora thanks Sheila for her offer to go and shut down and sell their home. This triggers the extraordinary sequence of letters in which Dora remembers her home in the finest detail in order to advise Sheila on the disposal of it and its contents. It is as though she is writing a farewell to each object and the memories that surround it. At first the closing down occupied a three-way correspondence between Dora in England, Jim in Canada and Sheila in Zambia, with letters taking at least a week each way, but then Jim sensibly decided to leave the practical details to Dora. So, from September, Dora's letters become weekly rather than monthly and contain both detailed advice and an outpouring of grief over her losses. The repetitions in these letters, and some small contradictions, reveal a woman in turmoil still trying to be helpful and to retain her grasp, from a distance, over what was happening. The detail that Dora summons up, as well as her inquiries about who received which of their possessions as gifts, also suggest a novelist's need to be able to visualise precisely how everything happened in relation to the place and people she knew.

What emerges in the last letters of the year is that Dora is wracked by uncertainty about where they will live in future and, most immediately, where her household things should be stored. As she longed to settle somewhere in Africa, it seemed to her most sensible to store their goods locally. Jim, however, was reluctant. Dora often remarks on the difficulty of discussing these issues with him: 'My wishes clash with Daddy's about America. I feel lost with the sense of not knowing where to be. Meantime – wait a while' (letter 16). And a month later, 'But then I don't know Jim's plans for sure – nor my own! I find it hard to discuss at all. He lives from day to day so relaxed. His return to Toronto is not yet fixed, though he expects it' (letter 18). And so the home she had created in 'Kintayre' was dismantled with their future still undecided.

1.

> Hotel Ambassador
> 1737 Cambridge St
> Cambridge 38, MASS, USA.

> Sunday, 20 January 1963

My dearest Sheila,

I'm longing for a letter from you. Your last was in answer to mine on the island, and I wrote, as I hoped in time also for your return. Some books I sent to Muriel. I guess you were very busy when you reached home putting things in order. Tell me [about ...] Muriel and John – how are they? She writes about a Little Mermaid Theatre – a nice title. You'll be soon plunged into theatrical activities. But don't give up your open air idea. If the Mermaid is to be so miniature, there is room for an open air plan, too, less ambitious than Maynardville [in Cape Town], but worth trying, if you do a Shakespeare especially. If. It's a big 'if', isn't it?

Behold me in the land of Universities – New England. The Boston area (to which Cambridge belongs as a suburb) has about 10 University Colleges. Harvard is the oldest in America, about 350 years. Every day I walk through a community of University buildings across shining glassy plots at the moment, for that's what happens to the rain – it freezes over. Every day Jim walks a few precarious yards to Mem[orial] Hall, which houses the psychologists. It's a hideous old red-brick building with many passages. Jim has a room to himself and 2 electric typewriters. My fingers fly when I type. Have you ever tried one? Every day I go to one of the several libraries where there are said to be 5 million books. I'm bewildered by the riches at my disposal (I have a ticket) and wander down to its underground regions, down six flights and then get lost in the labyrinth. I've found all Marx, for one, in Russian too, and all the writers you can't get in S.A. including Tabata's books. There are thousands of periodicals and papers and I'm even reading S. African ones.[10] I can hear you remarking: Can't she give them a rest? Actually, I'm battling with a sickness called home-sickness and the libraries keep me alive in every sense of the word. I feel excited at the leisure and opportunity to study – strange as that may seem.

---

10 Dora Taylor had begun to gather information about the relatively unknown opposition groupings in South Africa (including NEUM) so that officials and politicians in Africa, Europe and North America, and scholars such as Gwendolen Carter (see letter 3), might be better informed.

I should explain to you that we are living in an extremely expensive flat (k. and b. and one big room) in the hotel, and I cater for our food and washing as Jim was making expenses even greater eating downstairs in the hotel. I find food costing much the same as in London, less than I thought. We could also have rooms at a much more reasonable rent, but this has one great advantage, being practically next door to Mem. Hall. But I hate one room. I hate it badly. Shopping is done in one shop only, a supermarket round the corner, the door of which opens on its own as I approach with my small load. One other shop I enter – a book shop. Or rather, I've found 2 paper-back book-shops. Here I spend hours till my back breaks. As in the library, students stream out and in all the time. Every firm is turning out paper-backs galore, on science, philosophy, physics, sociology, literature, economics as well as all sorts of phoney subjects like American democracy, sex life etc etc. Here too, I pull out books like one gone crazy with wine, and I try to put most of them back! You'd think from this situation that America was highly cultured and literate. Some of these books confirm the fact that they are not. For some people are deeply perturbed, for ex, at the biggest crime figures in the world, among its youth. Boston, New England, is a hot-house of highly competitive Universities, and cannot be at all typical, least of all of the 'Deep South' where attitudes approximate to S.A.

We are confined to hearing radio from New England stations which provide a lot of music, much to Jim's pleasure. I miss English T.V. the English voice and English standards. The T.V. supplied in the room is an impossible instrument. The people I find most kind, from the day I arrived in a dock-strike and spent a day getting here, a small distance away. Jim meets folks in the lab, but otherwise we are extremely alone. Jim knows only one couple who invite us. By 'kind' I meant the kindness of folk in bus or train or street. So you can understand how I turn to the libraries. I've come across the book I already mentioned by Felix Greene.[11] So we'll send you a copy. It had a different title in the English edition. Jim has been re-reading it and so I've got 2 copies [...]

Our plans for return [to South Africa] are not yet fixed. The lease of the house finishes in Feb. I'd like to return now, but Jim wants to take the opportunity to attend a Psych. Conf. in Washington before leaving – in August when his time expires. I don't think I'll stay that long.

---

11 The author of *The Wall has Two Sides: Portrait of China Today* (1962). Greene first visited China for the BBC in 1957. He wrote other socio-political studies of American imperialism, drawing attention to the distorted reporting on China and Vietnam in America.

How are you all? Is Colin fine and fit for his job? I guess he's both glad, and sorry to be back. And tell me about Colin and Peter – and your diary – and your painting – and your own self. <u>Write soon</u>.

Our warmest love,
Mummy.
PS. Do tell Muriel and John how pleased we were to receive New Year greetings – and Michael and Doreen too in Hemel.

2.

>Hotel Ambassador
>1737 Cambridge St
>Cambridge 38, MASS, USA.

>Evening, 13 February 1963

My dearest Sheila,
Our letters crossed as they so often do. I wrote to you on the 20th Jan. and yours of the 13th Jan. arrived only on 28th. Now letters from S.A. take only 5 days. Perhaps the storms in England explain the delay in part. I was sure glad to have your letter for I had missed your ready pen. You need not envy us a visit here. You see, America is duplicated all over the place – Jo'burg for instance. And the corner of New England we are in is just as dull and provincial as most of England or Scotland. Cambridge is a suburb of Boston and everything has a shabby look – except the supermarket where you buy food. There's not a shop I'd buy anything for anybody out of – except books. Then the ice-bound streets shut you in from going any place. The cinema I went to in Boston was shabby – because of T.V. – though we haven't a decent set in the hotel room. We did see a shadow-pale Richard II in a BBC production, as an extremely exceptional event we are told. I'm ever so lonely. But there is one jolly couple, once lecturing in Jo'burg, who come for us maybe once in ten days to take us to their house in Boston. Otherwise the feast of books in the library is a bit indigestible every day and all day. None of these petty complaints really tell you how sad I am. The intense cold together with too strong room temperature is playing havoc with me. I'm just recovering from a cold and now Jim is down with it. – I wish you weren't so far away. I had a letter from Doreen today to say that Michael is advised by the doctor to leave England. He is chesty and not strong. Of course they wonder where they should go. South Europe as aliens? No. I think Europe is going up in smoke between those two old corpses de Gaulle and Adenauer. They've been secretly helping each other in their own arms race for years. (My wide fact-finding project in the library confirms that one.) Where _is_ safe? S.A? Everybody expects trouble there soon. The laws out-Hitler Hitler. S.R with the tough guy Welensky? I almost think you are in a paradise compared with other places. The snag is, to be outside the mining community, and is there a place in teaching <u>anywhere</u> in the Copperbelt? Is Lusaka a possibility? Or Chingola? Do

young ones learn music there? Or is there a teaching post anywhere? (But not off the map.) As Michael is no longer tied to a city because of hope of an orchestra job, I think both can give to a <u>smaller</u> community with their music? Am I wrong? Doreen wants only to teach music. She hates the cold and longs for heat. So do I. I hate England. Never go there again! Except for a flying visit if necessary. They're a long-suffering lot, and now thrown out of the European Common Market alliance by de Gaulle. Michael is qualified, I think, to teach primary, not the youngest, but in between general subjects. But music is essential to both (to all of them) out of hours [...] There's no doubt that Salisbury or Bulawayo would give them more scope, but I'm scared of the deal between Welensky and Verwoerd. They move in the same direction, esp. when Nyasaland breaks away from the Federation [...]

Have you written to Doreen and Michael since your return? When you do write I wouldn't say much about M. not being well [...] Doreen has made her house look so nice. I'm sorry they've put so much effort and substance into it. They bought a good car, also, as Michael was left a little by his parents. Dear Sheila, give our love to Colin, John and Muriel [...] Kisses for the children.

Love – Your Mummy
Did you receive books for the children posted in Nov?
PS. How is Timothy John? Any snaps?
PS. Does Muriel prefer us to use street address?

3.

> Hotel Ambassador
> 1737 Cambridge St
> Cambridge 38, MASS, USA.
>
> 17 April 1963

Dearest Sheila,
What a long, long time to keep your Mummy waiting for a letter. Did you receive mine of 27th March? It probably means you are working too hard. Dear Sheila, don't. Not quite so hard. If you have not someone to help you now, do find him before the hot weather comes along. I insist. The edge of tiredness makes you just that much the poorer in relationship with others. You owe it to yourself – and them – to be more relaxed in order to give <u>more pleasure</u>. There, that's a little sermon, the fruit of personal experience. I think such a lot about you these days, thinking rather sadly over the past, I'm afraid, thinking how little we ever 'met', as it were, regretting the almost inevitable pattern between the generations. Children like to be on their own, free of parents who are supposed never to understand. And sometimes both parents and children are the poorer for not knowing each other. And then when they are grown up, and could maybe talk with one another – there's no time or opportunity. The pattern is being lived all over again with a new family. Little Colin, I think, needs your especial care. He has to be the tough little man, but he's sensitive and not so 'tough' inside. Things won't be so simple for him as for Peter – and he won't know why. By the way, now that his attitude has changed towards school, don't let him think that being top is the beginning and end. Do check that. Because he might start up a wasteful conflict in himself when he fails to be top – a terribly false value that is too much encouraged in this competitive world. There is pleasure in books, in knowledge, for its own sake. It's much more convenient, much less bothersome and every bit as useful just to be – say – in the first half dozen. And of course he'll go to the University! I couldn't imagine otherwise. You know, children go through phases in growth, mental and physical. A spurt and then a slowing down, and then a spurt. Even at 12 years one has no right to judge of a child's ultimate capacity. That's why the English 11-plus exam is just crazy. Pity he couldn't go to SAACS in C.T. I remember hearing it had a high standard, if that is the school that moved to beautiful surroundings in Newlands. I don't

know if the new educ. Bill will interfere with curricula. But time enough!

We had a letter from Muriel at last, oh, at last, saying they would like to come in October. Would it be for John's leave? She didn't make that clear. Say we'll be delighted. Jim returns on Pretoria Castle, 19th Sept (from England) but I must return sooner, though after changing plans, have not yet fixed new ones, except that I go to England at [the] beginning of June. And when will you come to C.T?

I have still to see your diary of the Seychelles, or is it a story? I got the Writer's Year Book the other day. To make money, buy some Women's Mags, saturate yourself with the kind of thing they go in for. The recipe is, alas, all too stereotyped. That is, know your market. Get an agent and he'll place your stories, some at 200 dollars a time! Easy! The American way. I really wish I could. I'm too damn highbrow. What about it? So you must take more time off. Don't keep your *Spotlight* at its new big size. Folks will love it just as much half or ¾ the size – and it won't kill you so much. As to stories, doesn't your library stock well known mags, and the *New Yorker* for ex? I remember a young woman in C.T. wrote a story about Coloured people – too thin and simple, I thought. But she got £100 for it! Nadine Gordimer started through them. They are sophisticated as a rule, and occasionally serious. The *N.Y.* of last Nov. had a long, long confessional auto-bio by the best known negro writer, James Baldwin: "Letter from a Region of My Mind" – brilliant.[12] But the women's mags are probably the better bet. If you like, I'll quote you what the Year Book says about markets.

Now for drama. The other evening I went to see a play by students, adapted by a young man from a Polish novel. It is called "Eighth Day of the Week"! Modern, tragic, in a few loose scenes, just on the floor in front of you, as it were! [*in the margin*: The play had several scenes, but with lighting, it was simple. I barely noticed props. It was all in the mood. A short play.] Props: a small table, bed, chairs, etc. Lights are on bed for one scene, then shift to another part of the 'room' for next scene. 8 characters, the chief a young girl and her boy-friend. It had the desperate, tragic air of most Polish lit. and film born out of the terrible war. But I liked it. You might not. I asked the author (director) to let me have a copy for your group. But of course it's up to you to use it or not. I did buy the little book of O'Casey plays, rather 'old fashioned', maybe, but possibly one

---

12 Baldwin's essay was subsequently published as 'Down at the Cross: Letter from a Region in My Mind' in 1963.

or two (one acts) <u>might</u> be useful. Did I tell you I'm exploring the writers of the Theatre of the Absurd? The comic-tragic mood (often boring and hateful) of the avante garde. Only in Paris could such writers ever have an opportunity to be produced. *Waiting for Godot* is perhaps the most tolerable of them all. But Beckett, Ionesco, Genet, are an eloquent phenomenon of the sense of futility and loneliness of the individual characteristic of the intellectuals of the West. Pinter's *The Caretaker* was a moving example. But more of them another time.

Next week I'm probably going to see Prof Gwendolen Carter who wrote a big book on SA. I wrote to her and had a warm letter back. She is visiting SA in summer. She is at Northampton, Mass, so I'll have a 3-hour bus ride. The weather is now lovely and I want to see the countryside. John and Muriel asked for a copy of Daddy's Book. Tell them he hadn't one left (except his own) so ordered one from Yale Univ. Press. Some time maybe you and Colin will have a look at it. It's tough! Sheila, do write soon. Kisses and best wishes for little Peter when his birthday comes. Our love to Colin and your dear self [...]

Your Mummy

4.

Toronto.

22 May 1963.

My dearest Sheila,
You'll be surprised at the address. Not only did I not sail on the Queen Eliz. today, but I'm further off from home than ever. But before explanations let me say how overjoyed we were to have your long letter and glad to know that you weren't running the house single-handed. I guess having the children will keep you extra busy, but believe me, it is a precious time too. That period of being able to influence them and give to them is all too short, as I now know. I am at this age all too prone to look back and blame myself for not giving you more of my time than I did. And 'time' is shorthand for a complex of things, most of them indefinable.

It is good that you were caught up by the remarks of others about looking tired. You must consciously husband your energies and others will appreciate you all the more for it. Dare I say you are a little too like me in using up energy and always being busy, when you don't really need to be? Your love of the theatre, confined to one channel, is finding expression in a part of the organising side <u>essential</u> to the expansion of your little group, but I don't see why you should pour effort into the editorial venture as well as the secretarial. I mean – not so much. Others should take turns (as when you were away) or share it with you. And certainly cut it down. I was trying to think what book would be useful for you to quote from, to help fill space each time. Some book like Stanislavsky's with a quotation about acting or an actor or playwright or play. Or quotations from Shaw's reviews. This needs a library of books on drama to draw from, and I suppose you haven't got that yet. Or a book of reminiscences. I suppose the Gielgud book I gave you isn't very suitable. A 'Do You Know?' column might be an idea to use.

And now it is not far off from your birthday. The enclosed is just to let you get something for yourself – with our warmest love and best wishes.

Now I am writing from A.S's house in Toronto. They emigrated from that beautiful home in S.A. all for the sake of their precious little daughter, G. They did not want her to learn the racial prejudices that poison human relationships in S.A. That is why, also, they gave her an African 'nanny' while A.S. and H.S. were out working long hours. A specially well-educated woman whom G. was fond of and whose photo is now in her room in Canada. Do you remember the beautiful home they had near Kirstenbosch? They lost £5000 in selling it. Now H.S. has acquired a very well-paid job in an insurance company (procured on a visit beforehand) and after a year of painful settling down they are in a beautifully furnished house (the old furniture) in a pleasant suburb of a town that is still growing up on Lake Ontario. The wrench wasn't easy, for a Jewish community always has extra close ties with one another. They landed in the depth of winter and A.S. suffered the way I did in U.S.A. from the over-heated rooms that are a part of the life here. Every house is automatically fitted with central heating, which you cannot easily control if it isn't your own home. Of course its grand compared with the English freezing conditions, where they don't know how to keep warm. The large continent produces extremes of climate. The summer is sometimes as hot as Durban, which means Daddy will have a taste of it at its worst, in Washington.

To explain further how I didn't sail on the agreed date. Daddy is in a hotel which is now in the hands of the University and its restaurant is already closed. The room costs a fierce amount and to have to go to a restaurant and take taxis every day in addition would be exorbitant. At least I ease matters by looking after the domestic arrangements. So I'm extending my stay till July, in the hope that the agent will contrive to get me a place on a boat in spite of the tourist rush. I should be back at Doreen's before she leaves on 29th July for Italy and Jugo-Slavia. I shouldn't go with them. It is best for them to have a camping holiday by themselves. And besides, our house in C.T. no longer has a tenant. Indeed, if this continues, I wondered if John and Muriel would wish to go sooner to C.T. The snag is that Daddy is determined to stay on to the Psych. Congress in late August. As it is a rush-month, he sails for S.A. only on 19th Sept. and arrives only on 3rd Oct. The problem is what I am to do in the interim. As I told you, a lot of papers etc. lie waiting for me to see to at Doreen's. The future is very uncertain and I should leave these in some order. The two latest laws in S. A. are so violent that the situation in S. A. is an unhappy one[13] and I'm advised not to return alone now, as I originally intended. I think I'll just stay in Doreen's and Michael's house while they're away and either return a little earlier than Daddy to have the place ready for John and Muriel, or wait until he sails [...] I'm longing to see you all, but I don't

---

13 The General Law Amendment Act of 1963 allowed police officers to detain, without a warrant, a person suspected of politically motivated crime. He/she could be held for up to 90 days without access to a lawyer.

think we can allow ourselves the luxury of the same flight as that of the outward journey. I'll live in hope to see you in C.T.

You may remember that I planned to return to England when Daddy was to set out for a special conference of psychologists at Cornell Univ., Ithaca, N.Y. Well, the day after he left I sent a telegram to say I'd cancelled the boat, and now, of course, it would have been ungracious not to come on with him to the S's who had expressed disappointment at my not delaying sailing, in order to see them. I took a long bus ride (a day) to Ithaca and found it in the glory of Spring. The University is situated on a hill and near a river and woods, and the scattered buildings, with trees and lawns, look lovely. But what a crowd of 'petty' barbarians I saw when I went to have tea in their cafeteria. They look very different from the over-dressed students at C. Town. And different from the Harvard graduates too. <u>They look 'beatnik' with jeans, out-hanging shirts, rat-tail hair etc.</u> (some of them) but are at a more advanced stage, taking Ph.D., quite a number of them married. They are allowed married quarters, I believe [...] We stayed a day over the conference time and spent a pleasant afternoon with kindly people. That is what we are discovering. The public image of U.S.A. in radio, T.V. and newspapers is something we dislike, but individuals in different walks of life are kind and pleasant. This must be more or less true of every nation. We travelled by bus from Ithaca to Buffalo, and thence into Canada and along Lake Ontario, a pleasant drive to a pleasant city of rather more than a million people. Daddy is giving 2 lectures while here. We return to Cambridge in a week.

I should tell you that there has been a thaw in Cambridge, as it were. The coming of Spring meant not only beauty of greenery, but I've been meeting people just a little more and of course going to some lectures and one or two local plays – not enough. There was one amazing coincidence when the author of one of my favourite novels, *Fontamara* (1929), turned up at Cambridge to lecture. He is Ignazio Silone, the Italian author. It happens that I turned the novel into a play of 11 scenes, considerably adapted, called "Bitter Waters." It is about the peasants of Fontamara and has both humour and tragedy. More than a year ago the young friends of mine in Durban, Z. and E., stencilled and ran off the play without asking me. I told them we could do nothing with it before receiving the author's permission to adapt. But since coming to England, I did nothing about getting hold of the permission because I had half-a-hope of going to see Silone in Rome and telling him <u>why</u> I adapted his novel in S. Africa. Then

I put the whole matter out of my memory, on coming to U.S.A. Well I attended his lecture, in French (understanding little) and then spoke to his wife, an Irish woman, and she introduced me to her husband. It ended with them granting me permission to proceed with production (which I <u>don't</u> actually visualise under present conditions. Nothing needs funds and willing support and co-operation as much as play.) And I am sending them a copy of the play when they return to Rome at the end of June. At this same lecture, I got talking to my neighbour, who said his subject was philosophy. He lectures somewhere in the Midwest. After he saw me successfully approaching Silone, in spite of the crowd, he greeted me in congratulation, as it were, and we got talking. I just remarked that I thought the existentialist philosopher-dramatist-novelist-professor Sartre, was no true philosopher. So what did he think, since it was his proper field? It turned out that he had recently written some paper on this very question. I hadn't discussed the writer before with anyone, but at least it was some pleasure to exchange an opinion. And then on another evening, a young woman from Glasgow, a research worker with some firm in Cambridge, was keen to know about S.A. and on another evening she invited me to meet two young keen historians. The Rs in Boston (who were once a few years in Jo'burg) want us still to meet a headmaster who is interested in S.A. Did I tell you I wrote to Dr Gwen Carter, who lectures in Northampton, Mass, and is the author of *The Politics of Inequality: South Africa since 1948*? I gave her the benefit of a little bit of knowledge I had, to correct what she said about the Non-White movements […]She wrote warmly back and proposed meeting me, not here, but in S.A. in August – or next year as she is writing at present. She travels through Africa gathering information about the new African states and has written some other book on the subject.

Then I got round to revising 3 stories Doreen sent on from England and the Rs suggest offering them to the *Atlantic Monthly* in Boston. Here I have <u>extremely</u> little hope, but it is one small reason for completing the job before returning to England. So the U.S.A. has offered something new and interesting after all. It is a question of time and circumstance before meeting a few folk. Prof S. and his wife are most kind and friendly to Jim. He is at the head of the big psycho-acoustic branch of Psychology at Harvard. Jim has had charge of a group of Ph.D students for a weekly seminar and the students proved a most lively bunch – from all over the world, including Korea. S.R. (who lectures at Boston, close by Cambridge) says the average youngster coming up to College is as bad as any he encountered at Wits, but by the time any reach Harvard it's a worth-while group – the pick of them all.

I'm deeply anxious about the situation in S A. Indeed we don't know what to expect when we return. All is uncertain. The legislation is wholly fascist and asking for violence. A violent Nationalist African group is committing sabotage and made it possible for the government to come out with an act that deprives White as well as Black of habeas corpus rights. All the world protests, at U.N.O., but does nothing. The suffering dwells in my mind constantly, so that I can't sleep. The worst aspect is the fear that pervades the country, so that even correspondence is a matter for anxiety.

Among the many, many hours I have to myself, I talk to you as never before, wishing we knew each other better. There is a capacity for thought and feeling perhaps more sharp than ever before, but along with it a great tiredness that is such a contradiction of this vitality. And then I wish I weren't so cut off from you all. I think Jim will 'last' much longer than I because he really has a far greater capacity for taking care of himself.

I hope books, etc. have arrived. Give our love to Colin, John and Muriel and all our grandsons. Write soon!

[*In the margin*. Once more, love and best wishes from us two. Do find out exactly when and how John and Muriel might come to C.T. Let me know soon.

Your Mummy]

5.

Cambridge, USA.

Wed. 26 June 1963.

My dearest Sheila,
We were very glad to have your letter a week or so ago. The temperature here is running 93 plus and humid, so I'm just about managing to move at a snail's pace. You'll be surprised at me changing my date of sailing yet again, this time to 10th July, Queen Mary, arriving England on the 15th […] Daddy may go back to Toronto for 2 months (on invitation). At a medical lab. there someone very much liked his book and if the authorities agree he'll be there from Sept. But nothing is fixed. If not he goes to Jeannie's when he arrives in England at beginning of Sept. (after Conf. at Washington.)

Sheila, dear, your possible search in another part of the world, necessarily limited, is not a step to be taken without a great deal of thought and calculation, as indeed you and Colin well know. You see it is our 'fate' to live at a time when there are political and economic upheavals, and more to come, pretty well everywhere. So when you try to calculate – where best, where secure? there's no answer. To have a good, well-paid job is an enormous blessing, esp. when you are faced with the education of the children. I confess I have pictured your set up in N.R. as a small 'paradise' compared with Southern Rhodesia (where trouble is certain) and sinking economic position of poor old England, and mining in a bad way. (Of course I know you don't readily consider England in your survey.) South Africa is headed for trouble. Where isn't? We try to follow the political moves throughout Africa, and N.R. might pull through provided it isn't affected by the convulsions of S.R. if its government pulls out of the Commonwealth. [*in the margin*: (But we really know very little!)]

I can well imagine how infuriated Colin is that he is not getting the promotion he so well deserves. And how much he deserves it! The fools know it too. Yet place that vexation against the <u>security</u> he has, for you and the children. If Colin should feel he just must have a look round, can he make use of a short leave to do so, or is information about jobs in the world available on the spot? Or would he take unpaid leave? But hold on to his job? I'm sure you would be happy in a job, Sheila, for the sole purpose of collecting a fund – for the boys' education. It would give you a thrilling feeling in fact. I look round at the frantic busyness of younger wives (some, many of them, students) running a flat with no domestic help whatever, running to classes, lectures etc. etc. It is the norm here, and in England, and most other places. It is <u>too</u> frantic in fact, and I think of you and Muriel as privileged to escape the hurly-burly of it. But if you could take on a job for a specific purpose, and still have domestic help, then I think Colin would realise that it is worthwhile.

If you should come to C. Town, Sheila, instead of having a well-paid job on the mines, our home is there for you. But here's a warning. I can see that Daddy, now free, does not want to stay in S.A. The situation there is truly grave. He dreams of the U.S. (but there's no sign of an offer to a man who, after all, is retired.) England is backward on his branch of Psych. Indeed Dr. W. (once of Jo'burg) this year took a year's unpaid leave from U.S. to try to set up a clinic in England. This needs money, lots of it. He has not succeeded but goes back to a salary of about £8000 in U.S. – very different from a man retired. So for the next year we don't know our fate – or indeed after it, either. Somebody has suggested retiring to Swaziland, a good climate and investment pouring in – but Verwoerd breathing fire in anger at not being able to make Britain hand it over. After Muriel and John, and, I hope, you, have a breath of the sea-air in C.T., it may well be that we should sell the house if we can? Altogether it is going to be a year of change. I'm probably going to Swaziland when I return in August. C. Town alone would be too lonely. Sheila, I have several times posted books to you, to Colin, Peter, Ivan. Did they not arrive? <u>Write soon darling</u>.

[*In the margin*: My warmest love to you and Colin. Ask 'naughty' Muriel to write.

Daddy sends his love to you all and to John.

Your Mummy]

6.

[*post mark, Hemel Hempstead*]

Monday, 19 August 1963.

Dearest, dearest Sheila,
The days are timeless when you are alone. I had your letter (noted in my diary) at the beginning of August and here I have allowed all these days to pass before answering. I had Muriel's letter too. They have not been happy days, though I've been so tired, I welcomed being alone. And besides, it was only reasonable that Doreen and Michael should have their much needed revel of summer sun by themselves. Poor England seems to have settled into the ice age for good. We had one fine week after my arrival and that is all. My appointments with the dentist have been pretty grim for me – he ordered all my teeth out. A friend of Doreen's took me there last week and brought me back. I had new ones at once. No joy, but I manage to bear the nagging pain with tablets.

I have been busy since coming to England. Not 'busy' exactly, but the time has been an anxious one. Tabata, Jane and Mr Honono, a teacher from the Transkei who was under house arrest, have escaped from S.A. Tabata himself escaped by a hairsbreadth. The police kept guard over his house till midnight. At each place where he stopped, in Durban, in N. Natal, the police had been a few hours before. Mr Phahle, one time lecturer in Fort Hare and now an exile, teaching in Manchester University, approached Amnesty [International] and Christian Action the week of my arrival. They help those known to be political refugees, from any part of the world, provided they are of proven standing. A plane had to be chartered from Manzini, Swaziland, to Tanganyika, and they pay half the cost. By a small miracle, I had visited a headmaster in Boston, a friend of our friend, Prof R, and had given him a copy of Tabata's book on Bantu Education. He himself told me something of what is happening among the Negroes in U.S. (very similar in the South to S.A). He is wealthy and is committed to helping the Negroes. And he gave me a sum of money that almost met the sum required by Amnesty for the plane that was to take five people to Tanganyika, our friends among them. They arrived last week and were well received. But along with this news comes the news of the kidnapping of a young doctor Muriel may remember, a friend of Neville Alexander (who studied in Germany). His name is Kenny Abrahams. He had his first practice in S.W. Africa, where his young wife came from. He escaped into Bechuanaland, but was seized last week by S.A. police and taken to C.T. A deputation of angry liberals has asked the colonial minister to explain. Neville Alexander is in jail. Dr W's brother, a lawyer who defended in the Treason Trial, was in jail under the 90 days detention law, without charge and without trial. He escaped with others and the newspaper reports a big police hunt. His wife has now been arrested. You can imagine how all this means we must leave S.A. I should go back and see to the sale of the house etc. I don't want Daddy to go back. His plans, and mine, are most uncertain. He would like to set up in a clinic with Dr. W in London, but he has to find backers with money. He might ask for another temporary post in U.S. But I don't want to return to the U.S. All is in the melting-pot, my darling. But I still hope to see you and Colin and my little grandsons before I'm many months older.

I talk of melting-pots. But what of yours? I wonder and think about you both a lot. Are you staying on? Where else will you find security? But I'm sure Colin will act as he sees best.

Do tell Muriel our news and give John and her my love.

Daddy is at the conference in Washington this week, then goes to see the Ws in Charlottesville in South [Virginia], then off to Toronto for two months [...]

I'll be writing to Muriel and John when I get some daylight on what my plans should be, concerning S. Africa. It isn't easy to know what is best, or what is possible.

I sent on your message to Doreen, and she'll let you know about their photographing trip to Yugo-[Slavia] – sometime I guess! I've had 2 little notes, and cards from the children, just to keep me from feeling too desperately lonely. The cat and I are very fond of each other.

Sheila dear, tell me how things are. My love to you and Colin.

Your Mummy

7.

75 Marlin's Turn, [*Hemel Hempstead*]

27 August 1963.

My dearest Sheila and Colin,
I hope I'm not late for little Colin's birthday. Have you heard, yet, if he can go to the good school you mention?

I have sent off the usual books, books, books, not at all satisfied with the selection available in the town of Hemel. By the way, I tend to assume they more readily handle small books than the heavy 'annual' type. Am I right? Divide the little bundle of books as you think best. I hope the boys exchange.

Enclosed find a small contribution Daddy and I want to send you to 'celebrate' little Colin going to 'big' school. It will be useful for uniform, books, or something. With all our hearts we wish him a happy birthday. Kiss him for us.

I'm feeling very lonely and sad alone in the house. My teeth add to the desolate feeling – and English wintry summer days. I've lost my booking with Travellers Club in Sept. and Trek [Airways] also tell me they are full up. This is because my plans are difficult to finalise. I'm trying to find out if I can return to S.A. and settle our affairs. The latest arrests, and the expulsion of refugees from the Protectorates are disturbing. The As – now in Manchester – came to see me on Sunday and they know all the Jo'burg people being arrested. Goldreich, for example, was interested simply in the drama and took part in producing *King Kong*. But he has made the situation far worse for himself by escaping while held under the 90-day detention law – without warrant, without trial, only on suspicion.[14]

Daddy should be finished with the Washington Conf. by now and will be on his way to Toronto by the 1st Sept. I'm expecting a letter any day. Doreen and Michael and the girls have been staying a fortnight at Dubrovnik and thrilled with the experience of dancers (folk-dancing), the scenery, the sea etc. Doreen writes up her diary every day, it seems, in

---

14 It was later revealed that Arthur Goldreich, 1929–2011, was a member of Umkonto we Sizwe (MK), the armed wing of the ANC. With Arthur Wolpe he bought the farm 'Liliesleaf' outside Johannesburg in 1961. It became the secret headquarters of the SACP and MK. He was arrested there in July 1963, and escaped from jail in August that year. He later settled in Israel. *King Kong* was an all-African jazz opera first performed in 1959 with Miriam Makeba in a leading role. Goldreich is credited with 'scenic production and costumes' for that production.

preparation for articles, with photos, on their holiday.

Give my love to John and Muriel and Ivan – and a special hug for little Peter. How I miss them! Be good to yourselves.

Love from Mummy.
[In the margin: Is it alright cashing a S.A. cheque in N.R?]

8.

Hemel.

16 September 1963.

My dearest Sheila,
Of course your letter arrived the day after my sad epistle. I'm sitting in Euston on one of my rare visits to London and waiting till I can go to my appointment. Your letter relieved my anxiety in more ways than one, first about you and Colin, and then as to my own plans. It is a tremendous kindness on your part to offer to go to C.T. to clear up our affairs. This duty weighed heavily on me. I could not imagine any hand but mine handling our books and deciding what should be thrown out, what given to others and what kept. That is our biggest problem of transport. But friends here gravely assure me it is not safe for me to return in the present situation where Whites showing any sympathy are being seized. The situation is actually one of 'cold war' already. The sooner we clear up the better. I'm actually afraid of what might happen to our assets, such as they are, and am asking advice today. But of course Daddy has his lawyer and I wrote to him (Daddy) at once on receipt of your letter as to the best order of events. I think the more quietly we proceed the better. I have written to the house agent [...] to say we don't want the house re-let after end of Sept, when the present 3-month tenant leaves. Daddy may write to you direct, but you may be sure I'll let you know what he thinks as soon as I hear from him. When can you go to C.T? Can Colin spare you? Make your 'visit' as <u>short</u> as possible. Could you get an excursion, perhaps? I don't know the S.A. Airways facilities. You must decide. Of course travel by air and let me know the fare. I can send you a cheque at once and any other expenses you can let me know later. Daddy may get the lawyer to give you the right of acting for us. I just don't know the details of business. This is only a preliminary letter. You will perhaps enlist the help of Mr. E. over selling any furniture. One doesn't get much. That is why I'd like Lizzie [their domestic worker] and her daughters or son (?) to have whatever of my things would be of use. The bedroom suite and one of the wardrobes for ex. (That is the big bed now stored in little room.) The single and ¾ beds should fetch something, and dining room suite and couch and chairs in sitting room. Oh dear, my heart aches a little at the clean sweep. Any mattress that is none too good for sale, be sure to let Lizzie have [...]. There

are kitchen things too. But I'm getting into too deep waters for a short letter. Mr. E. has a few things of ours, our precious records and machine. Mrs. Z. has silver etc. and special books. Do not ring her. Go to see her in the evening. Already she has told me not to write to her because she is afraid. (Just like people in Hitler Germany.) My thoughts are with her often. She was so devoted to us all, especially T.

I think the <u>sooner you go</u> to S.A. the better, as soon as I hear from Jim what to do and as soon as you can make arrangements. You cannot know how much all this offer of yours means to us.

Forgive me for my few words.

My warmest love to Muriel and John. What do they say about losing their holiday in C.T.? Alas they'll have to forgive us.

My love to Colin and your own self,
Your Mummy.

9.

Hemel Hempstead,
Herts.

Sat. 21 September 1963

My dearest Sheila,

You may have received a letter from Daddy and what I say is redundant. However, I'm sure he would not mention the details about the house that I must try to remember. He fully agrees (though sad) that our home is no longer home and must be wound up <u>as soon as possible</u>. The government is moving to make a law confiscating the property of refugees. We don't fall into that category at all, but if there is much of an exodus, property may be frozen (ie. assets). Daddy has written to his lawyer [...] He has already requested a power of attorney to be sent to me here to sign, so that he can handle what I have as well as Daddy's. Of course the main part is Daddy's because last Dec. he received his life's savings that had been paid automatically from his salary into a Univ. fund, plus a contribution from the Univ. This [the lawyer] is looking after till Daddy should decide what to do. I'm not sure what I have. There is what is left over from my job[15] all these past years (£500) and the rent from letting the house since last March to Sept. this year, with 2 months deducted, I think, when house was not let [...] R.M.S. Rondebosch (Main Rd) may have the car. Daddy says you should use it. He has had it looked after while we were away. Remember we bought it only 6 months before Daddy left, after the accident. It cost somewhere about £240, I think. Try of course to get a fair price for it. Daddy may wish R.M.S. to sell as the simplest thing to do. I can't be sure it is <u>insured</u>. You would have to check that before using it and insure while there. I'm mentioning all this because all Daddy has touched upon is, the power of attorney; you having the right to act for us in everything. If necessary, the money from sale of house and furniture would be put in your name, if by any chance our total assets exceeded the amount we are allowed to take out of the country. I can hardly think so, but I'm ashamed to say I don't know what we have. I left the country before Daddy's life-money was cleared up, and as he was being paid in U.S. and we thought we'd be back, money-business was not discussed between us.

    I'm concentrating of course on <u>contents</u> of house. I've just discovered

---

15 With the Junior Literary Society

some lists. I had to give the house agent an inventory – very rough, I'm afraid. He (or Mr. E.) has key of house, 'linen cupboard' and little room to the right of passage; back door and garage. He might be the one to sell the house. But ask some advice first. (Lawyer? E.Z.?) Its value was reassessed for rates. Perhaps lawyer will know. I hope Mr E. will help you sell lounge furniture, carpet (£50 when new), dining room furniture, beds, wardrobes, etc. We bought the stove new from him a year or 2 or 3 ago (£40); frig (£40); washing machine is older. You might ask E.Z. over to see if there is anything she wants to buy, or knows of anyone. I doubt it. I want her to have a good thing as memento from us. Always <u>give</u> away to one friend or another whatever is likely to go for practically nothing. Many kitchen things, etc. can go to Lizzie and family; and any mattresses Mr. E. just does not want. (Also any suit of Jim's.) If rugs won't sell, give away, or keep if you can have some things packed separately for you and Muriel. I believe the railway allows you so much as part of luggage when going by air.

Daddy thinks only of his records, gramophone with precious loudspeaker and record cabinet. He wants these sent. I wonder if they can. Get advice. These are at Mr. E's. I want a footstool (at E.Z.). The barometer (of his father's) I'll ask Daddy about. And electric-clock (in lounge). Maybe sell this or keep it for yourself. There is a microscope in box (Muriel's). Take for Ivan.

I don't want you to have a public sale. Our household goods are too old-fashioned. I want other people to have benefit of many odds and ends, not a junk-dealer buying up a lot for 10/-. We have not a single piece of 'special' furniture except the 'Buchan' chair. Sell it if you can. It means nothing to me. The ghosts of the house are gathering about me – pictures: Daddy, by Anne Fischer.[16] Take it for yourself. (It may be on loan at Psych. Dep?) Muriel's well-framed picture. Take it to her. Van Gogh – yours? Renoir – girl – Doreen wants it. Picture of Coloured children (if still there) by V Desmore, give to Livingstone School, Lansdowne Rd. (near Lizzie's).

---

16 Fischer was a German Jewish refugee who became a well-known portrait photographer in Cape Town in the 1940s. There are two portraits of I B Tabata by her. She was briefly married to Bernhard Herzberg, a committed anti-Stalinist socialist who knew the NEUM leadership well.

One 'valuable' original – Bodmer. I'll ask Daddy.[17]

When Jane G[ool] left home, she sent my few things to Nurse Gool […] She has: Encyc. Britannica, with stand. Sell or give away the stand, I suppose. Could you transport books for us – or Colin and Peter? I'll ask Daddy. Paraffin heater – sell. She has a small radio. She may have a copy of my novel: "Rage of Life." But it's not likely to have been noticed in general folding up of goods. It does not matter in the least. There is a copy in U.S. Again, let E.Z. go over lists with you, in case she wants to take something over […]

E.Z. has: <u>1</u>.Silver tea-set. <u>2</u>.Cutlery. 3) Carvers. 4) pillows, towels. 5) Sheets, pillowslips. (Pack for me.) A white bedcover (double) keep for yourself or give away. 1 Glass decanter (give to E.Z?) (Or keep for yourself.) 1 Holland glass cheese dish (keep for yourself). She has 5 boxes of <u>books and papers. Pack with our other books that we want</u>. This book business is your biggest headache. Be <u>ruthless</u> in discarding, esp slim volumes of verse of no interest to anybody. (But one is by myself about the age of 20!) Keep it if you want it. For me keep Shakespeare, Dickens, R.L.S., Shaw, Ibsen etc. etc. Nearly all those in lounge – except those useless vols of verse. But <u>keep</u> for me 2 copies of Wilfred Owen's war poems and 'New Signatures' (c. 1930). Keep all books on teaching English Lit; criticism and grammar; on prosody; plays, take any for yourself. Daddy wants all psych books, except some to be given to the Psych Dep. Some <u>are</u> in the Dep. He'll let you know. I just cannot remember our books. When in doubt write to me. If any seem useful for Livingstone School, give them. If not, throw away. Of course keep any you fancy for you and Colin, or Muriel. 'Classics' I want, like Goldsmith, etc etc. The big 'Parnassus' of poetry; English plays in 1 volume; 'Palgrave' little collection of poems. All dictionaries; Roget's Thesaurus; classical dictionary; Bullfinch's Fables. Anything suited to Colin or Peter, or Ivan, keep for yourself. <u>Bring all books together</u> and superintend the packing. I think medium-sized boxes should be used to avoid breaking anybody's back unloading at dock or anywhere else. Of course, empty the smaller boxes that are at E.Z's (but one is big and heavy) and mix with other stuff. Perhaps do this job of bringing books together

---

17 This is a portrait of the Swiss-born Dr Frederick Bodmer who lectured in German at UCT and was the author of *The Loom of Language* (1943). A colleague of J G Taylor's, he gave the portrait to the Taylors in 1939; it is now in England. It is by Irma Stern, 1894–1966. She was born in South Africa, studied art at the Weimar Academy and was associated with the German expressionists. By the 1940s she was an established painter in Cape Town, achieving national and international acclaim.

near end of all your work. But begin discarding early. It's such a big job. Sell book-cases.

The little room is full of boxes. Their contents are hard to decide upon. Wherever we are, we need cup, plates, a few glasses, some small kitchen utensils. Michael says he did have some cups packed. But again, be decided by the cost of transport against value. We have too much glass. Could you pack some separately for yourself? 1 half-doz blue cups would do for us, and ½ doz plates, ½ doz glasses, bread plate, old bread (serrated) knife. And any other dish etc. you think possible and not adding too much to burden of transport. An expert must do this of course. We have heard too of books, even, arriving all sodden, having been left at docks. Could H. give you advice and help? He has a set of old Fr. records due to be returned. Give him some memento from me, from the house.

Blankets and travelling rugs, any <u>decent</u> bed-cover, quilt, sheets, etc. pack and send. But if there are decent double-bed sheets, keep them for yourself. Towels, pack, or give some to Lizzie. In big trunk in 'linen cupboard' is some rubbish. Give away, but keep 4 pillows for me. Take others if you wish. Pack among them (?) a nice Swedish tray. A small wine tray, keep or give away, if you don't want it. Give others to Lizzie and family (?) Mr E. may have some of our blankets. I cannot remember. Pack also a mattress cover, if good. Give away others. Pack curtains on door – for yourself. Curtains? A pair may be at E.Z's. Give away except perhaps for 2 that seem new, and good. (Sitting-room, or front bedroom.)

Always give away when you cannot hope to sell, or keep. I mean, if we cannot get a fair price. Give the Rs something, as well as E.Z. Give Mr E's maid something from the house. She is not a poor person. I believe E.Z. has a big, wide thermos (or at Searle St?) Keep for you if you wish. Don't pack <u>thin</u> blankets. I see in my list 'Head of a Madonna' behind trunk in linen cupboard. Is it Muriel's?

Garden tools, ask EZ if she wishes any. Sell or give away the rest. Electric kettle (?)

While in S.A. address cable or letters to Doreen instead of me [...] Get all help you need for packing etc.

Will Muriel and John holiday in C.T.? If so, they could perhaps transport some things you want, if you leave them at E.Z's or Mr E, <u>if</u> they are willing.

<u>Don't</u> stay in house alone. My heart will be lighter for you if I know a friend is staying with you, or you are staying with a friend, as the house

gets untidy. We paid phone to end of year. I wrote to house agent making sure house let ends at end Sept. Consult lawyer first before saying anything to house agent about selling. I must ask Daddy if you can draw money in S.A. as you need it. But first your 1st calculation as to your trav. expenses etc. Let me know <u>very soon</u>. I'm assuming you can cash cheque (S.A.) at your bank. Some of my own money is in a savings account (to be drawn within a week when necessary.) The rent is being paid into it. The rest is in a current account. My £15 a month now received from Jun. Lit. goes into it. I'll write ending my job.

<u>Doreen</u> would like the set of <u>Jane Austen</u> books. Also she should have the 2 vol Oxford Dict. Let Michael have ballet photo unless you want it. Muriel should have the <u>Rodin book</u>. Sewing machine – to Muriel? Floor polisher – Doreen would like it <u>if</u> not too heavy to transport. It is new.

As to turn-table, Michael thinks it could be taken out and old H.M.V. box discarded. Discuss with Mr E. maybe. The loud-speaker unit can go in box by itself, I suppose. As to Electric-clock, is voltage the same for N.R? The one in dining room is failing. Scrap it, probably (if it is still there.) Probably Ency. Brit. should be kept with its stand, esp. if Daddy suggests you keep it for the children.

If you can, give me a preliminary list of books where you are in doubt about discarding. Give Muriel some she may wish. I can't remember, esp. where books are duplicated.

Let her have Ibsen maybe, I'll keep the separate *Doll's House*. Let me have books in German and French, unless the latter seem too many. Then give me the best. You should keep the wooden figure from Indonesia and your 'dancer'. 2 small carved figures are Muriel's. Sell tall lamp-stand. I do hope Mr. E helps you about sale of furniture. Ask advice before getting anyone for final packing. This transport business will be very expensive. A big question: <u>Where</u> to send? We don't know where next we shall be, maybe Africa. In that case, to send all to London would not be reasonable. Daddy must try to find out. He tends to live very much in the present and has never before been called on to consider these practical problems.

I keep remembering more small things: a small yellow coffee set, for ex. Keep for yourself. Some small practical things in kitchen-ware we would need in a flat. To buy all again would be expensive. If at all reasonable, pack a few, but be guided by problem of bulk. You see, we've never moved before so I don't know from experience how ruthless we have to be. (I don't think Muriel and John, if going to S.A. should go till they see how the situation turns out on Dingaan's Day, 16th Dec. Emotions are high at that celebration.)

I'll write soon to our Muriel. How is she? Give John and her my love. And to you and Colin. Doreen and Michael add theirs too.

Your Mummy.
(Holland glass sweet dishes for you).
P.S. I hope agent checked his inventory. Details on enclosed paper were not part of general inventory given to [him].

10.

[*no address*]
Sunday, 29 September 1963.

My dearest Sheila,

It's out of my hands to know whether you can go to C.T. sooner than the 9th. I'd like it to be, but it could only be a matter of days. For I wrote to Daddy last <u>Monday</u>, telling him to arrange the sending of money to you, cabling if possible. 'If possible' because I assume it should be a S.A. cheque to conserve what we have here, not knowing when the other funds from S.A. will arrive [...] If Daddy can't cable this amount, but acted <u>at once</u> on receipt of my letter, you should receive letter on 3rd or 4th Oct, only. Another way is to send cheque to Colin for whatever outlay there is, if you should by any chance leave earlier. I wait his reply as to <u>where</u> to have things sent, though there are many things to do before you need to know. Doreen suggests that all we keep should be sent to you, on assumption of our possible settling somewhere in Africa. This depends on how urgently Daddy has tried to explore such a possibility. I'm in great doubt. He has been so busy and happy in Toronto, he is not likely to have thought ahead, till now.

Let me stop here and say how proud we would be to have our 7th grandchild! Please do tell Muriel to think of baby first and not drive herself with love of the theatre in the heat. Be firm on this, if you can. It's most important. Now some other points that come to mind. I'll ask Daddy what he might expect for the house. But I did say consult lawyer first. We had it painted up outside when we left. Inside is O.K. (if not ill-treated). But the lack of hot water in kitchen is a mistake on our part. If somebody soon enough took the house, they might take stove and frig, but don't wait too long to try to sell these. Consult me whenever you are in doubt about books etc. If it's possible to pack without inordinate cost some basic things in decent crockery, etc. that we have to re-buy wherever we are, do so. And I'd like you to have anything that you fancy. I'd hate to see them sold for nothing. There's a yellow coffee set (and jug or teapot?) Keep it for us or you – again depending on feasibility of packing. I wish I could ask any people who have had to go to a distant destination.

Could you send me our French dict. and idiom book (small and pale green) if still extant. Keep *Treasure Caskets* for the children. The later books might feed Peter's voracious appetite for a little. And all the introductions are my writing (8 books). But I only came in on helping to collect material from Bk. 3–8. Keep any book on Africa and history. Is there anything you think Colin would like? Of course preserve my Gorkys and lit. crit. by Russians of 19th C. and Babel's stories – the last may be at E.Z's (?) Please give me another address. Perhaps the Ms? I'd much prefer you to stay with a friend, as paying guest if possible, unless you occupy the house with a friend, once you are collecting all the stuff together. <u>But not alone</u>. I wonder if Lizzie or a daughter could help you in any way? She may be too old [...]

I've asked Jim where it is best to cable him. Don't hesitate to do so when there is need. See that every expense for you is covered. I've asked Jim about Grove's (music) Dictionary.

Warmest love to you and Colin and Colin and Peter and Muriel and John and Ivan, from us all.

Your Mummy.

[over]

P.S. I think the 2 fat tomes of Oxford Dict. are too big to send separately to England. Better keep them with our other books that have to be sent somewhere. I cannot trail all my 'classics' around with me. Keep what you think will be of use to Colin and Peter in a few years time. If by any chance I want to teach literature in Africa – I can then borrow from you! Do ascertain where the microscope is. Muriel should have it, and any plays she wants. There is a shabby Daumier book (pictures and cartoons), paper cover among music bundle. Keep for Muriel if she wants it. It is good satire. Discard music, but I'll ask D and M if they want any book of <u>scores</u>. There's a book of [short] stories by Farrell. Discard. Keep books on American lit. for me. As I said, maybe your biggest bundle is books and papers I mentioned before. I want all if possible. Doreen says to take the Renoir out of frame, as the whole is too heavy to send. She sent it in a roll. But your picture and Muriel's have such lovely frames, could they be brought by someone travelling from S.A. back to N.R. in the summer? Keep the Irma Stern also for us.

Be sure to convey my warmest feelings to E.Z. Would she write? I feel sad about her. I'm not sure if you should say goodbye to W.G. She made no response to letters last year about Muriel's wedding, and a letter in Dec [...] She is closed in herself I fear. But if you decide for old time's sake to see her, give her greetings from us. Ask where M. is.

The Oxford Dict is probably at Nurse Gool's, at back of Encyc. There may also be a small washing machine, but if packed off with J's things, forget it completely. The typewriter is <u>not</u> there. I'm running off to post. Once more – our love.

Mummy.

11.

>78 Marlin's Turn
>Judebridge
>Hemel Hempstead
>Herts, England.

>Monday, 7 October 1963.

My dearest Sheila,
I returned last night to find your letter and Daddy's waiting me. Daddy, contrary to my expectation, sends <u>me</u> a cheque (English) to cable to you. Now I'm hastening to cable to you, to N.R. […] £100 to cover your fare, and praying it will be in time. Your suggestion is a sensible one, about cashing a cheque in C. Town. Pity Daddy didn't do this direct. Now I'm enclosing a S.A. cheque for £100 […] It'll be terrible if you cannot get money at once! […] Actually, I'm counting on the lawyer giving you at once whatever you need from Daddy's account. Daddy has written about this. It's just that I'm not sure if you may not have to wait a few days for the machinery to move. I sincerely hope not. We don't know value of house. We don't know if it's wise to trust the agent […] to suggest a price or to get outside advice first. You'll be judge of that. You'll know already that neither Jim nor I are 'up' in business matters. We rely on you completely to do the best for us. I think you're right also, to sell our car privately, if you can. From my long letter to you in N R you'll know the answer to most of your questions. I'm so anxious to get this letter off that I'll mention other questions later. On no account auction our house and contents, which are both so unfashionable. Knowing Mr. E. enables us, I hope, to get rid of furniture privately. Mrs. A advises me, from her own experience, <u>not</u> to sell (or give away) all smallish household goods needed by us anywhere, crockery, kitchen-ware etc. Pack and send if not quite unpractical, the amounts you think 2 people need. Don't you dare talk of buying anything! Keep all you want and can transport. Blankets, sheets etc. We'll need 2 each if in Africa, 3 for one and 2 + quilt if in England. Take any others. Don't give any away. We need mattress covers, too, for 2 beds.

    Dear lass, live with your friends if you can. Not alone. But not in hotel unless necessary.

All our love
Your Mummy.

Cable if you can't get money at once! Daddy leaves communication now to me. He wants to keep the barometer! I think all should be transported to <u>you</u>. [*in the margin*: I think of ourselves as not being in England. This is terribly hard to decide. Daddy wants you to write out lists of his books to ask him which to keep. A big task.]

12.

London.

Wed. 16 October 1963.

My dearest Sheila,

How glad I am that you have friends to help you straight away. First about your abode. Are you to stay with the Ms and not have to be in Kintayre at all? Probably that is best. The agent [...] wrote to say that the house was the worse for damp. (It does not surprise me.) We had it all painted outside last year before Daddy left. And inside has good paint now on all the walls. I believe, too, that a new back door was made. But nothing keeps the weather out from that side in winter months.

You don't mention books, which I think is your biggest problem. Daddy writes about making lists of his. I think this is asking too much of you, unaided. Anyway you'll do your best. I would like you to make a preliminary run through of the shelves, casting out where you're sure we don't want to keep any. Then list some where you are in doubt and let me know. Don't get packers in till you have checked all household goods and are ready to say: pack these, etc. Did you consult Mr E. on Daddy's request for his loudspeaker, cabinet, records, etc? But remember this, he himself is not practical. You need others to tackle the packing of Daddy's records etc.

I'm terribly bothered about not knowing <u>where</u> we'll be. Daddy did say 'send to Hemel' before he received my letter suggesting all should go to you. Now I'm waiting a reply, but he does say that I should give directions to you where needed and not both of us from now on. All the same, it depends on whether he has any chance at all of being in Africa and that cannot yet be decided. I'd like if possible to find out the respective costs of transporting from C.T. to England (by boat) and by train to you. I feel we could best leave our books, bedding etc. and some crockery etc, with you and then only take what we need wherever we are later. Some things I'm sure you should take over for yourself. Or is our stuff going to be a burden to you. Oh, I do wish I knew exactly where you can send. Perhaps some blankets, sheets, towels etc. (<u>not</u> mattress) should come to London if we are forced to stay the winter here. The difficulty of deciding makes me want to delay the summoning of packers. Maybe this is wrong. I assume that the house and contents will be insured up to the last moment of transportation. Can you give me an idea of possible costs, from those who have experience. Can you sell the carpet? Daddy suggests asking D.S. if he wants the Irma Stern. (He'll be in the phone book.) I don't want to 'give' it away as it is the only picture you should ask advice as to its value. It might be quite a lot. D.S. is well off and able to buy it. You know how paintings acquire artificial value. The same applies to the Kibel.[18] Did you ask Muriel if she wants it? Be sure to give our warmest love to E.Z. She has a lot of our more precious books. Find out if I can write to her. Remember us warmly to Mr E. I hope he helps you a lot. Remember to ask H. to take some memento from us (if he wants to) – and E.Z. There's an old Scottish Buchan chair. Should you sell it separately or would E.Z. like it? I don't know if it is of any value. Probably not.

Do take care of yourself. I believe the lawyer can let you have whatever money you need. Keep in constant touch with me. How long do you think you'll take?

All my love,

Your Mummy.

---

18 Wolf Kibel, 1903–1938, was born in Poland. He came to South Africa from Vienna in 1929 because of ill-health, and is said to have introduced expressionism to the local art scene. The painting referred to here is of a group of children in District Six.

13.

London.

Tuesday, 22 October 1963.

My dearest Sheila,
You seem to be doing a big job expeditiously. What a labour – to list all the books. But first let me reassure you about the letter posted to me on the 12th Oct. I also received 2 yesterday and the cable this morning. I was overwhelmed with business in London yesterday, so could not stretch out the hours to answer your many questions and put some of my own. I just managed to write to Daddy. The remarks and instructions may not be in order of importance. I'll do my best to cover everything. The paramount question I'm quite unhappy about – <u>where</u> to send our stuff. What is your opinion? I certainly don't want anything to go to a storage firm anywhere. We are not taking out a load of furniture, but basic necessities in crockery and bedding – and then those books. They are a burden, it's true. But I picture you taking over some in any case, as if a small inheritance to you and Muriel. Some will be discarded altogether. On second thoughts, the 2 vols of Oxford Dict. should be sent to London, but don't send anything separately to Doreen. It can go together. And she <u>does</u> want the frame with the Renoir! I cannot make up my mind about the Bodmer picture. Can you give me advice? It's light in weight, but its value might increase with time. If you have already spoken to D.S. that's all right. We are not all that keen on making money out of our only 'collector's piece' – by keeping it. If you have not spoken to him we might keep it after all. It's just that I have difficulty in picturing where we shall be in the next year or two and have taken a rather fatalistic attitude to the break up of our home. I must not lament it when others is S. Africa are suffering far greater pain. But it does make me think of death, with its relinquishment of all one's little possessions. I have not many pretty things, but I do want you to keep what will give pleasure or be useful: the decanter, and the tinkling glass cheese dish, for ex., and leave us a minimum of glasses for our own needs. There you <u>should</u> pack separately what you can keep. About the encyclopaedia, give up the bookcase part, I think. It would be too costly to send it to you in Bancroft. I have only one proviso, if by any chance I should teach in Africa and need the books for reference – I might borrow them from you! By the way, there is a completely blank (green) book beside the *Treasure*

Casket (which is for Colin and Peter.) You could use the book for your secretarial work in Bancroft. The Junior Lit. answers I kept with the idea of making a book out of them. They are light, but bulky. What do you think? I don't think I'll <u>ever</u> get round to compiling that book. I'm not sufficiently interested. What about leaving them in E.Z's keeping?

E.Z! How glad I am that you have made friends. Perhaps I should not have hesitated to write. I will, sometime soon. She <u>must</u> give up toiling in her garden, but our house would be a poor exchange. She should have a smaller house. Now about the books etc. with her. <u>Don't</u> pack them separately. Packers are not interested. Let all that stuff go together with the rest. I assume Daddy is letting the Department have quite a lot, but if you feel like keeping a few for Colin or John, don't hesitate to do so. Has Daddy indicated what he wants packed? As to the books etc. at E.Z's, they should not go in separate little cartons as they are now. I assume they would be packed in bigger lots with the others.

Here's a small problem: we once put papers, <u>etc.</u> that we wanted to keep, in the garage, in a box with straw and other odds and ends, and under obvious rubbish. Now I just <u>cannot</u> remember if it is worth keeping or not. Perhaps not. Can you try to judge if it is? If there should be several copies of papers, for ex., keep three or 4 copies. If there is correspondence, certainly keep it.

Now to the load of '78' (old recording) records. Did you ask Daddy? They're a big weight. I don't think he should expect to cart those round the world – unless one or two special pieces. Perhaps Mr E. would take them or the College of Music (?) – if they'll have the gift. Have you kept the younger (Anne Fischer) picture of Daddy? K.D. has the later one. He can keep that in the Department. You speak of K.D. handling Daddy's books. What is kept by us surely joins the general pile for packing. Daddy now says: send records and cabinet and amplifier (ie. all his recording apparatus) to Doreen's. That suggests he really thinks of our base as London. I just don't know what is best. The items he lists really cover the only 'furniture' we are keeping. Yes, now we are at it, keep table lamps and pack. There's a tall one can be sold (if possible). Pack good curtains. Either Mr E. or E.Z had our long cream curtains (fawn) sent to them after cleaning. (Did you find footstool at E's?) I don't think Lizzie can possibly buy our washing machine. It should not have been left broken. Couldn't you have it mended? It is worth selling – but too big and heavy to transport to Muriel. Her own small one may be at Nurse Gool's. [*in the margin*: Ring up first

[…] Jane had it for years and took great care of it. Find out about this. Their home, too, has been broken up. By all means have it sent to Muriel – unless a new one would be cheaper. I'm very surprised she hasn't one. Yes, give Lizzie my sewing machine. Miss Craig gave it to me as my wedding present in 1926 – £5! Did you find a few odd books (one on Medieval times for Colin or Peter) at E.Z's, left at last minute. I cannot picture coat or hat. Give away, I should think. Open locked case. It's not a good one (?) Pack sheets, pillows, etc. except those you wish to keep. It seems to me I <u>should</u> keep enough for a visitor to sleep wherever we are. I always did. So maybe keep only double-bed sheets for yourself. (But decide on this.) You know the first tenant asked me to leave sheets and blankets for her […]

[…] Daddy should consider whether to transfer any [money] in your name, rather than leave any in S.A. […] But I guess this is best in [the lawyer's] hands. Yet I'd like to know if more can be transferred a year later, if sale of house pushes our total assets beyond the amount that can be transferred. You see, before long this sum is what we'll have to draw upon when we travel as Daddy's pension is not generous. That prompts me to question the choice of packer for our modest belongings: books and household necessities […] Now I may be taking up a wrong attitude. I just want you to <u>make inquiries</u> as to various packers and their charges, instead of taking Daddy's word in such matters – if you know what I mean. If you have already fixed with them, of course leave it at that.

About the green carpet – would you like it? Or is it quite unsuitable to your furnishings, etc? I think (but feel so completely inexperienced) that it is a big item to transport. In cold England, it would be useful – if we stay. Do use your own judgment on the problem. (I guess I'm suspicious of the cost of total transport precisely because we have never had to do it before.) On the other hand, this cost has to be weighed up against re-buying stuff of all kinds, wherever we may be settled. We should save ourselves unnecessary re-buying. I feel you are so much more practical than I am. Cannot you help me to decide? I'd like to keep the old Chinese rugs and any one that is not shabby – but again, we'd not need much, so keep any that you think useful for you or Muriel. Don't forget (to mention small matters) that we need some kitchen ware wherever we go, if not too bulky (or old) to transport. About E.Z's wanting desk and dressing table. Are you giving her the dressing table? Is it good enough?

The microscope – isn't it at E.Z's? I wouldn't like it to be lost. It's Muriel's.

The old French records (H's) were at Nurse Gool's. They may have been sent off with Jane's furniture. They were too old to be good.

I'm not interested in the old Kintore picture. Give it away. Part of the ugly old bedroom suite is in the pantry. Would you like the old Scots chair? If not, sell, if possible, or do whatever else you want with it.

About books I think good enough for Z. (E's husband). Ask her – or him. But keep what you or Colin or John or Muriel want. I cannot recognise by memory: Phil. Classics for English Readers. Send if in doubt.

Do you think EZ would be willing to take charge of those many Vols. of Hansards – ie. Debates? If not, discard. We used it to take passages out of them. Do you note from a quick glance any that are marked with pencil – if so, maybe send one or two. But <u>don't</u> spend time on this.

Do you think our stuff should be sent to England. Not knowing our plans, I feel so completely uncertain. If we did have to stay winter in England, we should have blankets, sheets, etc.

My dear, I wish you didn't feel the sadness of all this. My heart is with you.

All love from
Your Mummy.

[*in the margin*: How is Colin?]

14.

[*no address*]
8 November 1963

My dearest Sheila,

How wonderfully you have managed everything at home for us. I have no words to say how much it means to us. It must have been hard for you to decide how to divide things up. Now it is difficult for me to guess whether to send this letter to Bancroft or C.T. There are all sorts of little questions to ask but I guess I ought to let them wait:- about what you found useful in glass-ware etc. etc. I'm amazed at the auction of the house. I'm amazed at how you have made it look attractive. I just don't believe it will fetch what you say. Is the furniture sold <u>with</u> the house? Did Mr E. not handle any? What did Lizzie receive? And E.Z, what did she fancy? Is it possible to transfer the proceeds to England, to Daddy?

I continue to be amazed. I didn't realise how the lump sum he received at the end of his years at the University was being invested. I feel queer and conservative about that. You see, we never before had any to invest – except once in our green youth we 'bought' some trees that seem to have died in their first shoots! I find it difficult to adjust myself to the idea.

No, the Bank had not replied to my letter. I expect word any day now. I wouldn't like Daddy to tie up any more funds. You understand we'll need money for travel as well as living and the yearly University sum is pretty small for to-day. About the car. I think you should just take it over. If it can fetch only £100 and seems still good to you, it seems a pity to 'waste' it on other people. I have not had a reply from Daddy yet as he must be busy organizing his last visits before sailing on the 14th. Did he tell you he has had an offer of a further six months in Toronto, beginning next April? I'm so terribly glad he is at last receiving the appreciation that is his due. I don't want to cross the Atlantic again, but I urged him to accept this offer if it materialises. Meantime he could stay in Europe and continue with his next book. Getting rooms in London is monstrously difficult, but it will have to be done.

It saddens me to think of our home being made nice before it vanishes for ever. It is like a woman whose face in death somehow becomes touched with the beauty of the days of youth.

Be sure to write and give me more details when you get back. Tell me how everyone is? What have you left for Muriel? What books would <u>she</u>

like? Why does she never never write? Is she well? She must take more care against tiring herself, especially against the present heat in Bancroft.

By the way, it's a belated thought, but did you check to see if the house agent regularly paid in the monthly sums? I guess that will appear on the forms I receive. Did you find Muriel's washing machine – and her microscope? What is all transport likely to cost? I know landing fees on this side are large. My mere travelling trunk for example, costing £7 from C.T. cost £15 before I received it several months later.

Do write soon again. Give my love to <u>all</u> at home. I hope you are not tired.

Dear Sheila – Mummy

15.

[*no address*]
13 November 1963.

My dearest Sheila,
I have received your long letter but received it only after some days because I was away. Hence the delay.

My first thought is for our little Peter. He must have missed you. That makes me sad. I hope your return [to Bancroft] helped to make him better. You must feel strange now that your labours are over. I assumed you would not stay once the machinery for winding things up was settled. Yes, the house is not likely to fetch what it should, because we were foolish not to have hot water in the kitchen. I was tempted to tell you to have an attachment fixed to the kitchen sink (I see many in England) but it would have caused delay. What a problem this is with Daddy not knowing where he'll settle! That means I'm no nearer saying what to do with the 3rd load. What about your <u>own</u> plans? My wish is still that it should go to you – perhaps at the back of my mind is the thought that <u>you</u> should really have all we are not likely to need for what must henceforth be rather an exile existence, now here, now there. Yet I don't want to place on you an unwanted burden. I'm still forced to ask you to help me make the final decision. If you could get a Rhodesian firm not too startlingly expensive (as compared with transport by boat) keep the stuff. If not, send by boat. But I already mentioned that the price they quoted in C.T. for my trunk, for ex. was only half what I finally paid on delivery of it at Hemel. Dock fees were high. But perhaps the firm includes this cost (??) The firm which took over in England for paying dock dues, transport, etc. had entirely different papers. You see, you and I are still in a quandary.

About the transistor. I can guess it was sent with Jane's stuff, but I'm vexed about the microscope, which is Muriel's. I didn't think it <u>was</u> there. I thought it was at <u>E.Z.'s</u>. If I was so foolish as to leave it in the little spare room, which the tenant at the last moment asked me to unlock because she wanted it for her baby at night, it may have been removed. Was it not in the inventory? Did you get Muriel's washing machine? And the 2 Vols of the Oxford Dict. at Searle St [the Gool family home], with, I believe, some copies of a play of mine, "Bitter Waters", based on Silone's novel "Fontamara". (I have only one copy in England.) It was at the back of the Encyl. Brit. Did you take it, with the stand for it? There is little indeed in the old house to give you and Muriel pleasure, since the furniture was sold. Was this separate from the house on day of auction? Was it a poor sale? Who got the car and for how much? You do not say. Did Daddy not write about it? I'd like to know what you gave to H., E.Z, H., Lizzie.

I'm glad you saw W.G. How was she? I was sorry I didn't ask you to see Mr S. [at the Junior Literary Society], to whom I wrote saying I wasn't returning. I suppose they did put into the bank every month my princely £15!

When you have time you'll give me some details of how things are disposed of, I'm sure – a purely personal desire to know if <u>you</u> have anything you really like.

I'm sorry you could not stay for a breath of the beauty of C.T. I dare not think of it. You will let me have your poem one day. Be sure you do.

No, I <u>don't</u> see myself settling in cold England. But where? Flats in London are fiercely hard to get. By the way you may have found in the cupboard a plaque of Lenin (looking like Smuts). What did you do with that? […]

Tell our Muriel I will write soon! Daddy arrives in England on the 19th Nov. He has been moving around so much that I don't yet know if he's going straight to Jeannie's or to Hemel. We'll be together there.

Dearest Sheila – my heart is full. Forgive my lack of words. Give my love to big Colin. How is he? Kisses to little Colin and Peter. My love to you.

Mummy.

16.

"Invershiel", Blandford Road
Corfe Mullen
near Wimborne
Dorsetshire.

24 November 1963.

My dearest Sheila,
Your promised letter is late. Daddy and I are at Jeannie's [Jim's sister] and can begin to discuss our problems – but are no nearer solution. His heart is set on returning to Toronto, where he is so far appreciated that the Head of the Dep. suggests wangling another temporary period, from April to October – not yet fixed. I hate going so far away from Africa and I'm mighty sore at the thought of not being in England to meet Muriel and John. In fact, at this moment I cannot accept the idea. I've suggested to them to try to come earlier, esp. as it is also a question of enquiring about jobs. Universities, etc., would be closed from July to October. I did not mention this in my letter. But it's probably a different kind of job John is looking for, which is most likely actually in Africa itself, where so much exploration for minerals is going on. Can't they take a short holiday meantime? Isn't there some place you mentioned in S.R? But they must take malaria tablets.

The suggestion is to store for a while in C.T. what you are not transporting. How much would it be? Tell me. I fear having to transport from N.R. with no railway near ie. if to somewhere else far in Africa, or to England. If I took rooms in London, then I'd want some stuff, esp. if Muriel and John came. But – but – Daddy expects me to join him if he has the Toronto job. So you see – no daylight on our problems, yet. My wishes clash with Daddy's about America. I feel lost with the sense of not knowing where to be. Meantime – wait a while.

How did you find everything at home? How is Peter? Big Colin and little Colin? When does Colin go to school? Are you sure he can 'take' it? Have you found out about its quality? Boarding schools can torment children, but also do good. Is he not too young?

Tell me much more about the house affairs. I believe there's a letter from the lawyer, saying the house is sold, but I haven't seen it yet. Did the auction cost a lot?

Had the car deteriorated? What did you find out about transport through a N.R. firm? What was it to cost compared with boat? I've not heard from E.Z. yet. I must write. I wish we had not so many books. I once thought of bequeathing our library to a non-white community – but how? We cannot cart them around. Did you take only a few?

I've still to consider if I shouldn't take rooms in London now Daddy is here. It is too much for Doreen. But – so cold in cold rooms in London – if we can get them! I find it hard to discuss problems being in Jeannie's house. Jim seems quite unaware of them. He lives for the moment. You can imagine the position in S.A. Universities, when his student, […], has got his job in C.T. Tell me about sale of furniture. Did Mr E. help? How is he? I feel sad that Daddy has not written to him. He was counting the weeks for his return. Did you meet E.Z's daughter? Or did she hide away as usual? How is Muriel? She seems worried about Tim? Isn't October the worst month for heat, and she would be extra tired? […]

Daddy sends his love to you and Colin. And I send an extra share. Good night my dear one. (over)

Were you able to include what you were taking to N.R. as part of your allowance by train, though you yourself flew? Of course the cost of that is on Daddy. Was there anything left of the £100 to cover it?

By the way, I don't even know what the house brought. Yes, the Bank sent on the money, but Hemel was remiss in not letting me know. I looked in amazement at the sum, till I realised that the accumulation of rent for the house added up over a year and a half. Having always lived with a narrow margin left over, I'm now uneasy about investment – so old-fashioned am I. I distrust the whole business, aware of the danger of political upheaval. The murder of Kennedy, for ex, sent the stockexchange crashing down. Hail is crashing on the window as I write. It makes me wonder where, where are we going to be.

Doreen too is golden-hearted in welcoming us through all our comings and goings. But I feel that it's not fair that she should have both Daddy and me over a long period. She leads a very busy life.

I have completely forgotten a Xmas is coming!

Write soon. Once more – my love.

Mummy.
P.S. Daddy has made no move about job in Africa – or research, I find.
P.S. What is your opinion of the plan to leave stuff in C.T. for at least a few

months till something turns up? [*squeezed into margin*: Tell me if you don't agree.] I'm vexed I can't get this letter posted till afternoon. We are off the map here, much more than Hemel.

We return to Doreen's this week. I'm heart sore at the prospect of putting two continents between us again. The years are passing.

Daddy has had a most interesting time, but is now due for a rest.

I have not discussed with D and M at all about stuff [*continued in the margin*] coming here. They'd have no room either.

17.

Hemel

30 November 1963.

My dearest Sheila,

Your long, long letter was sent down to us at Poole after I had posted to you. Your letter brings home to me still more what a responsible job you carried out, what with deciding about auctioning, beetle trouble (alas!) and the neglected state of house and garden generally. I guess the sum-total of expenses, esp. dispatching, will seriously lessen the assets, but is all part of the upheaval of wrenching away from S.A., no more than other folks go through. It's only a disturbing expenditure as compared with the sober mode of living up to our modest income over the 34 years in the one house. One wonders why we accumulate 'worldly goods' at all. We could all live much more simply than we do. Our uncertainty of abode from this time hence-forward makes me realise this. Possessions just become a burden – except food, clothing – and even the books and music we need become hard to dispose of.

I find myself wondering what you did keep for yourself, and Muriel. It seems terribly little, though you give me no details. For one thing, I'd much rather you had had the car (remember only 6 months in Daddy's use) than the Ms. They got a bargain! Aren't you having the carpet, etc. sent at once? I'm surprised at you not taking the small book-case for ex. I'm quite sore at what I see in the 'sold' list, all of which, of course is public robbery. I mean by that, my darling, that I can't understand why you didn't take (for ex.) electric clock, occasional tables, flasks, wall mirror, teapots, round stools. (You gave them to me!) I would gladly have kept these for myself, even, (rather than sell). Mercifully, I retained no detailed picture of all these possessions in my mind, and with all the books and papers uppermost in my thoughts, I just couldn't remember what to tell you to keep. It's this devastating list that makes my heart bleed. I'd have given them all away, if <u>you</u> didn't want them, rather than see a crowd of strangers snatching them. As you say, the big newer things went for crazily little. The new electric stove had cost £40, and the old-new frig, also £40. I'm surprised at Mr E. not taking them, since he knew their value. Rugs and bed-spread could have gone to Lizzie, which means to members of her large family. My darling, don't think I'm blaming you in any way whatsoever. I <u>fully</u> understand the need for the auction of tables, big chairs, etc. etc. You just could not waste time with folks trotting in and out, or with advertising. This was the only practical way. It's just that my whole attitude to selling is confirmed by the legalised robbery of the auction. I really meant it when I said: Give away, rather than sell. I weep for example at the thought of a flask H. gave me. He himself might have used it. Or you. Oh, why were you not willing to take such a small but useful thing? And those small tables you gave me. How that hurts. They would not have been hard to pack. Dear Sheila, don't be cross with me. I'm tasting the sorrow of the break up of a home, which usually happens after one is dead, and then it doesn't matter. It's <u>not at all</u> the small return for the things I cavil at. That is nothing. It's the sacrilege of vulgar hands stealing things given to me, by you, by others. These are without price, indeed, outraged by selling. Oh, dear Sheila, my heart is too full to express it properly. I've lost a home and yet I'm most hurt over those little tables you gave me! I really cannot understand why you did not give them to someone, or yourself or Muriel – or me! I know of course you don't need them. [*squeezed between the lines*: (Later, I see you have the electric clock after all. I'm glad. Is it the one in the lounge?)]

What does 'collection glass £1.1' mean? What was it? What cups are referred to? Did you not take any? Is the carved chair, the old Scottish chair? Didn't E.Z. want to take it? What is meant by 'green carpet'? You surely kept the big lounge one.

I'm glad H. took the brass table. Did you give E.Z. the dressing tables? I'm glad she has the Taylor 'heir loom', the pears picture done on glass, I think, by your grandma. I still think the books left over will be considered worthless. Where are they? Could they still not be handed over to Nurse Gool, for example, to give (or throw) away? They'd fetch 2d like the things in the house.

I'm completely puzzled about the microscope. I wish I'd taken it with me to Rhodesia at the time of departure. Tabata, alas, thinks I did not leave it with him. We stuffed a lot of things in the wardrobe (unlockable) in the little back room and meant to leave the room locked. Only at the last minute we were foolishly soft-hearted and allowed the tenant entrance to it, for her baby at night. I guess anything could have been taken from that wardrobe. I just cannot remember what was in it and probably did not take an inventory of its contents. Did you find in linen cupboard <u>small</u> carvings of Muriel's former husband? Queer, I've completely forgotten his name. Don't worry about the Lenin plaque. It doesn't matter.

[...] I did not know the nature of all your expenses in C. Town. Were they covered by [the lawyer]? You must not lose a penny over all you have done for us. You have given what money cannot repay, but at least you cover obvious expenses. <u>Be frank about this</u>.

Did you ever find out about the possible transport of goods by a Rhodesian firm? Was it too expensive in your opinion? What shall we do? Daddy waits with complete confidence for confirmation of a further spell in Toronto, from April, and he expects me to go too. This I don't look forward to. Meantime, rooms are almost impossible to find in London. (D.P., for ex, has been searching for months. She lectures at Birkbeck and lives alone.) Doreen says we should not face winter in London in what would be poor (cold) conditions, but to stay on with her for the time.

Tabata, Jane Gool and N. Honono are in Dar-es-Salaam in (at present) very poor circumstances and we feel we have to help them. Jane's furniture was put into hands of a firm that went bankrupt and their possessions are stranded in Jo'burg, also including the Oxford Dictionary and copies of my play, presumably (which they stored at back of Encyclopaedia) and the little radio set (?) Also the money Jane had on retiral cannot be taken out of Swaziland to Tanganyika. Some way must be found.

We've had no further confirmation of sale of house for <u>£3,000</u>. A letter (note) arrived when we were at Poole and Doreen thought she sent it on. (It said house was sold.) We cannot find it. Did the buyer you mention take it? It seems a good amount. I wish I could decide <u>soon</u> where to ask things to be sent. What are your plans? Will there be decisions soon? In that case we could not saddle you with books.

[*in the left-hand margin*: Do you know, I've forgotten Xmas is at hand, and I've nothing sent for the children! (By the way, I do hope you kept the Children's Encyclopaedia and well as the Britannica – and others?) I'll write soon again. <u>You</u> write soon, too! And your poem – it is to me beautiful, something to treasure.

How is Colin now? How is Muriel? Aren't they taking even a short holiday? They need it. Daddy and all send their love. And I.

Mummy.]

[*in the right-hand margin*: P.S. Enclosed is for Peter and Colin with big hugs.]

18.

Hemel.

18 December 1963.

My dearest Sheila,
Happy greetings to you all! I'm wondering if you have received all my letters [...] We had [... Muriel's] lovely card yesterday. I posted a photocard of Jenny and Cat at piano yesterday to her and John. Perhaps I should not have put cheques in letters. Is it convenient from England? A money order would be better.

Tell me how Muriel is? At this period, with another little one coming soon after the first, a mother is rather drained of strength. I find myself worried by their launching into a holiday right in the middle of the local invasion of European resorts. Accommodation is scarce and dear and everything crowded, unless you find a place off the beaten track. Expenses in Italy and Switz. and France are shocking. In Spain it is still less, but it is not so reasonable as earlier, and the rush is great at that time. I rather fear that they will be disillusioned as you were. English climate can be <u>anything</u> – 'winter' for them anyway. And expenses are high here too. I'm wondering what <u>kind</u> of holiday John and Muriel are looking for. Ideal is sight-seeing, <u>if</u> you haven't children. Europe is full of riches I long for you to see too. Venice, Florence, Rome, etc. The Rhine, the Tyrol. I'm wondering if Innsbruck as a centre is not possible, but one would have to book places in a 'gast-house' well beforehand. The Tyrol was not so shockingly dear when I was there – 8 years ago!

Tenting equipment would be fun, and Doreen and Michael have de luxe equipment, but they'll use it for sure in August. It cuts out those frightful hotel bills. But one has to have a car.

I'm wondering how (or if) I could help. Rooms in London are fiercely hard to get, but if I knew their plans, I might try well beforehand to find rooms a bit out of London – not so far as Hemel which is very inconvenient, as you know, except if one has a car.

But then I don't know Jim's plans for sure – nor my own! I find it hard to <u>discuss</u> at all. He lives from day to day so relaxed. His return to Toronto is not yet fixed, though he expects it. I don't want to go and miss Muriel and John. But I find I cannot talk about it. I'm desperately longing to see you all. But travelling is such an expense if I go to Toronto too.

Do try to have a talk with Muriel and John. Doreen could have Ivan if that would help. <u>I would gladly help</u> but feel unable to talk it out with Jim. I cannot even suggest <u>where</u> to have our stuff sent.

I miss a letter from you, Sheila. Tell me how you are. And Colin? Did you have the stuff for you sent to Bancroft? Don't speak of <u>not</u> keeping the carpet.

Sheila is there something special you would like? We could send it or a cheque for it. I want you to have some 'memento' for all you have done. I hope you did not think my expression of <u>sadness</u> over the auction cast any doubt over my knowledge of the magnificent job you did for us.

Do write soon.

I had a card from H. yesterday. I'm sending to Victory Farm because I don't know his address. […]

P.S. I write to you about Muriel and John because I'm so afraid they do not realise the difficulty of travelling at that time with children, and the great expense of living in Europe, at all times.

We send you our warmest love to you all my darling.

Your Mummy.

P.S. I had a beautiful letter from E.Z. full of appreciation of you: an understanding of what I live for – and a great sadness where she herself is concerned.

19.

[*no address*]
Xmas Day, 1963.

My dearest Sheila,

I'm sure you are remembering us this day, as we are remembering all of you. Here it is bleak rain, not even white snow. The pall of grey from morn till night deepening slowly into dark from about three o'clock onwards prompts me to feel Britain ought to be left to its sea-mists altogether, unless science diverted to the welfare of man contrives to clear the heavy pall from out its skies. Above is blue sky, as I found when I was on a flight. You dated your letter 13th Jan. a date uppermost in your mind. How much I can understand your feeling about Collie, and just when he is becoming a more thoughtful person, as I guessed he would, watching his little face sometimes. Do be guided by your impressions of the school as to whether it is best for him. There is a crude tradition in the 'best' schools to 'toughen' a boy, with teachers turning a conservative and blind eye to the behaviour of boys to one another, – a British blind eye. For all such traditions – suited to the general mass – I have the strongest suspicion. The values are false. That does not mean the school in S.R. necessarily carries on the tradition. Probably not. Much depends on the knowledge and broad-mindedness of the teachers. Did you find his local school poor in teaching, and is he encountering companions with all too much of the Rhodesian attitude to things? Yet I would have said that your home influence and the encouragement of all that expansion of knowledge and interest through books, etc. would have made up for the deficiencies of the school. John and Muriel must be faced with the same problem for Ivan.

My dear, Daddy and I feel you should have the transport paid from the account controlled by the lawyer. I'll write to him. It would be a poor kind of 'present' if you had to pay all that for transport of goods. I mentioned last time – what would you like as a special gift? This can be it if you like. And oh, you didn't need to enumerate the stuff at that auction. I feared that after I had expressed my sadness that you would misconstrue my concern. It was purely a sentimental regret.

It's very thoughtful of you trying to get Mr E. to look after our stuff. I'm sure he won't, because his partner won't. Have you any idea how much it costs per month? I bring the matter up to Daddy and his answer is 'I don't know.' Life has been simple for him. Now in such a situation, his habit of not looking ahead is painful. Leave him in peace, as he was in Harvard and Toronto, and now reading here in Doreen's and Michael's home – and all is well. I'm afraid I'm in the opposite state of mind. Going to Toronto for half a year complicates the situation very much, <u>if</u> it comes through, because it delays the decision of where to settle. It cannot long be with Doreen. It's not fair on them. I cannot bear readily the English climate. I would like Nairobi, if we could get there. That's why we find it impossible, even now, to decide where to send the stuff. From your home to somewhere else in Africa would be extremely expensive. To bring stuff here and then back to Africa, likewise. I persuaded Jim yesterday at last to <u>write to Mr E</u>. He has not done so for months, though he already sent him records for himself and him! We'll wait at least for his reply. Let us know at once if he replies to you. Jim thinks, by the way, that he took the microscope over to Mr E. to examine his gramophone needle. Did you mention it to him, by any chance?

I wonder if Peter will dip into the Encyclopaedia B! What have they had for Xmas? I left an attractive small book on the Middle Ages at E.Z's. Did you take it for anyone? How I miss you all. I cannot bear an idle existence. I'm kept very busy as it is, writing letters in connection with our friends in Dar. Prof. Gwen Carter (U.S.A.) has asked me to make a complete file of all the literature of the All-Africa Convention etc. in S.A. This means quite a lot of work. I'm also 'brushing up' my French. I had been in communication with Prof. Carter (who knows S.R. and his wife, our friends in Boston) in U.S.A. Then she went specially to see T. and Jane when in Swaziland and had long discussions with them. She wrote to me a few weeks ago asking for these lists. She wants T. to write. She has written (among other books on Africa) *The Politics of Inequality*, on S.A. since 1948. She has asked me to meet her while in London. I have quite a friend in Fenner Brockway, M.P., who is trying to get a passport for T. He has proved most friendly and kind. But all in all, I don't do nearly enough work. Helping Doreen is only incidental.

We have had such a day of little present giving! Slippers for Daddy, a pen for me; a dictionary for Michael! Books and toys for the children. You know, this is most unusual for us. How has it been with you all? Give our love to Muriel and John. And to your Col. and Collie and Peter. [*in the margin:* And much to you

Your Mummy.

What is the name of the school in Bulawayo? I'm just over-anxious for Collie. I know you're doing what you feel is best.]

Dora Taylor's life and letters after 1963

Differences between Dora and Jim troubled her as their exile began, although she remained affectionately respectful and loyal to his wishes. She did not want to leave Africa, but he did; he took the loss of 'Kintayre' with equanimity, but she could not; she needed to know what the future would bring, particularly if they would return to Africa, but Jim did not plan ahead, preferring to live 'day by day' as she puts it. She tried to come to terms with their differences in temperament, sometimes by adopting Jim's sentiments. For example, when she writes in letter 17 that 'one wonders why we accumulate "worldly goods" at all' she is echoing Jim whose attitude was (as he wrote to Sheila in October 1963) that 'Worldly goods don't mean an awful lot to me and I've been without a lot of my treasured possession for a long time now', but her letters reveal that the severance remained painful.

When it looked as though Jim would indeed get the opportunity for research in Toronto that he wanted, Dora's reluctance to return to North America was shaped by her own dread of the extreme loneliness that she had already experienced there. Her desire to go to somewhere in Africa (she thought that Zambia or Kenya were possibilities) had a practical as well as an emotional source: other NEUM leaders, particularly I B Tabata and Jane Gool, had, as she reports in letter 6, successfully escaped from South Africa and she could now hope to work directly with them once again.

Loneliness was a near-pathological experience for Dora, and her letters after 1963 indicate that her efforts to grapple with it are still mixed with memories of the home that she has lost, the place that was made meaningful by her writing and political work as well as her family obligations. In early 1965 she writes to Sheila:

> You know, don't you, that we live through others, or die. If I could not exchange even words and thoughts with you, if you did not love me or understand me at all, part of me, the living part, would die. So is it with the devotion I give to what I believe in and the work and thought I constantly give to it. It is literally a way of life. Not 'happy' because too much suffering is involved, but because one gives the best of which one is capable it is a source of life. Likewise Daddy, constantly evolving his thoughts on his researches – well, he is happy. We are two dedicated, but lonely people. True, he meets his colleagues and talks with them everyday, while I – I work in my own way – and talk to you all in far distant Zambia.

In the 1963 letters, Dora's loss brings on poignant thoughts of death, as when she writes 'I must not lament [...] when others in S. Africa are suffering far greater pain. But it does make me think of death' (letter 13). Two years later, the link between her loss and dying is still leaving its traces, as when she asserts that 'we live through others, or die', but now she begins to hope that work, the 'source of life', will once again be available to her through the NEUM. Given this prospect, the immediate question of where their possessions should be stored becomes part of her emotional need to return to Africa. Once again, private domestic matters, personal psychology and public political options are inextricable in her daily life and thoughts.

In March 1964 Jim went to Canada to take up the research post he had been offered at the Defence Research Medical Laboratories in Toronto and, after visits to England and Zambia, Dora followed him. Once again, Dora's loneliness threatened to overwhelm her. She writes in September 1964:

> Can you picture me alone all day in a big impersonal city, in a room in a huge hotel and now in a little 2-roomed flat looking out on a wall and with the sound of cars swishing along the road every second [...] As Daddy lives in the lab, it isn't human [...] It is a terrible loneliness. Daddy realises it too. He says financially we can manage – I mean for me to visit Africa. But that does not remove

the problem of leaving him. Best of all is his happy condition of work, and his 'chief' so friendly. But at what a price for me. I see no simple solution. I break my heart every day [...]

I am a sentimental being and yet feel that my feelings have no right to exist. And they are desperate feelings. I check them (I try) by remembering what young Neville [Alexander] must be suffering on Robben Island, for example, or Mabel K. with one month in solitary confinement without trial, without charge and released without knowing what she had been guilty of. T. and others are in Lusaka and I know I could be the 'secretary' as of old. At present I feel shocked at my uselessness, shocked at having so little opportunity to be normal and meeting other human beings. A big city is absolutely ruthless.

Dora tries the familiar remedy of checking her personal misery by thinking of others worse off than herself; at other times she lifts her attention to world affairs so as to see her personal life from a larger, more analytical perspective. In a letter of October 1964 she comments on the political changes in Zambia and the labour disturbances with which Colin has had to cope on the mine, but is evidently still dealing with her own loss:

> my thoughts are on the change-over in Zambia and my heart goes out to Colin in the labour difficulties he is encountering in increasing difficulty. But there is no one person or persons to 'blame'. We are all at the centre of mighty forces that produced the 1st and 2nd world war with all its colossal destruction and the consequent upheavals ever since, all over the world. The change over in the Congo, for ex. is fraught with turmoil precisely because of the vast mineral wealth involved which the U.S. wants to control under cloak of U.N.O. Belgium and England up to now had the huge profits, but the U.S. wants a share. The turmoil there is not because the African is different from those in, say, Ghana. There, vast wealth was not at stake. The U.S. is controlling Angola too, where mineral potentialities are being explored. All this is far too brief to be at all adequate. All I know is, we as individuals are part of the big problems of transition. Our losing our home in S.A. is part of that. I try to be 'brave' by cherishing what is dear – you and the children.

Six months later, her circumstances have changed somewhat and Dora feels able to hint to Sheila that she has in fact found a fulfilling task. The seeds of what would unfold are evident in letter 6 where she recounts the escape of Tabata's party with the help of Amnesty and her own 'small miracle' which enabled her to contribute to the funds needed for their flight. From that moment, a web of contacts comes into play: her scholarly contact with Professor Gwendolen Carter; her work with Amnesty International in helping Tabata's group escape from South Africa; and her addressing the [Neville] Alexander Defence Committee (ADC). In April 1965 Dora reports that she is going to New York to speak to the ADC which has 'succeeded in getting the subject [of Neville Alexander who is back in solitary confinement on Robben Island] taken up at UNO.' A month later she indicates that her departure from North America may be delayed, but does not tell Sheila why, except to say that the ADC has agreed to 'extend its work to include our folk [...] They were moved by my eloquent story of the long political struggle and deeply impressed by T's writing, some of which they wish to publish.' To assist the publishing project, she has been asked to provide a summary of Tabata's *Education for Barbarism*. Then Dora allows herself to admit what must have been a painful irony for her: 'So I have been of more assistance to them all out of Africa than in it.'

While Dora was delaying her return to England, Sheila's third child was born in Zambia in September 1965. It would have been a momentous event for a devoted mother and grandmother, but Dora, despite a telegram suggesting that she go to Zambia, confines herself to a letter in order to convey the joy that she and Jim feel. In it she asks whether the suggestion that she should come 'was ... because of my [earlier] letters?' and she comments, 'I express feelings too much, I'm afraid, and then I regret that I hurt others by expressing too much, because then I take heart again and make myself very busy.' Her self-criticism occludes exactly what it is that has enabled her to 'take heart' this time, but she does allow herself to say that 'there is something I've undertaken to do which will hold me actually in the U.S. a bit, when Jim is in England. But I am coming to Africa before I'm much older. On this Jim has agreed.' Her caution comes from habits of secrecy that she had learned as an activist in South Africa, and so she does not even hint to Sheila that she has been working with the ADC to arrange a lecture tour of the US for I B Tabata. The other story that Dora's letters do not tell at this time, probably because she was so profoundly diffident about her novel-writing, is that she had been submitting scripts of *Rage of Life* to publishers in London, without success.

Only in an October letter, from New York, when all arrangements have been concluded and Tabata has safely reached the US, does Dora give Sheila a full account of what will continue to keep her away from Africa. Her letter is worth quoting at length for its characteristic note in which pleasure in her own achievements in serving the political interests of African people is tempered by her diffidence and her sense of family obligations:

> It is not at all as I thought it would happen, and certainly not at this time. Yet it is all due to my efforts. I told you months ago about my work on behalf of the <u>A</u>lexander <u>D</u>efence <u>C</u>ommittee, branches of which are in W Germany, England, Norway, US and now in Canada. This is to help the 11 young ones and their dependents who were seized along with Neville Alexander in 1963. Well, my eloquence to a group here in May (remember) so moved them that they have undertaken an enormous venture, a tour of some of the big cities and universities of the US by none other than T. I never, never thought it would come to pass, but he was granted a visa to tour and lecture under the auspices of the ADC. We have most devoted friends here (as a result of my May visit) who waited till the winter university term should begin. Of course it is now completely out of my hands. But they are so impressed by T's writings and now by his presence that not only have they made elaborate preparations for meetings across the country, but they want to publish all he has written. At a reception given for him, publishers, professors, members of African embassies etc., attended and he is interviewed for radio etc., a rather overwhelming experience altogether. If only it had not come to fruition right now when I dreamed of flying to Africa. But unfortunately my presence is needed, for in the very little spare time, T is extending his book *The Awakening of*

a People. You know from of old how much I can help with this [....] I am going to Boston to look up files in the big libraries for the book. Also, at the big libraries here. I can hear you scolding me sadly. Indeed I would have wished it to happen at any other time, but once having set a machinery in motion, I ceased to have control over it. T. flew via Accra (to discuss there with ministers etc.) and stopped a night in London. Great was the rejoicing in Hemel [Doreen's home], something Jim had been hoping for but not expecting, for it was all finalised after he left for England. That is why I didn't find it possible to speak or write about it to anyone [...] But, Sheila, I do think and hope you will understand. It is a rare and unexpected thing to happen and is actually the fruit of my labours. It may not prove easy or plain sailing, but there is a certain 'climate' here today that makes many people eager to hear an authentic voice from Africa.

Tabata's lecture tour covered over 20 cities and many universities and was a great success, although, as Dora began to note in her letters, it was not likely to bring in the funds that the Unity Movement needed for its work in exile.[19] Elated by Tabata's success, Dora is also satisfied with the work for him that she is able to do in Gwendolen Carter's collection of material at North-Western University, and in other libraries in the region. In her last letter of 1965, Dora tells Sheila that Jim's temporary appointment in Toronto has come to an end and that they are preparing to return to England. The closing of this chapter of her life is not as painful for Dora as was the loss of 'Kintayre', and her tone remains buoyant as she comments, 'It is easy to fold up our tiny domain here'.

Dora's movements during the next year, 1966, are determined mostly by the Unity Movement's effort to gain international recognition and by the fresh work on *Awakening* that she has undertaken with I B Tabata. He travels frequently between Europe (including Hemel Hempstead) and Lusaka, where he is now based. In July Dora is in Zambia again, visiting Sheila and Muriel and their

---

19 After Nkruhmah was deposed in a military coup in Ghana in 1966, the Unity Movement again found itself without a financial backer, and still without recognition at the Organisation of African Unity.

families, and while there undertakes for a brief time her old role of secretary to the Unity Movement. But when the group of exiles is beset by internal strife, her hopes of a more permanent occupation in Zambia come to nothing and by November, Dora, after a noisy send off from Lusaka, is back in England. There she finds that Jim is not well, he is 'feeling physical effects of sclerosis, but is saying nothing'. Dora's political work is now confined to an attempt to run a branch of the Unity Movement in Britain.

Dora and Jim built a comfortable flat attached to Doreen's house for themselves and there they lived for the rest of their lives. Jim died first and Dora a couple of years later, in 1976. Although her life had stabilised, and she remained energetically devoted to family and the cause of justice and liberty, she did not ever regain the centred and productive life that had disappeared with her home in Cape Town.

Bessie Head
(1937–1986)

Bessie Head's life and writing

When Bessie Head left South Africa for Botswana in 1964, letters became her lifeline. She had experienced rejection in South Africa and now she found herself a stateless, friendless refugee in her new world. With only the barest official recognition of her presence, and knowing no one in her new country, she had to rely on the exchange of letters for confirmation of her identity and her right to exist. She had, as she thought, no living relatives and so it was friends who supplied the everyday exchanges which mattered so greatly in her new circumstances. Once settled in Botswana, Bessie's life continued to be stormy and her letters give a moving insight into the means by which her daily life went on, as it had to, amidst crises. The creative as well as the destructive aspects of one particular crisis, her visionary experiences and her intermittent mental breakdown, are a powerful presence in the letters that she wrote to Paddy Kitchen.

Letters took on a practical as well as psychological purpose. Some written before those published here are addressed to the friends who had helped her leave South Africa, thanking them for their guidance and assistance and reporting on her experiences in the new context of Botswana (Vigne 1991; Cullinan 2005).[20] Soon after her arrival, it became clear to Bessie that she would have to try to support herself and her young son by writing. She had begun to have stories and articles published while still in South Africa, and so her letters to newer friends who might assist her also became an important feature of her epistolary lifeline. Besides writing, Bessie Head was an avid reader and a perceptive analyst of her world. Gradually, as

---

20 A comprehensive selection from Head's other correspondence is forthcoming from Africa World Press, edited by Linda-Susan Beard.

she established herself as an intellectual, letters became the means by which she achieved the vigorous exchange of ideas that she needed. Once her first novel, *When Rain Clouds Gather*, was published in 1969, she found abundant opportunity for this kind of exchange for the number and range of her correspondents grew rapidly. It has been estimated that at the height of her activity, Bessie was corresponding with some thirty people in various countries of the world (Eilersen 1990: 61). Her letters show her capacity to establish rapid rapport with people, some of whom she had not met and would never meet.

As she established herself as a writer, letters also became a kind of notebook for Bessie, and letter 67, where she questions Paddy Kitchen about a comment made 14 years earlier, makes it clear that she had an excellent memory for the details of her friends' letters as well as her own, and that she probably re-read them frequently. Her exploration of ideas in her letters had to be intuitively and carefully managed. When she tells Paddy Kitchen that one of her friends, Randolph Vigne, did not care for the kind of reflections on deities that she was sending to Paddy (letter 26), it is evident that she took care to identify and respect which of her correspondents would be responsive to each aspect of her many ideas, experiences and speculations, and explored these appropriately in her missives to them. This process was a kind of practice run for her fiction and became particularly valuable to her when she attempted, in her letters to Paddy Kitchen and others, to bring order to her visionary inner life while writing the novel she would call *A Question of Power*.

Bringing order to her papers was a somewhat easier task and by the time she began writing to Paddy Kitchen in 1969, Bessie, realising the value that letters would hold for her, had started a filing system for her letters, those received as well as those she sent, and for her other papers. She sustained this orderliness throughout her life so that, at her death in 1986, her friends in Serowe found an astonishingly full and invaluable record of her intellectual and emotional life. One of her Danish friends, Maria Rytter, has recorded that after Bessie's death she found boxes of papers under the bed when she went to help tidy her little house, and she recounts the moving of these to what eventually became the collection of Bessie Head Papers in the

Khama III Memorial Museum in Serowe (Rytter 2008: 3–9). There the letters were filed and catalogued by another of Bessie's Danish friends, Ruth Forchhammer. It is thanks to this work of preserving one of the most extraordinary literary archives in the region that further publication of some of these letters is now possible.

Early life

Bessie Head never knew her parents. As she says in the first letter here, she was educated in an orphanage after having lived until she was 12 with a foster family. Her mother was white and her father black, a combination which was officially taboo under apartheid. But the story that Bessie herself believed about her origins, which she touches on in this letter and tells more fully in *A Question of Power*, is not quite what subsequent research has revealed.

What is now known of Bessie's early life is recounted with a delicate empathy in the biography, *Thunder Behind Her Ears*, by Gillian Stead Eilersen. Bessie's birth mother had had a breakdown which contributed to the end of her marriage, and had already been hospitalised when she conceived her mixed-race child. The father's identity is still not known, but some years after Bessie's death the Birch family, her mother's siblings, did come forward to acknowledge that they were related (Birch 1995). Nellie Heathcote, the foster mother whom Bessie loved and had believed was her birth mother, lived in Pietermaritzburg where Bessie was born. Mrs Heathcote struggled to support her family after her husband died, so much so that a local welfare officer decided that Bessie should be sent to the mission orphanage and school that she mentions in her letter. This was St Monica's Home, an Anglican establishment in Durban, where Bessie would spend the next six years of her life. About 18 months after her arrival, when Bessie was expecting to go home for the holidays, she was abruptly told by the school principal that she could not do so, that her birth mother had been insane, and that her origins were 'a horror' – as Bessie put it in a piece that she wrote for Dulan Barber, Paddy Kitchen's husband – and would set her apart throughout her life (Head 1975: 108). As Eilersen comments, 'this gruesome treatment of a child, even by the standards of South

African society, is puzzling' (2007: 25). The racism reflected in the missionary's remarks was commonplace in South Africa in the 1950s, but her cruelty to Bessie was extreme and would help explain why Bessie reacted so strongly to the prejudice against mixed-race people that she and her own child, Howard, encountered later in Botswana, and why, having been 'cut adrift from the only moorings she had known' (Eilersen 2007: 25), the first thing she did in Serowe when she could afford it was to build a little home of her own for herself and her two-year-old child, Howard.

When Bessie Head turned 16 she decided to pursue a further two years' training as an elementary school teacher and to stay on at St Monica's. At that time the school came under the direction of Margaret Cadmore, who is depicted by name and with admiration in Bessie's second novel, *Maru*. In 1956 she took up a teaching post in Clairwood, Durban and in her spare time continued to read avidly. She became interested in Hinduism and, although she later rejected all religions, its influence is evident in aspects of her thinking on godly and god-like creation and destruction (see letters 38, 40 and 44). After 18 months Bessie resigned from teaching, determined to find a new career as a reporter in Cape Town. She was successful, being taken on for three months as a freelance reporter by *Golden City Post* and then appointed to the permanent staff; some of her experiences as a budding writer are present in her posthumously published but first-written novella, *The Cardinals*.

When she moved to Johannesburg, Bessie was employed at *Home Post*, a weekend supplement to *Golden City Post*. Among her tasks was the editing of the girlie romances published in each issue; another rather different one was the writing of two popular weekly columns, one for children and the other for teenagers. The latter, which had started off as an advice column for the love-lorn teens was modified by Bessie into an exchange of less stereotypical ideas. She began it with the jaunty salutation, 'Hiya Teenagers'. Its extroverted cheerfulness established the relation Bessie wanted with her readers and it seems to have worked well, for many young people wrote back to her. But this jauntiness has a forlorn echo a decade later when she greets Paddy with 'Hi-ya Paddy' in letter 58. This was the last letter she would write to Paddy during her breakdown and it inaugurated a six-year silence which she imposed in order to try to recover from the mental turmoil of 1974 and from what had seemed to her a patronising rejection of *A Question of Power* by her literary agent and her publisher.

Although it had its inner storms, life as a school pupil and trainee teacher had been relatively sheltered for Bessie. She had witnessed the impact on Nellie Heathcote's household of the Group Areas Act (they had to move once their suburb was set aside for Indian people), but it was not until she became a court-reporter in Cape Town and later witnessed political resistance in Johannesburg that she really felt herself caught up in the public, political turbulence of the 1950s. During the Anti-Pass Laws campaign, in which she was a peripheral participant, Bessie joined the Pan-African Congress and, although she swiftly withdrew from party politics, she retained a life-long admiration for the party leader, Robert Sobukwe. It was during this time that Bessie's volatility developed into periods of elation followed by sharp depression, that the many sides of her nature came into collision, and that despair seems to have led to an attempt at suicide (Eilersen 2007: 54). After a time in hospital, Bessie returned to Cape Town where she again worked on *Golden City Post*, but this was short-lived.

She also resumed her interest in left-wing political debate and in these circles met Randolph Vigne, who would later publish much of her writing in his magazine, *The New African*, and would be, largely through his letters, a mentor.[21] At this time Bessie wrote a cyclostyled news-sheet featuring local issues and the absurdities of the apartheid system. She called it *The Citizen* and sold it wherever she could. One of her places was the Stakesby Lewis Hostel in central Cape Town to which people from many parts of South Africa came for lodging.[22] There she met Harold Head, newly arrived from Pretoria. A few weeks later they married and lived in rooms in District Six. Then Harold took a reporting job with *Evening Post* in Port Elizabeth and

---

21 When Vigne left South Africa, he continued to edit and publish *The New African* from London. In letter 24, Bessie suggested a meeting between him, his wife and Paddy Kitchen and her husband, Dulan Barber.
22 For example, I B Tabata, the great friend and colleague of Dora Taylor, lived there for several years in the 1940s.

the family followed him. Howard was born in May 1962 (see letter 22 where Bessie explains her choice of name for her son). Not long after, when Harold was offered another job back in Cape Town, Bessie moved again but by now she seems to have suffered a feeling of growing instability in her life. She has recorded that when their Port Elizabeth friend Dennis Brutus was arrested and later imprisoned on Robben Island she felt such losses personally as well as politically (Head 1963).[23] The widespread arrests also had a drastic impact on the lives of Lilian Ngoyi and Dora Taylor, and Eilersen suggests that these were what contributed to Bessie's feeling that her life was a failure. It also led to her decision to leave Harold, and, presumably because she had nowhere else to live, to go to her mother-in-law in Atteridgeville, outside Pretoria (Eilersen 2007: 69).

This move proved stormy too, and by early 1964 Bessie was desperate to get away. She needed a job to support herself and Howard, and had seen an advertisement for teachers in Botswana (then Bechuanaland). She applied for a job and for a passport. When the South African authorities refused the passport, she appealed for help to Patrick Cullinan and his wife Wendy. Her only recourse was to take an exit permit which meant that she could never return to South Africa. By early March she had accepted a post in Serowe (having had to look on a map to find out where it was) and, a few months before Howard's second birthday, they left.

Although Bessie's immediate reasons for leaving South Africa lay in a blend of personal and political disappointments, and although her escape was precipitous, she also believed that her move was a positive one. She hoped to fulfil the belief she had in Africa's age-old tranquillity and its capacity to provide her with a place where she could dream freely and profoundly. Years later, when she looked back on her journey, she wrote that having 'survived precariously, without a sense of roots, without a sense of history' in the slums of South Africa, she knew that she needed 'an eternal and continuous

---

[23] A poet and political activist, Dennis Brutus was imprisoned on Robben Island from 1964–65 and then placed under house arrest. He went into exile in 1966 and was president of the South African Non-Racial Olympic Committee, which would achieve South Africa's exclusion from international competition. He returned in 1991 and died in 2009.

world against which to work out [her] preoccupations [...] a deep commitment to people, an involvement in questions of poverty and exploitation and a commitment to illuminating the future for younger generations'. Although much personal turmoil followed her move to Botswana, Bessie Head felt that she had found what she wanted. She epitomised the sense of stability that she found in a timeless scene of a 'yard where a tall slender woman pounded corn in a stamping block with a long wooden pestle, her bare feet partly buried in a growth of summer grass'. She records turning away from that yard to gaze where 'the land lay in an eternal, peaceful sleep, the distant horizon hazy and shrouded in the mists of the earth' and thinking that 'the dwelling places of all the tribes had been, for ages and ages, just such small, self-contained worlds, busy with the everyday round of living' (Head 1984: 278–79). It was a version of this regulated, self-contained, everyday world that Bessie Head was able to bring to life for herself when she built the house she called 'Rain Clouds'. Her description of its building (letters 20 and 21) captures some of the rapture she felt when in touch with the dreaming land, and her account of seeing the Builders' Brigade pupils at work conveys her recognition that her desire to illuminate a 'future for younger generations' could indeed find practical fulfilment.

The early years in Botswana were not easy. Her teaching job in Serowe ended in a disastrous confrontation between her and the headmaster. Then, at the home of Patrick van Rensburg, the founder of the Swaneng Hill School (letter 21),[24] she met an agriculturalist called Vernon Gibberd who was running a government-owned experimental farm at Radisele, south of Serowe. She was given permission to work and live on the farm. Although her stay there lasted only a few months, what she learned about raising crops and vegetables in a drought-prone country provided her practical skills

---

24 After Van Rensburg had left the South African diplomatic service and his country in order to combat apartheid, he and his wife settled in Botswana and asked for permission to 'start a secondary school where it was most needed. The Bamangwato Tribal Administration granted him a plot of land eight kilometres outside Serowe' (Eilersen 2007: 84). Head outlines the distinctive features of the school he founded there (letter 21). Vernon Gibberd was an agriculturalist from England who was 'convinced that the disadvantages of drought and poor soil could be counteracted scientifically' (Eilersen 2007: 95–96).

which she used for the rest of her life as well as with much of her material for her first novel, *When Rain Clouds Gather*, including the figure of an agricultural officer whom she called Gilbert Balfour.

It was the appearance of one of the first short pieces that Bessie Head published from Botswana, 'The Woman from America' in the *New Statesman* in August 1966, which opened the way to her first novel. She had moved to Francistown, one of Botswana's official gathering towns for refugees, when a letter from an editor at the American publishing firm of Simon & Schuster reached her. On the strength of the *New Statesman* piece, Jean Highland invited her to submit a novel and, when Bessie mentioned her lack of resources, arranged for her to receive writing paper and a small advance. By this time, Bessie had also met the British novelist Naomi Mitchison who was deeply attached to Botswana, and the Bakgatla people in particular, as well as knowledgeable about crop production. They embarked on a lively correspondence, which rested on two topics that also became central in Bessie's letters to Paddy Kitchen – gardening and writing.

Working closely with her editors, Bessie completed the first draft of her novel in just under a year (Eilersen 2007: 110). She wrote and lived in a 'humble two-roomed wooden cottage [...] with corrugated-iron roof and large veranda. It lay in the sandy no-man's-land between the black township and Francistown [... It] was supposed to be haunted [... but,] quite unaffected [Bessie began to collect] some pieces of furniture and basic utensils [in order to] make a home for herself and Howard' (Eilersen 2007: 104–05). Published in early 1969, *When Rain Clouds Gather* was an instant success, especially in the United States, and it was the subsequent sale of the paperback rights to this novel that gave her sufficient money to build the three-roomed house in Serowe where she would live for the rest of her life. But this did not happen until further disruptions had propelled her out of Francistown back to Serowe, and she had written her second novel, *Maru*.

The trouble in Francistown arose over Howard who was being bullied at school and told that he was not a real Motswana but a 'coloured'. He was a well-integrated child who grew up speaking

Setswana but was nevertheless rejected by some children. Upset by their racial taunts, Bessie took him out of school and turned her thoughts to Swaneng Hill School where he was already known and socially accepted and where she knew he would get a good education. Patrick van Rensburg agreed that Howard could attend the primary school and at the beginning of 1969, just days after holding an advance copy of her first published novel in her hands, Bessie returned to Serowe. It was not an easy return, for many rumours, particularly about her sources of money, were circulating. This was because neither the refugee allowance nor the United Nations grant to study agriculture that she received were familiar resources to the villagers, and many people assumed that she had a hidden lover who supported her. She was publicly humiliated on occasion, and compelled to leave the house she had borrowed. Distress led to Bessie's first breakdown and brief hospitalisation but, curiously, because her collapse seemed to the villagers to demonstrate that she was crazy rather than 'loose-living' (Eilersen 2007: 130), a much greater tolerance, but still not a wide acceptance of her, followed. Then she was allowed to rent a small, traditionally built, round hut in the Sebina ward of Serowe and there she lived with Howard while writing *Maru*.

The letters to Paddy Kitchen
When Rain Clouds Gather was published in New York in March 1969 and in London two months later. Reviewers were enthusiastic and Bessie began corresponding with several new friends as a result. Among them was Paddy Kitchen, a London-based novelist and reviewer, who had written about this unusual novel for *Tribune* under the title 'The Way to a New World' (Eilersen 2007: 131–32). Paddy came from a wealthy family located just outside London; she was offered a place at Cambridge University having been a brilliant pupil at school. She decided, instead, on a secretarial course which would prove fortunate as it enabled her to fend for herself when her father lost his money. She worked for an advertising agency and, in the evenings, as a hat-check girl at an existentialist nightclub – her step into bohemian circles in London. After work on a magazine,

she became personal assistant to an architect and then to Robin Darwin at the Royal College of Art. These milieus provided some of the settings for her early novels which included *Lying-In* (1965), the novel about which Bessie asks several questions in letter 43. At the Royal College Paddy met the Guyanese painter Frank Bowling whom she married in 1960. They had a son, Dan. Their house in Clapham was known for its wonderful, overgrown garden for she was, as an obituary in the *Guardian* puts it, 'as sympathetic with plants as with people' (12 December 2005). When she divorced Bowling, she lived with and later married Dulan Barber, a thriller-writer and editor. She bought a 'dilapidated thatched cottage' in the Northamptonshire village of Barnwell where she created another magical garden and about which she later wrote a book called simply *Barnwell* (1985). It is in the line of social history in Ronald Blythe's *Akenfield* and Bessie Head's *Serowe: Village of the Rain Wind*. She successfully combined fiction with journalism and biography, was a literary critic and, later in life, the art critic for *Country Life*. She died in 2005, having been a life-long socialist.

As a result of her review of *Rain Clouds*, Paddy was asked by the *Times Educational Supplement* to interview by post the unknown writer from Africa, and so began a correspondence that would last, apart from one break, for the rest of Bessie's life. Paddy's article appeared in September 1970, about a year after their letters began. It was one of the first published accounts of this extraordinary woman, her appealing subject matter and distinctive ideas to reach a British readership.

Bessie's first few letters have been lost,[25] but the earliest ones here show the verve and trust with which she responded to the idea of being interviewed by post, and their opening exchanges about 'wizards' were clearly fun for both writers. When Bessie's letter opens, 'It all depends on the wizard, of course!', she is laughing at Paddy's

---

25 In the published interview, Paddy Kitchen quotes the opening lines of the first letter that Bessie wrote to her: 'Thank you for your letter of August 27th. The thing with me is that I have no husband at the moment, therefore I have a lot to say for myself. If I were so fortunate to have a husband, be in love, I should forget all about the world and spend a great deal of time kissing. Knowing my nature, the gods condemned me to a long life of celibacy in order that the world might progress. It's not much to my liking' (Kitchen 1970: 36).

earlier response: 'sleeping with wizards in the night-time' would be 'enchanting – in the best sense of the word!' which she quotes in letter 25. But Bessie also had to be scrupulously honest about herself and so, again in letter 25, she warns Paddy that their game is one she could take only so far, even within the playful possibilities of letter-writing.

The major topics of their letters were established rapidly: Bessie's new house; her own garden and the Boiteko vegetable garden (a communal project for the villagers that was near her house); her writing and reading; and her child. She and Paddy began corresponding just as the building of Bessie's little house was nearing completion, and her account of it fills her letters with joy. But, while her house gave her the first anchor in life over which she had some control, Bessie did not want 'Rain Clouds' to be simply a refuge, and particularly not a fortress.

Cherished objects were important to Bessie but she cared about them for the memories of people with which they were imbued, not because they had monetary value. The anguish that Dora Taylor expressed when her household goods were sold had a similar source. They also shared a sense that besides one's family, friends were what gave character to a home – particularly those who came in order to share their studies and writing. Bessie said that the people who had worked on her house 'added a blessing to it' and that she wanted her house to be the kind of place where 'the most lovely people on earth' would 'enter' (letter 21). As a writer, she also wanted her home to allow her to continue to be 'the universe' rather than being a house that would reproduce 'family life with all its narrowness'. In this spirit and at its best, the writing that she did in her house, the fiction just as much as her letters, expressed the unconstrained self of her imagination as well as being a means of reaching out to others.

Gardening was one of the means through which Bessie was able to sustain her daily domestic life amidst its storms. She put it under the rubric of 'practical matters' (letter 26), but in writing of the plants and creatures of her gardens she was also presenting her psyche. Desiree Lewis points to 'Head's linking of the everyday, the ordinary, the 'profane', with universal experiences, politics and spirituality' and of 'the moral and spiritual import of what conventionally seemed only personal or small, silent and marginal' (2007: 84). When Bessie reports (letter 37) her discovery of a spinach-beet (for which Paddy had sent her the seeds) that was 'still green and clinging to life in the near desert which is my garden at present', Bessie is transmitting a metaphor for her own life at that moment. The plant had gone unwatered for nine months; Bessie herself had recently returned from a lengthy stay in hospital after a breakdown. She and the plant are, against the odds, surviving.

Gardening, like the weather, can be one of those anodyne topics which strangers find safe when they first correspond, but this was not Bessie's approach to letter-writing and nor was it her attitude to gardening. In the Boiteko project and through her own seedling nursery, gardening became a practical way of entering and supporting her new community. From her first account, she makes central the friendships that gardening afforded her, an outsider, with the village people as she records her pleasure in feeding those who had worked with her transplanting onion seedlings (letter 22). This link between cooking, nutrition and gardening is strong from the start. Her technical interest in vegetables and herbs, which began at Radisele with an introduction to the science of crop yields, informs her accounts of which kinds of vegetables survived Serowe's frequent droughts. But her systematic practicality is always linked with her idealism, as is evident in the enthusiasm with which she told Paddy about the self-help gardening project. High on her list of its benefits was the dignity it brought to people engaged in communal work and trade (as with the building of her house), and she loved the quiet atmosphere of the Boiteko garden where women undertook voluntary work as equals. Her weather reports convey a similar combination of technical and psychic significance. For example, she evokes both the psychological effects of the failure of the rain clouds to deliver the promised rain, and the practical importance of what she herself has had to learn about horticulture in a region with a pattern of brief and unreliable rainfall (letter 43).

As vegetables were part of her interest in nutrition and the villagers' health, it was inevitable that she would have to engage in developing their taste for new varieties of food – getting them to accept, for example, that sweet peppers are a good source of Vitamin C (letter 26), or, in what proved a forlorn hope, encouraging them to grow cauliflowers. When she found that the Boiteko garden had become the centre of a new communal craft and trade centre, her delight is palpable (letter 38), as is her sorrow (letter 60) when, after a year away, she found that not only had her garden gone wild but all the projects that had grown up around the Boiteko garden had disappeared, leaving the buildings to the white ants.[26]

Her disappointment leads her into the only account in her letters to Paddy of her Serowe book which, she says, gave her pleasure because it recorded the 'genial and expansive' world she had known there. This is the book in which Paddy Kitchen is included in the dedication. In some ways this is a curious dedication. Paddy had been important to the writing of *A Question of Power*, and Bessie, saying that she had 'much to thank you for during this time of correspondence' had asked if she could dedicate it to Paddy (letter 44). But the confusions and delays around publication were so great that this intention seems to have been overlooked. So Bessie was probably making up for the omission in 1981 when *Serowe: Village of the Rain Wind* came out. From another angle, the dedication was apposite in that Giles Gordon had earlier discussed the idea with Paddy (letter 58), and it was prophetic in that Paddy Kitchen, partly inspired by Bessie's writing, would also write a socio-historical study of a village.

Although Bessie resisted the label 'feminist' for her writing, protesting and chuckling over the student who wanted to apply it to her work (letters 65–69), she gives a strongly gendered account of garden work. When she reflects on her difficulties in organising and giving instructions to men in the Boiteko garden, she contrasts their behaviour with the 'free and easy' way in which women could cooperate (letter 26). She found the instruction needed by women so 'natural and effortless' for her to give that she was led into a generalisation which at other times she might have qualified. She

---

26 Serowe's expansion in recent years has meant that what was the Boiteko garden has disappeared under the car park of a shopping centre.

observed that while women carry out 'the basic show of how the world runs on oiled wheels' because they have both 'brains and [a] clear head', social mores require them to 'perform unobtrusively' without due recognition for what they do. The person in whom her judgement was most clearly embodied was Bosele Sianana, the 'particularly terrific woman' (letter 38) whose silent, regular companionship while working in the garden helped Bessie to steady herself, especially in times of crisis. It was this woman who, despite having had little formal education, had learned to speak English through talking to Bessie and who became so good a linguist that she could act as her interpreter when Bessie interviewed villagers for her *Serowe* book.[27]

Reports on gardening fade from her letters after 1980 (the year that she and Paddy met in London), partly because she was able to travel abroad much more once she had been granted Botswana citizenship and so had less time for gardening, partly because the research she did for her historical novel *A Bewitched Crossroad* took her to Gaborone for a long period, and partly because her worries about Howard's future once he had finished school began to loom large in her letters. But if gardening fades, Bessie's rapport with the natural world does not diminish, and she reports on matters like drought through the behaviours of birds rather than the details of her garden. She tells Paddy that they had been through 'a silent summer' in the absence of birds and that it was so hot and dry that even the 'insects could not come out of hibernation' (letter 71).

Bessie's letters do not ignore current affairs in Botswana or on the world stage. She has plenty to say about the aftermath of colonialism in Africa, the IRA bombs in Britain, her sympathy for the Jews in history, her interest in China, and, locally, what was happening now that a post-independence generation was in power. As she becomes more of a citizen of the world, which is not the same as her earlier wish to be universal, the distinctively personal flavour of the early letters fades a little. Thus she can move swiftly from her pleasure in finding buds on her guava tree, despite the lack of rain, to reporting

---

27 Bosele features as Kenosi in *A Question of Power*.

a scandal around murder and sexual escapades among civil servants in Gaborone (letter 71). The gossip leads her to reflect on what she sees as the 'dead, silent marriages' that were a 'disaster ... both in African custom and tradition as well as the stress of the colonial era'. While she says that she had handled the matter inadequately in her first novel, *When Rain Clouds Gather,* her judgement on dead marriages is one she writes with supreme effect into her short story 'The Collector of Treasures'.

In writing about writing, Bessie reveals herself to have been a very perceptive reader, and her comments often indicate the attentiveness she required of her own readers too. Her tastes were eclectic and, in the realm of fiction, what might be called highbrow: the Russian novelists Pasternak and Dostoyevsky, and the early hero of her literary life, D H Lawrence. But late in the correspondence she also reveals a delight in detective fiction (prompting Paddy to include Dulan Barber's books in one of her regular parcels) and, in a comment that would have been unusual at the time, says how much she loves discovering the local life implicit in recipe books from 'out of the way' places' (letter 78). In another example of her capacity to read below the line, she sends a horoscope for Marie Antoinette to Paddy advising her that if she can overlook the mumbo-jumbo she will find a very interesting portrait of the woman. The letters show that her love of music was also intense, if not as broad as her reading: Miriam Makeba, Odetta, Nancy Wilson, Oscar Peterson – musicians in the African-American line of jazz-blues. Paddy evidently shared these tastes and encouraged Bessie to appreciate new performers through the records that she sent from London. Like Bessie's Howard, Paddy's son, Dan, hoped to make a career in music (letter 62). While Paddy became a reputable art critic, easel-painting seems to have been one taste they did not share. This may have been simply for want of opportunity on Bessie's part, for her love of the Boiteko-project pottery made by Peter and Christine Hawes (letter 51) rests on a strong visual (and tactile) sense, as does her questioning the scene on the paperback cover of Paddy Kitchen's novel *A Fleshly School* (letter 23).

Bessie delighted in the criticism of her novels that Paddy and

Dulan Barber published (letter 43). In return, her own comments on her friends' writing are warm and perceptive, while they often have the selective focus of a craftsman. For example, in letter 40 she elects to comment on the musicality of the prose in *Lying-In* because it was a quality for which she strove in her own writing. When it comes to Chinua Achebe as a modern African writer, she turns her attention to the context of his fiction (letters 43 and 53). It is in her delight in great writing for children, however, that Bessie fully reveals how responsive and how sensitive her enthusiasm for the writing of others could be. This should be set against her disappointment over the general dullness of children's books that featured African children (letter 33): 'no fun, no veering, reeling imagination in fun and mischief and adventure'.[28] She took a robust delight in these qualities in the William books (in Alice's ability to control William's boyish assumption of superiority, for example), in Pooh's innocent egotism, and in the strange world of *Alice in Wonderland*. She and Howard lived those books as they read them together, and she extends their pleasure to Paddy when she types out long passages from the William books (letter 41) so that her friend too might howl with laughter.

Bessie Head was a wonderful short story writer, as some of the letters here indicate: the account of the Christmas picnic with chicken while the duck burnt at home (letter 42), or the account of how she found time to read Paddy's guide to the *Poet's London* (letter 62). This latter story, in which a back injury allowed her to skip to the front of the queue for a government water-tap as well as giving her an opportunity to read the book, is echoed in Bessie's later story of being able to read *Barnwell* 'amidst household tragedy again' (letter 74). In the later letter, she is more amused that an accident should, once again, allow her time to read her friend's book than she is concerned by her injury. But detachment was not always present, especially not when her psyche was under attack. Bessie had had to fight too hard to survive through her writing to tolerate anyone threatening her interests – as with what she knew was the illegal

---

28 Bessie made some exception for Naomi Mitchison's *The Family at Ditlabeng*, which she sent to Paddy's son, Dan (letter 40).

publication of *Maru* in Zimbabwe (letters 79–82). Even less was she able to tolerate the initial rejection of *A Question of Power* by her agent and editor (letters 46 and 47). There were two points on which she was, understandably and rightly, very touchy: if she felt patronised as an African woman, and if she felt indulged or pitied or dismissed as a 'mad' woman. Hence her fury with her agent, Hilary Rubinstein, and her request to Paddy that she help in rescuing her manuscript (letter 46).

Bessie's letters to Paddy about the ideas in *A Question of Power* are among the most intense that she wrote as she tried to give order to the intricate weave of vision, fantasy and quotidian experience within which the clashes of the god-like characters are told.[29] As she explains (letter 40), Bessie began writing this novel as two separate stories, the part which she called 'Theophilus' was about the gods, while the other, 'Summer Flowers', became the story of the gardening done by her protagonist, Elizabeth. Head told some students who visited her with their lecturer: 'There're two sorts of persons in me. There's a practical person: I love the everyday world and the things that people do with their hands. Then there's somebody attracted by the mystery and riddle of life' (Gardner et al. 1989: 8). As the fictional work progressed, she felt she could not convey this double strand in herself in two separate stories and so she endeavoured to portray them more accurately as interwoven. Their exposition in her letters is often easier to follow than are events in the novel where matters are dramatised rather than explained, and where the protagonist, Elizabeth, is often left bewildered by her nightly visitations.

While her novel-writing enabled her to treat her nightly visitations as potentially enlightening, in daily life Bessie was not always able to do this. At times she feared that the evil she witnessed in her visions might be generated from within herself, and she feared that she was

---

[29] The terms for discussing Head's novel, and for the experience that she charted in it, are problematic. Bessie was hospitalised and treated for mental illness on more than one occasion and she draws on these episodes for her novel. But terms that come from western accounts of madness ('paranoia' and 'hallucination', for example) do not countenance or accommodate the creative effort and analysis that went into her writing, and, as Jacqueline Rose has argued, their use is 'precarious' (1994: 408) when the judgement (or diagnosis) is a cross-cultural one. For this reason, rather than hallucination, 'vision', 'visitation' and 'visionary' are the terms used here.

confusing her visions with events in the outside world. Later she realised that this applied particularly to her suspicion that people were plotting against her because she was regarded as 'filthy, tainted, a half-breed' (letter 31) and to her belief that a distinguished leader of Botswana had been murdered and that another had instigated the murder (letter 35). Because of her confusion, she felt compelled to ask Paddy to destroy her letters (letter 55); fortunately for us, Paddy sheltered within Bessie's permission to preserve the gardening letters and seems not to have destroyed any. Bessie's final, quiet but heartfelt, comment on her time of tribulation is that while she could not undo any harm she might have done, she 'longed not have lived it' (letter 59).

Although Bessie's letters to Paddy are strongly autobiographical, the time gaps between them and her selectiveness about what she wrote mean they do not cover every event of importance in her life. Because of the breaks during 1973–74, and the long silence, after her hospitalisation, that lasted until 1980, these letters do not record her gathering material for her Serowe book and the volume of short stories, *The Collector of Treasures*, that emerged from it. Nor do they cover her momentous decision not to leave Botswana. Thanks to a Norwegian doctor, Marit Kromberg, who had worked in Botswana, Bessie received 'a genuine offer to re-settle in Norway' which carried many advantages: 'a free plane ticket to Norway; a living allowance for eighteen months while she was adjusting to the society; the prospect of citizenship; social security; good, varied educational facilities for Howard and the chance that he could become wholly integrated into Norwegian society; much sympathetic support for her as a writer' (Eilersen 2007: 190). Initially Bessie accepted the offer for she had often felt desperate to leave Botswana. But then, after completing her Serowe book she felt certain that she could not go. Her decision reflected her deep pleasure in her book, but it also reflected her feeling that having given the best part of herself to her adopted African country, she had earned the right to live there and would die there. It was only in 1979 that the government of Botswana granted her citizenship – this too is missing from her letters to Paddy.

Bessie's delight in children's books leads directly into her view of children themselves, 'What I am trying to put over is that children are fascinating, anywhere ...' (letter 33), and her knowledge that Paddy had a son just a little older than Howard encouraged her to write in some detail about her own child. Besides her pleasure in Howard's early abilities, his inventiveness, for example, and his gregarious nature, she clearly enjoys him even when relations between them are temporarily strained. Howard had to contend with his classmates' gossip about events leading to Bessie's first stint in hospital, and she reports that when he adopts their attitude that she is mad, she challenges him. After a pause to reflect, he replies, 'I like mothers' (letter 38); she relates his words with relish, sympathising with his difficulty and enjoying his steady thoughtfulness. Her ability to see herself from her child's point of view is often present when she sets out to amuse Paddy with her stories. Her understanding of Howard's profound 'distrust' of her also contains her detachment as a novelist who stands back to look at herself while observing human error or folly, and her insight also comes from her own blunders over cultural differences. She enjoys the fact that Howard could negotiate local custom intuitively and more adroitly than she did.

Within their broad interest in writing, their gardening and their children, Bessie and Paddy discovered, in addition, numerous small, shared experiences and tastes which strengthened a bond between them: 'Either you visit me one day or I visit you. That's certain. I should feel so comfortable in your house because our experiences and tastes are so similar' (letter 22). Their sharing so many little things 'enchanted' Bessie to the end (letter 79). In their children they found a particularly moving, as well as amusing, set of connections: both boys were football-mad when young and later each hoped to make a career as a musician. After her many celebrations of Howard in the early letters, these affinities must have encouraged Bessie to tell Paddy of her later difficulties with Howard once he had left school. Her anxiety over his future is particularly clear when she reports his refusal of a job in the bank that she had wanted him to take (letter 63); Howard was now nineteen and his mother knew how fierce the competition was for regular employment of any kind.

Eighteen months later, when he had gone to Canada at his father's invitation but seemed unable to take up the opportunities offered to him there, Bessie's frustration is evident (letters 65, 68, 72). But when he returned to Botswana, her affection is again uppermost as she makes the best of it: 'he is a boy with a very strong sense of belonging, so he is happy to be home again' (letter 73). In her last letter to Paddy, however, it is evident that their relationship has hit a new low and that Bessie is traumatised by his sustained anger against her. It is a letter of compelled, anguished self-defence.

Howard left Serowe, probably to pursue his music, and was not at home when she died suddenly two months later, in March 1986. Bessie's death was a great shock to all her friends in Serowe; they knew that she had not taken adequate care of her health but perhaps did not realise how seriously affected her liver had been by heavy drinking, or indeed that she had moved from beer to spirits (Eilersen 2007: 342). She died of an infectious form of hepatitis. At her request, Bessie was buried in the cemetery of the Botalaote ward.[30] It was then on the outskirts of Serowe, a site which 'looks out over the Serowe plain with the broad, sweeping vision that was Bessie's own' (Eilersen 2007: 345).

Howard died in 2010, but his son, Aaron, now lives in Serowe. Bessie's house, the centre which sustained her life's work and achievements, has been declared a national monument. The Bessie Head Heritage Trust, registered in 2007, is working towards restoring 'Rain Clouds' and turning it into a museum and research centre with accommodation and resources for visiting writers.

---

30 Head touches on the story of the Botalaote people in 'The Deep River: A Story of Ancient Tribal Migration' in *The Collector of Treasures*.

20 [*handwritten*]

Poste Restante,
SEROWE,
Botswana.

16 October 1969.

Dear Paddy,

It depends on the wizard, of course! I have indeed had some gorgeous dreams of being kissed. The impressions are so vague, though, I forget them. Also, my heart is so dispersed and broken down, I seem to have lost that feeling of the personal as though it's almost a crime. I once read a story about Jewish children in a refugee camp. A child was given a cup of milk. She said: 'Is it alright if I drink all of it?'

There is a rain that never stops. Beyond that I merely hope for that simplicity of heart called love. I'd not like to die like this because I really have no other treasures except a capacity to love people. Also, I have found that a love as found between married people must be honourable if others are to be included and allowed to walk in and out of the door. You see the ideal, when you have nothing. You see women with small, pinched hearts and the husband is a run-about.

My observations about women in Africa are not fixed, but flexible. Nor do I really mean black people, but mankind as a whole. D H Lawrence once wrote: 'Ye Gods! He straddles the narrow world, like a colossus!' The biggest, broadest view, is my heaven. If I am critical, I think it springs from a desire to <u>impose</u> the greatest and highest, on the narrow and mean. One often fights, bitterly, brutally but if the mean is overcome, I scarcely remember what took place. I only have a vague memory of a torrential outflow of words. Let the enemy shiver, repent and I am undone. Hatred is very reversible to the most intense love. I tackle people individually, regardless of their background. It's just that Africa has been my working area and particular types of people have stepped into my life. That a lot of them were extremely vicious and mean is incidental, really, like part of [a] job you don't like. In a personal way, destiny might have presented me with a lot of hell to remove the blinkers. There's the roar of the crowd. That's not for me. 'One road leads to fame and importance and another to peace of mind.' When you see so much evil in people, you also see that they are so because they are pushers and grabbers. I know myself well enough to know that I have a good share of human failings and had to choose: Not this, but that. Not the cheap, the sensational, but the straight and narrow road. If not, I should not be worthy of the company of the gods. Perhaps I feel I am not allowed to lose the privilege of associating with the gods – by gods I mean people who are humble, unpretentious and who, when presented with those two roads, prefer the good.

Men are often greater than women because, although they have a wider area of choice and the vehemence and power to commit evil, they often prefer the good. I think this way only because I have been loved by a few great men and it was they who preferred to love in silence. Great men are like Gulliver. They have a lot of ants crawling over them.

No, I do not inspire sexual jealousy. You have to have a reputation. A man is so valuable to me, he is like the kingdom of heaven which is hard won. And love is so powerful, it can make unseen flowers grow under your feet, as you walk. I'd find such a love but I'd hand it on to some other woman who was poor, because I am so rich, and free. The idea of accepting anything for myself, in this present situation of change and flux and strain does not come easily. I see the need of the other is greater than mine. But the day will also come when I'll be given a whole cup of milk and like the Jewish child say: 'Is it alright if I drink all of it?' Should the gods in my heart say: 'Yes', then some woman in that picture goes flying and I won't feel sorry. For one thing, the man will be extremely good and great and he'll have an ant. I've stepped aside for other ants but some ant is going to get it one day. It's only ants who hate me. I have a reputation for undoing them! I have never been disliked by spiritually noble men and women.

This letter is not typed because I am running up and down to a construction work where a small house is being built for me. I received a thousand pound advance from Bantam Books, New York, for the paperback rights on *Rain Clouds*. I am building a home with this.

My childhood and growing up were so haphazard. I took care of myself from as far back as I can remember. How I ever got born in the first place is a miracle. My mother was a white woman. Her family owned race horses. My father, an African man, worked in the stable. Before I could be born my mother's family placed her in a mental asylum. That's where I was born. She never came out and died there in 1943. People were paid for caring for me. I was harassed for a long time by a child welfare organisation, even though I had to do a lot of my own upbringing. The latter part of my life, from 13–18 was spent in a mission orphanage. It appears remote now, that is, if you survive all that. Besides, I would not be the universe had I had a family life with all its narrowness. I am happy.

Bessie.

21.

Poste Restante,
SEROWE,
Botswana.

(end of Nov) [1969]

Dear Paddy,
The upheaval in my life is too tremendous to mention. I impulsively ordered a name plate from a friend who wanted to give me a gift for the new house – part of the title of my book — *Rain Clouds*, but all the time I feel it should be HEAVEN. It is not so much a resting place for me as for some treasures I've carried around through years of a battered existence, number one being a collection of most of D H Lawrence who is the one great love of my life. I built a book shelf for him at last and the magazines and letters I can't bear to throw away. A house is someplace to put things you love intensely but my house is more than that. The building of it was a conspiracy, at the right time, of some of the most lovely people on earth.

You might have heard of Pat van Rensburg, the person mentioned in the dedication of *Rain Clouds*. He first started a high school, built on voluntary labour and donations. It is almost a town now, with electricity and water and my house is just a stone's throw away, outside the fence of the school grounds. He gave me a tiny piece of unused school land. The school is not only a school but a village development workshop. Most of the staff are I.V.S. and Peace Corp volunteers but what concerns me just now is a part of the village development project, the Serowe Builders' Brigade. A few years ago it started, to absorb primary school leavers who in former times worked for any bugger for only three pounds a month. From a straggling beginning, it has shot up to one of the most highly organised and efficient of all the projects the school runs. I went through the whole rigmarole of getting a house built, as not even wild horses could drag me from the construction scene. A school goes on all the time the house is being built because an instructor quietly calls out: 'K.B., change that to a continuous join.'

Even now that the house is complete, the instructors still walk over it for the purpose of making out progress reports and what not. While my house was being built, I joined the gardening section of the Serowe Farmers' Brigade. The two differ. The Builders' Brigade has Batswana men as instructors, qualified builders on a paid salary. The Farmers' Brigade has both white men and women. They are a cut above the general run of white people but the atmosphere is pretty dismal. They, unlike the Batswana instructors, despise the material they are working with. They despise me too. They have a way of totally talking over your head when they are with a white comrade, clearly giving the impression that the black skin can't understand anything, really. I hate working with them after what I saw on my building plot. Whatever I say about Africans and Africa, a black man or woman just never overlooks people. There is no high or low when people are working.

Compare this. The Motswana instructor: 'K.B., make that a continuous join.' The student quickly lifts the brick, chucks out the cement and carefully chooses a new brick. The instructor idly stares at the sky. Very little talk, only work and a murmured correction now and then.

The Farmers' Brigade, where I work. Shrill voice of a Danish woman who thinks she knows JUST everything: 'I don't understand these people. They don't know anything. They are so lazy. Phenyo, don't leave the manure on the top of the garden bed. The nitrogen evaporates.'

The result of this attitude is that the students often omit to greet the shrill, nervous wreck and back answer her or him left and right.

To give them a page of their own literature, these people don't know how to make love in the night time. It is not superior knowledge, because I also work with the students at the farm, and learn from them. The trouble with the white man or woman is his or her own sex organs but so God help me, I can't stand the racket. Just at this point I am trying to pull out of the Farmers' Brigade to join people who are working on the beginnings of a vegetable garden. They are just poor villagers. The site is awful. Nothing is moving. I attended a meeting this evening. There is no money for a fence. I like such a situation because I have learnt to pull tricks and poverty is my second name. I am at home in a situation where there is nothing and I force something to happen.

To get back to my lovely house. A German I.V.S. volunteer was the only white man around the works. Something was right with his sex parts, because they were surely African in design for so much harmony. He gave the impression of simply believing in goodness, in the simplest way, the way your old neighbour simply believed in the unchanging train service. I said to him, the day before he departed to Germany: 'Karl, each person who built this house added a blessing to it because I have met so many wonderful people, all at once, at the same time.'

I am touchy about this. I want it to be that kind of house where those kind of people enter. I am doing the last jobs myself to keep the memory of the way it was built and the people who built and the serious, intense, concentrated expressions of the students for whom a whole new life of dignity has been created. The students at the Farmers' Brigade have that same expression of concentration when they work but it totally escapes the eye of the shrill white woman. I don't know what they want but those shadows and shades are the most important sign of progress. I think that's why I just can't get along with white people no matter how hard I try. They overlook the humanity in man. I can be driven to a point where I could commit murder, in a blood red rage, because of the shouting, the shrill assumption that white knows everything and black, god how they treat a black skin. You count the time: 'I'll get away from them but maybe I have to do this job.'

I had some lovely dreams. Some white people whom I really loved used to appear as black people or with my complexion. I used to think that this was a sign to me to overcome any dislike I might feel as far as they were concerned. I write freely about this because I feel you belong somewhere among that group and then, deeper still it is not really the black skin my dream indicates but the goodness of the heart of those individuals – that above all they are perfect already.

Believe me, I run my show entirely on the word love. It is so vast, so broad and creative that I really don't understand anything else. About this, I am a one-eyed Jack. If I am sure I love you, I can manage anything. The trick is to be sure. Love is like a scientific instrument that measures and gauges all things. It sees through all things. It worries about the slightest imperfection until perfection is created. Nothing less. Your young friend might have nervous breakdowns over her painting equipment or some other vague ailment. I have had hundreds of breakdowns over love but I stick to the ideal knowing that it is attainable,

You asked me to mention books I'd like. Send me your novel coming out in January. I have a home for it, now.
[*ends*]

22.

Poste Restante,
SEROWE,
Botswana.

11 February 1970.

Dear Paddy,

Either you visit me one day or I visit you. That's certain. I should feel so comfortable in your house because our experiences and tastes are so similar. I used to drink quite a lot in Cape Town, wine. In Johannesburg, brandy and whisky, but here in Botswana I can only manage beer, a strong, black kind, but it hits my head so hard, these days, I hardly go beyond two small bottles. My nervous system is busted to bits with so much agony that I can't seem to stand much drink. I lose my concentration and get tongue tied. It amuses me that a small bottle of beer makes me reel and reel when I used to stay cold sober on a gallon jar of wine and straight whisky the whole night through in Johannesburg. I have a favourite phrase: Old age is catching up with me. But it might be more. The physical frame just can't take it. But I'd surely drink with you!

I have some sunflowers growing in my garden. A lot of village people are working with me now and not so long ago we transplanted onion seedlings in pouring rain, just last Sunday, in fact. It was a great day because the onion seedlings are going to bring us a lot of money when we sell them. That day too, I bought a fat chicken who made a terrible roar and commotion when I killed her. I thought: 'God forgive me, this lively little beast does not want to die.' I had to screw every nerve to kill her. She had a big egg at the bottom of her tum and enormous yellow ones inside and some just developing, so no wonder she made such an uproar. But the combination of roast chicken, transplanting onion and rain and some hungry friends made it gala day number one. Working with some of the village women taught me a few things about myself. I like giving out information and I find it grasped so quickly and easily. I thought: 'If people are respected, they learn.'

I am not quite sure where Guyana is on the map. Or the spelling is new. Is it Cheddy Jagan's country?[31] Somewhere in South America?

---

31 Cheddi Jagan (1918–1997) was premier of British Guiana before independence and president of Guyana from 1992–97.

My son's name is Howard. Not long before he was born I was reading a novel based on the life of a great American architect. The name stuck in my head, because the personality was so striking and he revolutionised American architecture. I had the name Howard in mind from the man in the novel but strange to say my old man here can make almost anything with his hands. He just looks and makes a reproduction and given enough material, he will just create and create and I live in such mess and confusion because like Picasso, he uses junk tins and anything at hand to create a picture. We got this on his report at the end of last year: 'Arithmetic and reading are very poor but he is very good at inventing!'

Another strange thing, the meanings of both our names tally so well, though I did not know it at the time. Bessie means: 'The oath of God.' Howard means: 'Guardian of the oath.'

I have had several dangerous accidents through my son's inventive ability. Not to mention falling over things inside the house, there's always excavations going on outside into which I always fall and a terrifying assortment of machinery, spare car parts, wooden wheels – anything with an outline or form, he can make into something new. I have lived always on the razor's edge of death with him, not knowing what I am going to fall over next. The only thing that keeps us from being blown into oblivion is that he still uses water for petrol inside his inventions but in a few years' time when he gets on to the insides of a real motor car, I'm dead. Or he, most probably he. I thought: 'Oh God, why did you send me a child like this, so hazardous to live with and at the same time deprive me of all male company so that I can't make another one if this one blows up?'

In despair I took to creating a little girl for myself. Her name is Alice and she originally came from a village in Ghana. She's in my son's reading book, which I stole and put on the D H Lawrence shelf. She just thinks everybody loves [her] and has big, luminous black eyes. I am enclosing a picture of both Howard and my imaginary little girl, Alice. It's all I have to comfort me at the moment but I have such a life where anything happens and I am sure to find the little girl some day, even if I adopt her. I really need to counter-balance sheer hell with some sweet, heavenly company.

You asked me if I'd like some books, once. That is, if you can find some for me. I have long been after: *The Brothers Karamazov* by Dostoyevsky (paperback with Constance Garnett's translation). Something strikes me about a similarity between him and Pasternak, that huge, chunky mass of philosophical thought, the fascination Jesus both had for them, but the originality with which they expressed that fascination. Also the same mystical theme. I feel that Pasternak was simply the re-incarnation of Dostoyevsky but this time with the genius so powerful, so controlled, so devastating. Dostoyevsky was uncontrolled genius, he got near to controlling himself in his last book, the *Karamazov* one but he is sheer hell to read other than in his first book: *Poor Folk*, where you find that same control. I have a set of some of his writings and they just swamp me, the overpowering emotion. My head can't settle in him but I read *Karamazov* from a library in one hell of a glow. D H is the only writer who holds me for any length of time and whom I re-read. Nearly everything he wrote was BEYOND masterpiece level and I'd be happy if you could get me a few items of his in paperback:

Look! We Have Come Through! (some early poems)
Sons and Lovers
Women in Love
Pansies (the poems published after his death) (I am a little confused here and the title might be *Last Poems*.)
    There is also a biography by his wife: *Not I, but the Wind*.

There is more about D H that my mind cannot fully grasp and control yet but to me, he is the most important writer for the swing of a new decade. He was a prophet and God of the future, without the usual vesture garments, the prophets have. They all went through some rigmarole of celibacy. He went through the reverse and came up with something I struggle to get hold of. There were his mental approaches to the spirit or soul which were just solid work and so rigidly recorded. I follow him that close as I have worked out almost everything along his lines and my writing goes the same way – it's solid, it's food and I can't put it down unless I know how it's done. I only haven't got Lawrence's permanent rhythm and music. I might get the magic of his emotional control. I have used people outside myself, to control that rush of feeling, but I can build up now, except that goddam music, the low-pitched key and the incandescent earth. It's way out. There's something loud inside my head, a hell of an orchestra. I can make a rhythm of that but it is a fearful racket. I swear I'll never top Lawrence on anything or care to but he is tremendously important for the future. Much of everything I wanted for sanity, I got from him.

You can't make a break-through with any bastard over Lawrence, the way I feel about him. They say Lecher. I don't like mentioning the importance of D H to anyone because they're such fools.

Sincerely,
Bessie

23.

<u>Please note</u>: New address
P. O. Box 15,
SEROWE.
Botswana. Africa.
9 March 1970.

Dear Paddy,

I have a Post Office box now. I used to pick up my mail from the Postmistress. It ought to encourage me to learn to ride my bicycle because it means I can get mail, even on Sundays now. I have fallen so often off the bicycle that what courage I had is at a very low ebb, just now.

Your husband's hair-do is very impressive, so new and unusual that I became a little dumbstruck, considering how I always have an opinion on everything. Please tell him that his originality in hair make-up has stunned me into silence. As for the little boy, he is an adorable sweetie-pie. The world is so strange these days and changing so rapidly that I looked hard at him perhaps thinking he was a member of my clan. Depending on where you are – in America they called me a Negro. In England they think it is polite to say African but the reviews were highly entertaining from that side. They thought I ought to be African but the word got round that there was some interference from another quarter so I could not be genuinely said to be African. I had such a wail of laughter of this that out of it I found the name for my clan – Sense of Humour. He is such a sweetie your little boy, like he has a lot to say for himself and is not at all put out by the camera or any of the problems of living. Those ships appear very close to the shore.

I have a present for your garden – some sunflower seeds from my garden. They were harvested recently and have been drying on the roof of my seedling nursery. I am interested to know if they will germinate there. An agricultural officer showed me how to send seed to another country. He said one must look for the eggs animals lay on the seed. That's what causes epidemics and disease. I don't think the insects have as yet caught onto the fact of what's going on in my yard, except for some very troublesome wild rabbits from the bush. A family consisting of a mother, father and several children devastate my seedling pots. I can hear them carrying on just past midnight but I like sleeping so much, I just groan and cover my head with a pillow. We are nearing autumn or late summer here so it is possible the sunflowers I send might just like the warm weather. They have made my yard look so beautiful with those big splashes of colour that I am going to attempt to grow some more during the colder periods.

All in all, the garden is a terrible headache, this summer. We are really having another drought. The cabbage leaves are getting cooked. The onions, which stood like tall, straight soldiers, have the ends of their guns, brown and dry, and I was experimenting with some gum trees and lost over 100 seeds. The only thing about being a gardener of kinds is that it brings one an awful lot of friends. There's an old man who buys seedlings in plastic pots from me. There's a Peace Corp volunteer, who was surprised by some of my technical know-how, into thinking I might be an expert and said: 'My, but you have a lot of toomaytoes.' I like the pronunciation of 'toomaytoes', so much. We are selling the 'toomaytoes' just now, at 5c a pound. An old lady, my neighbour, came to buy a half pound, while her friend wanted 1lb. They gave me a 5c & 2c. I rushed to record the sale in the book, I said 5c plus 2c equals 8c. Something felt wrong, there. I sat for some time and eventually came up with 7c! That's where my son gets his poor arithmetic from.

I eagerly look forward to the parcel you sent me. One night I was working out some ideas on Lawrence's poem, 'Not I, but the Wind', but I could not get so far with it, like perhaps I might be able to now. But that night I dreamt he shook hands with me and smiled somewhat. It gave me an odd feeling on waking up as I had been reading him for years and years. Why should he shake hands with me at twenty eight years and not when I first fell in love with him which was doomsday. I thought he might have had a special meaning in that poem and I shall get to work again on those ideas some day.

So harassed have I been by my garden and the hot sun and the way almost everything is getting burned that I have not yet had the time to get into your new book *Fleshly*. Are those just any people on the cover? I hope to send a word about it in my next letter.

The name of Odetta was meaningless to me until I looked through my file on Martin Luther King the other day. She [… and] Joan Baez sang at his rallies with their guitars. The Odetta girl has a wide, flaring, beautiful mouth. Is she as rich in tone and shades as Miriam Makeba, from my home country? You mentioned that you wrote a portion of a novel on Odetta's African Soul. We do so much alike. I wrote almost the whole of my new short novel on some love songs composed for Makeba by her bass player, Bill Salter. I have never heard anything like his music and just wonder who he was, i.e. Negro or what. The sorrow was so disillusioned, an end, but yet a quiet assertiveness of Salter's individual worth and genius. I thought he might be a white man. Black people are loud and too loud, especially that side and especially when you are looking for the shades and shadows as being the most important things.

There is only one black man who affects me as profoundly as Salter, the bass player of Makeba. He is Oscar Peterson, the pianist. That man can pick up any trashy song and turn it into real gold. I keep picking him up in odd places, but I have only one of his L.P.'s – The Way I really Am, he says. His other L.P.'s say, so oddly: 'I long liked the Duke' – So, Oscar Peterson Plays Duke Ellington ... or ... Oscar Petersen Plays Cole Porter or Nat King Cole. Like he's always loving someone and not himself. I looked long at his face. I really love for some as yet unexplained reason. One day I came across a hair-raising article about him in *Newsweek*. The writer said: 'I was wondering where Oscar was. (He left America.) I picked him up in this cheap bar in Paris. He was fat, sweating and had on a shirt not washed for weeks. I said: 'Hiya Oscar, what ya doing here.' He looked at me through drink-bleared eyes and said: 'So ya like me, do ya?' And I said: 'Yes.' Then he said, 'Buy me a drink.' I thought that it was a pity that such a great artist should go to the dogs like this ...

Do you know what happened to Oscar Peterson, by chance? Like I say, for something I can't pull to the front, I love the man's music. There is something deeper in those – Oscar Peterson Plays The Duke. Oscar Peterson is <u>the</u> American of Americans. He is so Americanised, he is really like a summary of all that's been going on there, even the cheap little reporter who thinks he knows why a man drinks and that decent people ought not to but he [is] a Negro, after all, without the discipline of a decent white man, etc. Oscar Peterson is so hopelessly and deeply that whole goddam country, a whole long statement of a story and he has the key to it. I wondered so much about this till I hit on the fact that no one sits in his American skin like Oscar. Every other Negro wants to be on the African kick with voodoo drums and what not. It's just a feeling I have but I have only one L.P. here and heard another so over and over. I think it was Oscar Plays Cole Porter or something like that.

Much love,
Bessie

24. [*handwritten*]

*[Undated on page one,
no address or salutation]*

[15 March 1970]

This hasty note is just to tell you that a friend of mine in London – RANDOLPH VIGNE, 3 Macartney House, Chesterfield Walk, London S.E.10 is very eager to meet you and your husband. I took the liberty of telling him you love me and usually anyone who loves me gets V.I.P. treatment from him because he is like a father to me.

Like me, Randolph is a refugee but with the difference of having been a considerable personality in Cape Town. His family must have kept their British links and slightly he is like Mr Finley[32] in speech – so much class. But it ends there. There's a humility that makes him belong anywhere – very much like the late John Kennedy in getting on with people – the same generosity of intellect, practical, quick moving, often amused by the insanity of mankind. He started a magazine in Cape Town called – *The New African*; for which I still write. He used to be the publisher's reader for Oxford University Press and also did some private research on conditions of Xhosa speaking people of the Eastern Cape among whom he grew up. He has a publishing business I think in London – books for children.

Mostly I thought of your husband, Dulan. Randolph might like him. I saw little of Dulan's face in the photo – but it gives a lovely impression of kindness and good humour. I sent Randolph your address. I'd be so happy for you to meet him; because I like people whom I love to link up.
Let me know,
Bessie
[*on a separate sheet, but probably belongs to this letter*]
P.S. Yes, the novel was based on the life of Frank Lloyd Wright – by Ayn Rand. It was the only beautiful thing she wrote; but it horrified Frank Lloyd Wright. It's Ayn Rand. I followed her up. She's brutal, pushy. Up till now there have been two great women in history – my mother and Madame Curie. My mother: She laughed: 'If one can pay the price for many – I am ready.'

---

32 Terence Finley, the Refugees' Welfare Officer in Francistown

25. [*handwritten*]

P. O. Box 15.
SEROWE,
Botswana.

7 May 1970.

Dear Paddy,

The enclosure is about wizards.[33] To tell the truth I am not really broad-minded enough to support an idea, perhaps an impulsive one you mentioned in one of your earlier letters – 'I think that sleeping with a wizard in the night is enchanting in the best sense of the word.'

You don't know what you might have to sleep with, and also one ought to ensure that the wizard's soul is good, else a damnation might result over which one has little control. First, I feel, wizards must have form, there must be communication to size up the wizard. Then, after careful scrutiny, I might agree about the enchantment of the bed. Wizards are too fearful a phenomenon for me [to] support blindly. I worked a little story, though, because I don't like prejudice in myself.

Bessie.

---

33 The enclosure is no longer with this letter in the archive.

26.

P.O. Box 15,
SEROWE,
Botswana.

26 May 1970.

Dear Paddy,

You may certainly do as you please with the 'Wizards'. I often write many small pieces like this for friends, sort of comments in spontaneous vein on the times. Most go to Randolph who puts them in the *New African* and they often arise out of my correspondence. I had to find another audience for God, though, because Randolph several times scolded me very sharply for wild and irreverent comments on God. He does not like them and I am only too happy to open up new territory as I have much to say about God, in a way people have not thought of, and to my way of thinking, if you don't mind me praising myself, God-like subjects are my true originality and also cultivate my sense of humour.

Let me get to practical matters first in case I forget them. Indeed, broccoli must be adapted to frost. One day I was putting out some cauliflower and an English volunteer asked: 'What's that?' So I said: 'Cauliflower.' And she said: 'We have something different in England and it looks purple' (and something about sprouts). Anyhow, the first cauliflower crop appears to be a failure and I have another coming along, very pampered, with a good packing of mulch to keep the soil permanently moist. The truth is a private wish for some lovely food I used to cook in South Africa, roast beef, roast potatoes and cauliflower in white sauce, seasoned with pepper. I don't know anything nearer heaven than that. Everything else about the gardening project is so honest and in earnest, except the cauliflower. Most times my vegetable book lists the type of vitamin to be derived from eating such and such a vegetable, so I say: 'We must grow that.' That is how sweet peppers got a head start among the women who work with me, not counting the fact that they took packet fulls of it home because it produces so much fruit. It is firstly Vitamin C. The poor husbands know about that by now because one day one of them came to buy some onions and looked across at the sweet pepper plot with a wide smile: 'Are those the peppers?' he asked, obviously knowing the history of sweet peppers from A to Z.

There is no trouble about tomatoes and cabbage which everyone knows and loves but cauliflower has never been around except for the elite and the difficulties I am encountering with the preliminary work will need a pretty tough argument to get it into the big garden. For one thing the seedlings are fussy too. They won't germinate or grow without a good deal of sunlight. Then, when transplanted they reverse that desire. Just forget to water that mulch-packed bed of cauliflower for one day and they fall flat on their faces as though they haven't had water for one year! 'Don't give me too much sun, please, I'm so fragile.' The first thing I did was to start crying. Then I started to reason: 'This variety I'm using is no damn good. That's why it goes on like this.' The seed firm in Johannesburg sent me an order form, so I changed from 'Hybrid Southern Cross' to 'Cumulus'. Then they advertised a type of Broccoli: 'St. Valentine' and I ordered one ounce. I thought broccoli, St. Valentine, might surprise me by growing here. It might be just that little bit which turns the tide, and I don't see why I should not dare. I'd also be happy to know if you know of the nutritional value of cauliflower, so I can surprise people into buying it on as large a scale as they are one day going to buy the sweet peppers. It will take away the fearful feeling of guilt on having ordered so much seed for such a nuisance vegetable. I thought I'd also enclose the draft of the order I made for vegetable seed so that you and Dulan can see what you are likely to get to eat from our garden, if you visit one day. Some other material enclosed too, a special method of bed preparation, and seedling cultivation. The work from my side, the massive amount of seedling cultivation is going well, but not so the preparation of the big garden. There are too many people at odds, too many small minds all pulling the wrong way, too many people who don't like or care about planning and organising. I might have one strong personality to make the hard work run smoothly because it has to be done by men and I don't like organising men because I haven't really a dominant personality but there is a little item worrying the nice gentleman at the moment. He doesn't see who is my boyfriend and he doesn't see why he should not be and I know that story so well and my own long and complicated explanations are unsuited to the action types, so I have been hard pressed to invent a boyfriend, or failing that, some very impressive reasons or casual attitude, or as I carefully hinted: 'I'm twice the age of your mother, my little boy.' But it is causing me real anxiety, the work in the big garden because I can say so much: 'I have the money for the fence. Please get the fence up.' Then no one bothers. The present organiser of the voluntary labour is a daft dumb-clut from Wales who is hard for me to get along with. There might be one life line in the mix up, a Motswana man, whose wife works with me, but I heard he was off to the new mining town, quite soon and I desperately need someone to carry the ball of the one acre plot and get things moving there. I know what's needed and built up the money for it, in advance and also figured out that the base work was good and massive seedling cultivation, but like I said, I just don't like organising men. For that matter, the women too, who work with me. The atmosphere is very free and easy. I say little, except: 'Can we make 100 bags of cabbage today and 50 tomatoes?' That's all they ever hear from me but they come every Saturday morning. For one thing, they know the work, blindfold. They gossip and have a nice time. Then there's some hot coffee or tea or a parcel of vegetables to take home. And they see the rewards of their work, twenty pounds now, for three months from selling seedlings. More, there's always something growing, thriving. Sometimes, curiosity is there of its own accord: 'Teach me this or teach me that,' and I like it that way, natural or effortless. The day I am doing something wrong I get such a constricted pain in my thought, it makes me think too deeply, like telling those dumb-clut men to go on with the fence and not start digging up the whole blasted garden without the fertilizer being there! It is at times like this that one thinks many bitter things about the male species, how they are really natural muckers around and that the basic show of how the world runs on oiled wheels was always performed by women. The tragedy of being female is that you always have to perform unobtrusively, not having such a loud voice, muscles, freedom of movement and what not. But brains and clear head are most certainly the superior possession of women. The other thing I really hate is that: 'I'll move earth and heaven for you, provided I make a break through somewhere.' It just makes me give up everything because there's something really impersonal in the end, that a solitude, self-imposed, is coherent because it is a part of an inner evolution and it ends there.

Randolph said he and Gillian had a 'delicious dinner' at your house and that both he and Gillian liked you and Dulan 'extravagantly'. What I know he likes is sensible atmosphere, so he must have found it there. If people are not sensible, he fails to tell me anything nice about them. The delicious dinner must have been some out of this world roast meat, I assume, and vegetables and perhaps some pudding?

Today, with the letter, came the parcel of Penguin paperbacks. I straight-away dived for the herbs and spices and sighed with relief. The good writer says that herbs and spices are very beneficial to the digestive system which removes a nightmare of my childhood. There were a long series of strange ailments, months and months of being bed-ridden with fevers. A doctor said it is spicy food and I was to be given no more, especially curry. Some Asian next door neighbours had their Divali celebration at that time and I nearly died because I like Asian food more than any other kind of food, especially the sweetmeats and cakes of Divali. I used to say: 'Well pepper and curry powder are like cigarettes. They kill you but you will die all the same, so why give them up?' Now I see that spices of every kind actually prolong life. This is heaven, proper.

I'd also just had time to look through the Lorraine Hansberry book: *A Matter of Colour*.[34] There is the very clear picture of the lynch mob and the clearest expression on their faces is that of the moron, the semi-literate, and so ugly and repulsive a group of people that 'lowest form of human life' so aptly applies to them, vacant, mindless object[s], without the slightest hint of aliveness or mental alertness. I have a very wide observation of evil and it is always like that, the activities are also permanently brutal and seemingly hopelessly insignificant, yet for such people they put up notices 'White Only' to make them gods. If it were only evil I had seen I could not compare the overwhelming beauty of goodness, which is so purposeful and significant, often humble and ordinary too. There is something else. The faces of the lynch mob were the faces of a vast majority of white people in South Africa, vacant, loose, open mouths [with] cruel, vicious expressions. You wonder who they are, what's the purpose and where they are heading, because they are the exceptions of humanity, not the rule. I also worked out something applicable to my own destiny, that one mis-step from me, will take centuries to straighten out, one error has no end to suffering and I don't care for a century of hell in my destiny. What of this mass of people, who don't think? How do they bear up under the retribution of centuries?[35]

---

34 Hansberry is best known as the author of *A Raisin in the Sun* (1959). The book Head mentions was published in England in 1965 with the subtitle *Documentary of the Struggle for Racial Equality in the USA*. It contains 124 pages of photographs which capture from the inside the experiences of those who struggled.
35 Several paragraphs about the dreams on which the missing piece, 'Wizards', was based have been edited out here. The letter ends abruptly, without a salutation.

27. [*handwritten on air letter*]

18 June 1970.

Dearest Paddy,
Short note to thank you for certain earthy versions of heaven. Indeed, all we see here is the sun. That's climate. In a year there might be 14 cloudy days.

Dulan would agree with you about meddling and muddling if he were a writer. He obviously does not know about effeminate men, 7ft tall, with weak sex parts who try to impersonate <u>real</u> males with good sex parts. <u>Effeminate</u> men are so evil, the source of hell and damnation comes to them, soon. This is going on in my mind while I dig my garden. Sorry a running battle is going on here with the devil! His name starts with S … (Satan).

Thanks so, so much. I must tell you about the class structure of my garden – the things for experiment like your parcel are top class. I shall grow the sunflowers in summer. The strong winds of winter knock them down. I am making a separate order of spices. At the moment I grow Geera [jeera: cumin], an Indian herb.

Sincerely,
Bessie

28. [*handwritten*]

P. O. Box 15,
SEROWE,
Botswana.

2 July 1970.

Dear Paddy,

You might have been puzzled by abrupt reference to Satan in my short note last week. I had a little time off from my job this side and sat down to bring him into clearer focus. For one thing he's like Matenge[36] – 'so profoundly clever as to make the innocent believe they were responsible for the evil.' I've got his head on the block. It's about to roll because I'm sick of being killed for centuries and centuries. Enclosed is '---' for Satan, the man/woman in pants responsible for all the suffering of mankind; the root cause, in fact.

Sincerely,
Bessie.

---

36 A character in *When Rain Clouds Gather*. The piece which Bessie mentions at the end of this letter is not in the archive.

29. [*handwritten on air letter*]

P.O. Box 15,
SEROWE,
Botswana.

7 July, 1970.

Dear Paddy,
Short note at P.O. to thank you very much for 'Gasbag.' More on 'Gasbag' when I read it at home. I sent you another of my 'God' pieces last week.

Goddam, but I howled with laughter to see the extract from my letter, especially the part about 'my little boy'. To tell the truth, he really fell violently in love with my book *Rain Clouds*. Mistaking the author for the book, briefly, he positively flew into my house. The following conversation took place: 'Where's the husband?' So violently and abruptly. So I said: 'How old are you?' So he said, truthfully: 'I'm 22.' So I said: 'I'm 33 in July'. He stared at the floor a long time and died quietly. Then he burst into life again. I said: 'My son, will you take care of me?' So he said, intensely: 'Willingly!' He helped my women's group erect the fence. Last Saturday afternoon I dropped down on my knees and put my head on the ground. I said: 'Thank you, God Tom.' Oh, I have acquired the most beautiful son in the universe!! More later, after reading 'Gasbag'.
Love to you and Dulan.

Bessie.

30. [*handwritten on air letter*]

P. O. Box 15,
SEROWE,
Botswana.

25 September 1970.

Dear Paddy,

I suppose when you have a break down nothing is coherent. I am so used to them, these long periods of darkness when every effort is painful. People don't think that 'the forces of evil' are real. So much has been lost. You know there's no garden anymore. A lot of people contributed to removing me from simple organising. They've done it for more than six years now. It's this 'coloured dog' thing. There's something else. My mind has temporarily snapped. I've had too much of the horror of the spirit pushed through my head. Evil remains permanently evil and cannot make anything beautiful. How does one live permanently the victim of a sterile, uncreative force?

The marjoram grows in tins. Thank you for the books, the article. I am so ill and broken down. I can't move.

Bessie.

31 [*handwritten on air letter*]

P. O. Box 15,
SEROWE,
Botswana.

15 October 1970.

Dear Paddy,

I wasn't working at the farm for so long but as an independent organiser of the work for a village garden. It was really Pat van Rensburg's project. He'd kept all his projects in the school. The new method of seedling cultivation and the deep trench garden were in use for some time at the school and my work was mostly educational. To a certain extent I made the first move for him with the garden. Village people did not want me, regardless of the fact that much was achieved in 9 months. You'd ask why? Then read *Maru*. To Africans I am a Bushman, filthy, tainted, half-breed. Just like the white man feels about black people. You aren't sure if you smell or not. They said they would work with a white volunteer but not me. I had a different kind of communication with Pat when I took on the work. He's also been through hell but you can't be what happens to you. You can be the results of hell. But I found a home for myself too as a Bushman, or Masarwa. So *Maru* really belongs to me.

Bessie.

32. [handwritten]

P. O. Box 15,
SEROWE,
Botswana.

10 November 1970.

Dear Paddy,

Thank you for your letter of 30th Oct. I've just received the money from *The Times* too and since the bank sent me two duplicates, I enclose one for you to see how they change money – R means Rand. Thank you very much for the money too.

I could not sell *Maru* at all in America. It made everyone there jump. A certain lady agent in New York, linked to my London agent, simply refused to hand it to the 'New Yorker'. I feel their reaction was a terrific booster for Giles. He's really gone to town on the blurbs. They are so damn good, nothing like I had for *Rain Clouds*. The man has really taken *Maru* for his own.

I lived in a hut while writing *Maru* and the goats used to just walk in. They live so much with people, they just walk in and smell everything; sometimes they sit down.

The marjoram grew so vigorously and profusely. I'd put down half the packet so I harvested the first crop and rushed to plant the next crop for some seed. I'll get about 2 spice bottles full from the first crop. I thought you might be a little short of marjoram and enclosed a packet.

The bush marrow is in the garden and the sunflower seeds have germinated. I put them among other things. It's difficult to get the Broccoli growing. All but three of my first planting-out died, so I thought I'd keep the seeds for cooler weather.

Howard saw the picture of Dan and asked to write him a letter and a story, which I also enclose.

Sincerely,
Bessie.

P.S. I noticed that should one belch after a meal containing Marjoram, one is very pleasantly reminded of one's dinner and the afternoon and surroundings are unusually happy those days. Must be a tranquiliser herb.

33.

>P.O. Box 15,
>SEROWE,
>Botswana.

>4 December 1970.

Dear Paddy,

Dan's letter was read through several times, till its contents could be said backwards. We had a little trouble with a fellow called Jason. He was his father's favourite son and one day he sent Howard a shirt, saying Jason sent it. Of course I was foolhardy enough to pass on the message to which Howard said: 'I must write a letter to Jason.' Jason did not reply. Another letter was sent, then a toy watch and a paper ship and still no word from Jason. The mail was eagerly watched: 'Did Jason write to me? Did Jason write to me?' So you can imagine the complete emotional turmoil in the household at the present moment. The spelling went haywire in agitation and full stops are left out. Also there will be no peace till the letter is posted so I hasten to include my letter.

He was given *The House at Pooh Corner* this year as a birthday present by a teacher at Swaneng whose little boys were invited to his party. That night I picked up the book, started on a few pages and howled so hard, Pooh hooked me. I often think now, that reading for children won't get anywhere unless the mother gets hooked first. After Pooh was literally EATEN with joy, I managed to dig up *Winnie the Pooh*, then two volumes of *Alice* and lastly *William – The Bad*. The year went by, on wings. The night times before bed were filled with Pooh songs ... 'I could spend a happy morning being Pooh ...' The main difficulty with *Alice* was to get the songs over. I could not put them to tunes as easily as Pooh's songs and then again *Alice* is so intellectual he missed half, except the Mad Hatter's tea party: 'Eh, stupid,' said the Mad Hatter. So Howard said: 'What's that? Read it again. Is he saying Alice is stupid?' (He had a difficult time starting school. There was too much fuss, fuss and he was at the bottom of the class and had to do extra lessons at home so he was very relieved to hear Alice being called stupid.)

Which brings me to children's books on children in Africa. I have several. They remain unread. The books were produced by American and British publishers, with the rule in mind – children there want to <u>know</u>

how children in Africa live. They are so dull, they stun the mind. The children go dutifully to school. Then they come home and dig the garden, herd the cattle, eat porridge from a wooden basin – every artist seems to get the utensils right and the mud huts as though they are already in the museums there, but it is so dull and the children are simply presented as beasts of burden, hoeing the mealie plot, and doing many other kinds of dreary work, with cheerful grins. Even Naomi Mitchison hit the same line with the books she wrote about children in Botswana – no fun, no veering, reeling imagination in fun and mischief and adventure, like the way Pooh hooks you from page one. In the first place, I am damn well convinced both Milne and Lewis and Richmal Crompton etc., associated with and loved really great children. People think of adults as great, often overlooking that children can be great too. Those authors drew their material direct from their models, certainly there was the Liddel girl and when you look at Piglet and you were a teacher, you say: 'That nervous little boy who took on the dangerous side of all the adventures – that's Piglet.' Also, the nearest I can come to affection for everybody like Pooh, is my son, also Pooh's flat, prosaic mind.

The style of *Rain Clouds*, the simplified version of English was really hailed, in America, as the book for the juveniles. I resented it, simply because one can't write to a particular audience and I can't help the simplicity of my style. It comes out straight with no tangles in the head. I was lucky to compare two audiences because the English audience, which follows events in Africa were more concerned with the contents and my own personality before anything else. Besides the public there is drilled into caring about poverty.

Well, *Maru* was first asked for by the juvenile editor of that publishing house, following the reviews. That's why you get that feeling that it nearly veers in that direction, especially Windscreen Wiper, the baby goat. Indeed my son made many a contribution there, most directly the story about Tladi, the African or Motswana demon. At the time of writing *Maru*, I had difficulty putting him to bed. He used to stand in the room, shaking from head to toe and eyeing every corner, fearfully. Eventually he blurted out: 'Patrick saw Tladi. David saw Tladi. Now Patrick said I am going to see Tladi tonight.' So I said: 'Who is Tladi?' So he said: 'It is very dangerous talk and I can't tell you.' I asked some adults: 'Who is Tladi,' and they averted their heads in embarrassment, so I got real curious and worked out my own tale. This Tladi scares everyone. Into the story he went.

Indeed, that reeling, imaginative style, so attractive in the Pooh and Alice books can very easily be re-captured in the African environment, except that Africa rarely provided an environment for me. It has provided an environment for my son alone. For one thing, unlike me, he is gregarious and fearless of human contact. I have always feared mankind. Due to this, he asserted his own personality and moved away, living three quarter part of a life that escapes me, except when he does the kind of things that make my hair stand up. One evening I could not hear him, for silence. I went into my bedroom and found him sitting on the floor. The vaseline bottle was open and he had smeared his face, hands and legs full of grease. I said: 'What are you doing?' He said, quite calmly: 'You weren't washing me properly. Now I'm clean.' Mothers here rarely wash their children, fearful of the drudgery of that extra bucket of water. When baby has to go out, he is grabbed and rubbed over with vaseline as a substitute for a bath. In any case he shines, so my son must have heard his friend's mother say: 'Now baby is clean.'

Indeed, there is a stability here and a [… conservative] outlook which my son finds very appealing. Everything is wrong with me but he does not criticize Batswana people as often as he looks critically at my words and actions and corrects them. Advice is given freely to what he really looks upon as a harmless lunatic. Once he found me with a huge bundle of mosquito netting I was fixing for his bed. He said: 'What's that?' So I said: 'It's my wedding dress.' So he said: 'When are you going to get married?' So I said: 'Oh, sometime.' So he said: 'Who are you going to marry?' So I said: 'Oh, someone.' So he said: 'Well, you can't get married here at home. You must go to the D.C.'s office the way Mrs Glackson did.' (The poor child has seen so many wild versions of human behaviour in this house, that he profoundly distrusts me. The expression of his face is always – she's like that because she does not know how other people live.) Every day I am given news – Oliver hurt his mouth, the other lady had a baby, the next door neighbour is getting married, Goabamang's mother beat him, Oliver's mother gave me an orange. (Oliver's mother so dominates his mind that he took to talking exactly like her – 'I'll have some m-eee-lk.' Oliver's mother comes from a part of England where they talk a strange version of English, pronouncing the words <u>extra-carefully</u>. And are very conservative in outlook because I can hardly get a conversation going with Oliver's mother about the universe. And she has several times eyed me uneasily.)

What I am trying to put over is, that children are fascinating, anywhere, and beautiful things can be written about them for them because they are as important as adults, perhaps even more. I might, if I live that long, get like Naomi Mitchison who loved her grandchildren so much she carried pictures around of them. Then I could produce a children's book, from memory but the anguish of my inner life is so high at present it is about all I can concentrate on – to steady myself, to keep alive. It is like a drowning rat grasping at every straw. Giles so urged me to write and the nearest I can get to at present is a re-working of rough essays I wrote to friends. He said he had talked with you about the possibility of putting the letters together. I straight-away cancelled the letters because often I wrote things, so on the verge of mental breakdown that they are not true reflections of my feelings. There is a very masculine side to me that does not care to cry, but only loves a <u>purpose</u>. I have much of that in articles pushed away from the immediate, which project my faith in the future and are often very gay and humourous. But not the letters. One tends to expose the real horror there. At present it's really like this, these people think I am a sub-human dog they can giggle at. But I have other things of vision and beautiful reflection and I prefer to work on that for the next book, alone. Because I believe in my own visions of goodness, if I believe in nothing else […]

To some gardening news. There is an error in the Cape Gooseberry Jam recipe I sent you. Please don't put the sugar in at the same time with the fruit. Boil the fruit first, for about fifteen minutes, then add the sugar. It brings out the pectin which helps the jam to jell, but if you put the sugar in straight away it makes a very thin jam. Now I think I have here the relative of the Cape Gooseberry. It is called the Tomato Ground Cherry and the seed came from America. It is almost impossible to grow in summer here and I have only one plant in the garden with fruit on it. The plant just dies like hell in the heat and the one that thrives was planted under the vegetable marrow you sent me. The Cape Gooseberry is slow, because it really establishes itself as a small tree but the cherry tomato, under protection, produces fruit like lightning which very closely resembles the cape gooseberry. I have still to compare the taste but the plant is almost the spitting image of the cape gooseberry. I'll send seed when I have some for your summer there, and you may have the quick production of the ordinary tomato, plus the sweet fruit of the gooseberry.

Also, can you track down the English name of the aromatic spice seed which has the Indian name of 'Jeera'. Again Jeera is almost impossible for

me to grow in this intense heat. The plant is so fragile, it gets scorched with the sun. I get the seed from a certain Asian lady at Swaneng named Mrs Ghosh but so much does she use Jeera in curry that she has to smile painfully as she parts with her spice seed. If I am sure the English name is Cumin seed or Fenugreek, I can order it myself from my seed firm in Johannesburg. It looks like Fennel and Aniseed but differs from them very sharply in taste. Now, I was introduced to Jeera in Cape Town where women have a totally different approach to curry because they use a lot of turmeric and whole spice seed. In Durban we used to buy our curry blended, then add, tamarind, garlic, ginger and the leaves of the coriander plant. I don't fancy eating whole coriander seed like they do in Cape Town but the memory of JEERA stuck and when I mentioned it to Mrs Ghosh she immediately knew what I was talking about. She obtains her spices at great difficulty but I saw in Rosemary Hemphill's books that nearly every Asian spice had an English name and in her recipe for curry she mentioned Fenugreek and I thought: 'THAT MUST BE JEERA!' Jeera has a heavenly taste in curry. I like to produce the spices myself so that I can push them through Pat van Rensburg's shop. Because women here don't have those kinds of things and the only way they will get to them is through Pat's shop which gets to poor people.
[*ends*]

34. [*Handwritten*],

[*no address, undated*]

Thank you immensely for the gift of William Books. They might arrive this coming week. I love the little fellow because he <u>creates</u> playtime all by himself. Also his version of English is <u>SO</u> terrific; basic, earthy, devil-may-care. I don't say I love William with sentiment. He's too unsentimental but somewhere in my mind he's a GIANT among children. Here we go again. I also read every book I could on him in my childhood. Funny how we did all the SAME things!![37]

Yes, McCalls, out of the blue, made an offer for *Maru*. Now, I ought to be a little flush as from January onwards with the McCall advance for *Maru*, plus a little in royalties from Gollancz. I'd like so much a set of the William books – by Rich[m]al Crompton – *William the Good, William the Conqueror, Just William*, etc. If you could either get them at an old books store or get a book shop to fix me up with 6 or so and the price and postage, I'd get the money off to you January. The William books are <u>invaluable</u> and I love him most of all the children's books. To have the William books in the house is the nearest thing to heaven. It was like that when I read *William the Bad* to my son. He listened with huge, round eyes. [*ends*]

---

[37] The two pages of this letter seem to have been mis-filed and probably do not belong together. The last page has been dated by an archivist, 4 December 1970 in pencil, but this repeats the date of the previous letter. It seems unlikely that Head would ask for William books to be sent immediately after thanking Kitchen for posting some.

35.

P. O. Box 15,
SEROWE,
Botswana, Africa.

21 July 1971.

Dear Paddy,

Thank you very much for your lovely letter. Howard is also a football maniac just now. In fact, when I came back I found a fellow I hardly recognised, independent like hell! He'd been everywhere he pleased and made so many friends and done things that make my hair stand on end. He took a trip to a village 36 miles away with a group of school friends, wandered in the bush for miles, then temporarily got adopted by a young volunteer who lives in a hut nearby and spent the evenings cooking the supper. They were eating just plain porridge. I don't see my son any longer, but Huckleberry Finn! He talks about Dan a lot because I said we'd go to England (the centre of his life is friendship). Dan seems to be a boy just like him.

In many ways I was distressed before the breakdown. You really had a funny correspondence from me last year because I kept on muttering my anguish aloud, saying weird things about war and devils and what not. The most important thing is that society did not treat me badly, especially since I came back from hospital. The trouble was where my mind was travelling, it was horrible territory full of evil images. It was like thinking out hell to its conclusion, which is eventually death on a large scale. It was too vivid, there was too much imagery and I was tracking down a kind of cruelty and torture that is the exception rather than the rule. There is a surface humour to the breakdown. First, there was a tremendous explosion in front of my very eyes, like hell was ending. I wasn't well enough to focus my mind on reality, the dead bodies lying around my inner vision appalled me. It was a game going on for three years. Half reeling I confused the inside with the outside and picked on one of the dead bodies. I said aloud: 'So and so has been killed by so and so.' I said this to several astonished people. They said: 'No, you [are] quite mistaken. No one's dead.' The trouble is, too many people were behaving weirdly, just at that time. I think they were watching the breakdown with curiosity. I had no defence, that's why I hit out so blindly, perhaps unconsciously trying to create defences. There are situations where no decision will help you, because you are really insane. My insanity is rather weird and confusing and it all came from the inside, not the outside.

The garden work I was busy on last year, kept going though I dropped out. There is a little shortage of water but there are onions, cabbages and tomatoes in the garden. In fact, the area surrounding the garden is a hive of activity, full of people busy doing things and buildings going up – a pottery house, beer house, shop and cooking and bartering of goods, very much like my village in *Rain Clouds*. There's only a jam making programme at my house each Saturday morning. I am dithering about whether to settle for that because last year I put all my time into establishing the big garden and did not write. But there's been such a complete break to the flow of my life here, that I am extremely uneasy.

A girl once had an awful love affair with a white man. He was a bad hat. I said to her: 'How could you?' She said: 'But it was a rich experience.' I could not see anything rich in it. I'm rather in the same situation today when I look back on my life in Botswana. It was a mixture of everything, both horrible and beautiful. I find myself saying that the horror was a rich experience. I haven't made it peaceful yet, like something you wind up and throw behind your back. I brood over it, struggling to assess its value. I started writing down some things. I call it my third book, but it is private material, private analysis of evil that haunted me. Did I ever resolve the evil or understand it?

So when you ask me my plans for the future, it is a question that fills me with panic. I know I ought to go away. How long, and how hard did I not try to leave this country. It was like I was held here till the grill or my fate was worked out. There's something gone wrong with my feelings too. Paddy, I had an appalling temper. I just used to flare up on the spur of the moment. There's something funny going on just now. I've had too many people say they love me. In the bad old days I would have reeled with joy but not now. I don't take my humanity and goodness for granted anymore.

It's like this. It's that matter of Satan. I saw too many in my nightmares, with swollen, distorted features. I used to say: 'DAMNATION!' I'm going through a mood now where my own Satan is coming into focus, which it didn't before. I keep on thinking: 'O God, will I look like those other fellows? Have I a long history of evil behind me?'

It's so difficult for me to plan the next step ahead. It's not like last year when so many plants grew in my yard and connected me to so many people. I keep on putting off the day I take up the work again because the breakdown affected all the people I worked with. There was a trust and friendliness there. It's not the same thing to be on the receiving end of pity for being in the loony bin. I found some of your Marjoram still growing in the tins but there's so little in my yard just now – a few desert trees, some gooseberry bushes and paw-paw trees. Otherwise I have just left the beds bare. So many interrupted melodies, I mean just work I did, not inner storms. There's something so wonderful about doing a job every day because it helps you to think ahead. I have a theory about each life one lives. When you are born to create something beautiful you are mentally prepared for the event. I used to dream like that. Failing that, you'd think blows would be easier to take in maturity but not just now. There's a troubled feeling that nothing was meant to be simple and straightforward for me. You feel like that when you have been taunted, tormented and tortured for a long time. It's like there's something saying over your shoulder: 'Yes, you bugger. You've skidded through danger at the scruff of your silly neck but if you don't break now, you will in another life. It's written in the stars that you're doomed.' It's a part of the brooding just now.

It was very kind of Giles to worry and want to help me. I know he should only be interested in whether I can write another book or not.

So you see how vague my plans are. I am writing but it might not be the third book.

Mrs. Moore is a wonderful woman. I went to her house the other day and talked. Life's been easy for her. She never ever had to worry about much except her old man Stan. She worries that he can't manage the accounts of the school, yet he was a teller in the bank. So she fusses with the housework, gets up earlier than he to do some of the accounts, teaches bookkeeping part time then helps him in the office. 'Stan needs me,' she said, 'that's why I help in the office.' I get the feeling that the old man would not be able to stand up on two feet. It's more or less what I am reduced to just right now. But the reverse. I'm like Stan. I'm not standing up on my two feet and I just wish I had a husband like Mrs. Moore. It's a bad spell I'm in, but I'm sure you would agree that Dulan helps write your books by just being there. I haven't got down to reading *Linsey-Woolsey* yet, though I started a bit just before going to hospital. There's a pain between me and everything I'm doing just now and I'm not really concentrating because it's so awful. It just hangs over my chest area like a permanent and insistent clamour. It's [a] feeling.

Yours sincerely,

Bessie

36. [*handwritten*]

P.O. Box 15,
SEROWE,
Botswana, Africa.

23 July 1971.

Dear Paddy,

Thank you very much for your lovely letter. I certainly don't over-value myself, especially now when I live at a very low ebb. It wasn't so much my surrounding world – but the dangers in which I lived, internally. I want to feel that I saw and thought all those things for a purpose – it was so rough and violent, inhumane. I think people too often get the platitudes of goodness – but not the torments of hell; which are harmful.

My correspondence with you last year was rather funny – so many wars and devils. It was like muttering bits of anguish out loud, then not saying the accurate things because I was broken. One good thing certainly survived the confusion – the big garden in the village I was working with. It has vegetables in it and people are working. Surrounding the garden are some new buildings – a shop, pottery house and beer house. Mostly it's to see how something can be made from nothing with people's hands.

I'm not feeling so well. The backwash of so many bombs begins to take its toll, at last. I really have no plans from day to day; partly because I feel everything I was meant to suffer has completed its cycle. I was like a millionaire who was forced to surrender his wealth at gunpoint; and start all over from scratch with nothing. I've begun a bit of dubious writing.

It was so kind of Giles to worry about me, especially as his main concern was whether I could produce another book or not.

God knows how I suffer at present. I laughed my way right through hell because the pomp of it was so funny. But I'm not such a tough guy like Al Capone – I'm crying.

Sincerely,

Bessie.

37. [*handwritten*]

P. O. Box 15,
SEROWE,
Botswana.

23 August 1971.

Dearest Paddy,
Thanks very much for Howard's books. We have started on Worzel Gummidge. We'd just finished Naomi Mitchison's *Family at Ditlabeng*. I was very surprised at the detail she collected on poverty, the inside stuff you really have to live through to know. Howard liked it because it's of an environment he knows and I wondered if Dan might like to know about Botswana, because it's a good picture of day to day village life of children, easy to read (Howard read it straight through). Could I send it along to Dan? There's a collection of children around the house just now because Howard has organized a regular football team. They all pick gooseberries on Friday because I give them a little pocket money. They pick so swiftly, with industry as though trained to work hard. It is a pity children in Africa are only represented in books at present as working hard. No magic playtime like Susan and John have; and dreams. I used to work hard too, when little and I wonder now where my dreams come from. Are they a foreign thing? What were all those stirrings of wonder and longings?

There's half a struggle to bury a dark world that lived side by side with love and light. I am afraid of it. But what sort of shape does the future need, because it grows inside a living individual. Someone close to me only liked my first book. People far removed – I am getting in the American reviews – like the second. The person closest said the people in *Rain Clouds* are 'real' to her. It is straight, prosaic stuff – *Rain Clouds* – God, do I only write about people working on development projects? I have two – the practical and the dreams; even the dreams were inclined to be practical but they were dreams. There's too much mystery in man. People are not only 2 dimensional – they are universes, stars and suns and planets and energy. A little of this view came out in *Maru*. I'm tortured because it had its nightmare side.

Mrs Moore handed me a nice letter from you; about your books. I like the title of the last book and feel myself very much a part now of the life of David and Elinor. The ending of *Linsey-Woolsey* is superb – but there is a distraction in my mind – it's the quality and power of the first book – *Lying-In* – as though, in there, the material is held together by the sheer power of the <u>writer's</u> joyous will. It's really a poem from beginning to end – nothing is out of place, disconnected, there is a humility, insecurity and tenderness – Vanessa jars on me in the other books – her comments are usually her irritations with people surrounding her, and Elinor is a complete puzzle to me – maybe selfish, neurotic and self-centred. I'd had time to go back to *Lying-In*. There's nothing to beat, for instance, the quality of the conversations between John Talisand and Vanessa and the high flying, lyrical passages on William – high flying, because he is so sharp, direct, human, ruthless, sane (and selfish too). None of the other people in the other books come anywhere near the stature of John and William. I liked John and wondered why he disappeared. I don't like Barnard so much. I write too so I know a little about the writer's joyous will but I feel it's all in the first book and the others tackle problems of people in a city like London that I am not familiar with – but they might be typical Londoners – not universal like William – that's where I get lost. The girl is a girl I'd know in *Lying-In* and the love situation – but then I am really quarrelling with a more select, exclusive atmosphere in the other books. I'd say they are white people talking to each other painfully – but I'd say the first book is talking to everyone. I even know passages of *Lying-In* by heart; they just settled in my mind.

I have to get another book finished quite soon or else I'll starve. But at present it's more than starving – my mental bounce, even the will to live depends on the typewriter – but what a see-saw ride I'm taking! God knows, no creation was ever made by a beggar but by a dreamer who knows his dreams are the right ones. I am astounded by some of the things I have written recently – crawling, miserable stuff – but still feeling towards the point where I pull the right thread and have everything going my way. Then my third book begins with earth and sky blending and drunken days and nights. I keep on telling myself that the out-of-condition state of the typewriter is just the right thing. I'm waiting to hear from a man who comes in to fix typewriters, then I say – by the time the typewriter is fixed up I ought to have found the right thread and got up off my damn, crawling knees. Being a worm isn't a bad thing, though, especially when you're clearing a lot of junk out of the soul.

Sincerely,
Bessie.

P.S. The garden work is picking up again. The other day I was looking around the yard and came upon an amazing thing. Your spinach beet (perpetual spinach) had been unwatered for 9 months. It was still green and clinging to life, in a near desert which is my garden, at present.

Would it be possible to send me a few packets of the Spinach Beet/Perpetual Spinach? I'd mentioned in my last letter that it survived the drought in my garden; and I am keen to put down a few seeds on one bed in the Boiteko garden. We are a little short of water and things that struggle to live like the Spinach Beet did in my garden are very interesting.

I was just looking through my notes and came across your seed catalogue letter and the instructions on how to grow and cook cauliflower. Unfortunately, the cauliflower programme fell to pieces with me but I hope to make a few seedlings. There's a fruit tree programme to start too because the Farmer's Brigade now has a forester from Denmark and things like grafting can be learned. He is at the moment concentrating on fodder trees for cattle and goats. It's the most interesting thing but it takes time to see how it can be used on a large scale. The first thing he said was that Botswana is a most depressing country for trees.

38. [*handwritten*]

> P.O. Box 15,
> SEROWE,
> Botswana, Africa.
>
> 27 August 1971.

Dear Paddy,

I hardly know where to start my letter. For one thing you seem to be just now the proverbial friend in need; such a lot of understanding sympathy! I'll get tangled in my own thoughts (that's made me throw away 2 typescripts after page 14 or so) so I think I'll maybe begin my letter with your question about the pottery, and also add a line from *Rain Clouds* – the remark passed by the old man Dinorego to Makhaya – 'A lot is happening in my village and a well-educated man like you can bring a little light.' For I suddenly wake up and find my village of Golema Mmidi right on my doorstep. People are just busy doing EVERYTHING. Last year the Boiteko project was only the garden and within a space of two months or so its expanded to a Pottery Brigade, Brewery, Tanners' Brigade, Weaving and Spinning Wool Brigade. The centre of it is a shop, not the usual kind of shop but a place where people bring the things they've made with their own hands. So the shop is a jumble of rough, home-made articles and some bags of corn, mealie meal, sugar, tea, candles – the only articles from outside. No money is exchanged in the shop. We have work vouchers on which are printed the words – 1 Boiteko (the equivalent of 10/-), 1 dirufo (the equivalent of 1/-), 1 serufo (the equivalent of 1d). We do a certain amount of work within our work brigades and are issued with a work voucher. I at present earn 3 Boiteko a week for making gooseberry jam, 1 day's planting in the big garden and for seedling preparation for the garden. With my three Boiteko I go to the shop; and see what I can buy or exchange. What I have been doing is building up a collection of the pottery work. The pottery brigade is run by a man and his wife named Hawes. They get the red clay from the hills nearby, then they have students who work with them, mostly young girls and they make thick chunky plates, heavy teapots, casserole dishes, milk jugs, chunky cups and glaze them. The plates are about ½ inch thick and heavy on the hand (I have 3 so far) but they look beautiful on the table and have designs on them invented by the students. This is the most exciting thing about the Boiteko project – that it has the potential to make people <u>inventors</u> and is a cross between people's own skills and the skills of the volunteers at the school. I have half my eye on the Boiteko project for the third book except that Makhanya isn't there any more, and without [a] Makhanya-type I've temporarily lost the tense, taut control I have in writing. Everything else I'm holding on to is so jumbled, often chaotic and intensely painful.

I'd not known about the Brewers' Brigade until I got home from hospital. My son introduced me to the organizer, a young man called Rod. The first few nights I heard nothing but Rod, Rod, Rod. Then Howard would sit bolt upright in bed and give the most wonderful interpretation of noises water animals make by a river, his black eyes round with wonder. Rod, while I was in hospital, had taken him for a short holiday to the Limpopo river, near the northern border of Botswana. He took a very dim view of Rod's diet and said to me indignantly – 'He gave me paw-paw and bread and butter for lunch. Do you call that lunch?' Rod lives in a mud nut nearby and also likes Botswana midday diet of mealie porridge and meat; of which Howard didn't approve either. He eats steak (meat is cheap) when we are flush and even when we aren't he doesn't notice a change because I simply stop eating and drink tea. So I managed to dig out Rod. He turned out to be a quiet, reserved Englishman with a sudden, startling, unexpected, weird giggle. It might be his youthfulness. He was just as indignant of Howard's behaviour as Howard was of his diet. He said Howard used to get under the table and tickle his legs all the time. Just as we were talking and eating and Howard interrupted, he reached out one hand, bonged him and said: 'Shut up.' The glow of hero worship in Howard's eyes was something to see. If I had done that he'd have sulked for an hour. Since I have come back he has been fond of remarking: 'The standard fours (his classmates) all say you are mad.' To which I replied: 'Of course, everyone knows I was in a mad house.' The very next day he came out with that 'you are mad', I turned round and said: 'Look here, you can take your things out of this house and go and live with Rod. I'll ask him.' He was stunned. He looked deeply thoughtful, then he said: 'I like mothers.'

Rod told me he had worked for a brewery in London and the reason he is here is that the organiser of the project, Pat van Rensburg, is particularly fond of beer, so beer is one of the top priorities. I seem to think it will go down well too with all the hard work that is being done around the Brewery. A kitchen/café is in the process of being built and also some showers and toilets. Then at the back of the garden there's a kraal for pigs. The pigs are being brought to supply leather for the Tanners' Brigade to make sandals.

The garden is really there today because last year the work I did was also done with a particularly terrific woman. In many ways other people were not there and we often worked for hours and hours in silence. It's very difficult to get such a harmonious click. 1970 was hell for me. I remember the first days. I was reeling. She used to turn up for work. I used to steady myself. Then the fence came out of it. And today long, neat rows of vegetable beds. Somewhere between the fence and the vegetable beds I was entirely swamped by the internal storm. But today I look at the garden almost as an evolution in the relationship between the woman and I. She is in charge of it. Something remained of the early effort; the pioneer struggle; though when I wrote to you during the later stages I was maddened, ill and barely alive.

About writing. I have, in a practical sense, the writer's dream. Giles is. So is McCalls. Two perfect publishers saying: 'What's next?' There are the years and years when no one would care. And now at 34, there's nothing else I can do. And there's a terrible storm of living behind me, the sort of thing that was coherent, of my style – a gigantic Jacob's ladder of tormented dreams; always demanding the impossible from me; in situations that were not noble. The lack of nobility eventually rubbed off on to me. One cannot help being part of each situation. I think back to times when life was simpler – that's 15 years ago; and I was 22. I one morning swallowed 50 sleeping tablets and was forcefully brought back to life; by doctors. The process was so painful that nothing ever broke me again because there's nothing so awful as being pulled back to life with stomach pumps and drips. It was that which helped me to survive the Jacob's Ladder I encountered in Botswana. The inside world of everybody is obscure. Mine was given a significance only to force me to destroy it. It was composed of Gods; some were real and approachable; some knew. Love is simple in many ways at least what one sees on the surface; the losses and gains, the stability of some people's married lives. But like the song says – we know nothing of the chemical forces that flow from lover to lover. It's like melting the intangible soul to the intangible soul for good or ill. In the soul within, its power and to me, most decidedly the shortest route to heaven (then I found out it's the shortest route to hell too) for by heaven I saw clearly that insistent love directed at a single individual over a period was like changing every particle of plain earth into pure gold. You get the gold, yes. But love has a strange side; 'I'll never let go of you.' What I meant by millionaire was that too many people were loved insistently, then I was faced with breaking the links. I know it happened on an intangible level but a tight network of evil had built up around me. I knew those lovers had not been created in milksop circumstances; the nobility of the inside people was too high. I was unprepared to find both hell and heaven side by side. The explosion of December was the end of it because link after link was broken. <u>I was so surprised</u> by a remark in your letter: 'The image of a millionaire surrendering his wealth at gunpoint is perfect …' Words like perfection, beauty, goodness so little apply to me just now because the way in which it was done sickens me. You think back on our people's Gods. They say beautiful, perfect things – they make their spiritual abdications in peaceful circumstances, they walk through life as celibate monks: 'harm none, love everyone.' And to a certain extent people try to reflect that as the idea of the good life. But I saw a world where the souls of God dream both good and evil dreams and these take on living form. That is the nightmare and unfortunately like Elvis Presley – I'm all shook up.

As I have said in the beginning of my letter, my village of *Rain Clouds* is right on my doorstep but a living reality. It's really nothing for me to knock off another 60,000 words by December, but these other things, the heavy drains on my physical resources, the deep pull inwards, keeps on getting between me and what I am saying, insistently, forcing me to write two books at the same time. The second typescript got so messed up because I half had someone moving, laughing, washing, working, and it was shot through by a sort of cringing humiliation. Each person knows their working materials – I think the shoemaker knows his sandals are coming out right – so with the first line of a book.

I'm just getting my typewriter repaired – the 'h' is so worn out it doesn't hit through on the paper – and I'm just pulling through a dark tunnel so Giles might yet get the book he asked for about the garden. It's certainly not going to be another version of *Rain Clouds* because, like I said, Makhaya isn't there any more. He even moved into *Maru*, the same type of stillness and control. Only Penguins noticed it because they told Giles *Maru* is too similar to the first book and its only when I find I haven't got my stock idea of what a male is like that I too agree with them. It never ever bothered me that Makhaya was the best dressed-up version of Bessie

Head; imposed on, dominated and agreeable to my vision because I could manipulate him in writing. I think it might be much more difficult for me to write about men from another view – with Bessie Head imposed on. To tell the truth, I've been doing so much introspecting these days – to pinpoint crime, to pinpoint weakness, that I think now of a remark passed by a volunteer friend from America, named Mike. He said – 'You come over very strongly. You bowl people over.' You can't see it when ¾ part of your life goes by in solitude. I couldn't understand him, but now I'm thinking back to what he was like, quiet, always waiting to hear something and moving at a casual pace. One morning, as I was passing his rondavel I saw him at the window spraying perfume under his arms. I was intrigued. He was spraying perfume absent-mindedly. I asked him what he's doing. He said: 'I am going to work.' I said: 'I mean you're putting on perfume like a girl.' He didn't say anything but he had a nice way of smiling or an expression of sort of worldly know-all wisdom.

I think, though, that there are subtleties in dominance. There might be personality dominance which is easily recognisable and which I don't have – but between a man and a woman there are shaded-down inward things and very precarious and delicate balances that decide a relationship – its quality, the strength it will unfold. It must be a combination of intuition and feeling because you can actually feel a person struggling with you, say, for instance for a kiss and you see the point at which the man realizes he isn't going to get it. That's where Makhaya comes in. I know he isn't going to kiss me; or I think I know him and arrange my balances to my way of liking. Funny, one can really do this with a lot of men. It's no harm because one does not or could not love them.

As ever,

Bessie.

39. [*handwritten*]

P.O. Box 15,
SEROWE.

14 September 1971.

Dear Paddy,

The string bag was made in our Boiteko shop. It is woven out of ordinary coarse string. The necklace inside the bag is a combination of seed from a tree in the bush and watermelon seed which has been dyed. But an example of what we buy and make.

I would have liked to send some pottery but the young man who works in the shop tells me he sent some to his parents in England and it arrived crushed.

Sincerely,
Bessie.

40.

P.O. Box 15,
SEROWE.
Botswana.

15 October 1971.

Dear Paddy,

It's lovely weather for gardeners this side! I'm typing this letter in between running out into my garden to plant pumpkin seed. We are getting a lot of rain. The big garden is stuffed with vegetables and the members of Boiteko, our project, keep a sharp eye on it. We take the vegetables to the store and cabbage and onions disappear in a twinkling. Talking about the store, I did some shopping for you from my Boiteko earnings. Someone told me he had sent some pottery to his parents in England and it arrived crushed so I bought you a string bag which you sling over your shoulder for shopping. I saw the girls wear it like that. There's a necklace inside the bag I posted made from the seeds of the Morake tree and combined with dyed watermelon seeds.

The Cape Gooseberry does need a lot of sunlight to produce fruit. It is possible though that the plant will not die. What I usually have to do this side is let them grow and fruit during the summer and chop them down during winter. They grow very high here, produce well for one season – my yard yields 10 lbs gooseberries each week from fifty bushes from about October to May then they run into long stalks with hardly any fruit. I cut them back but they start sprouting new shoots again and grow up into a new season of fruit bearing. I suggest you watch your bushes. Stack them somewhere out of the snow and if they need cutting down perhaps do it early spring. I'll send you the seed of its relative, the Ground Cherry Tomato. Treat it very much like an ordinary tomato for planting. It produces fruit much quicker than the Cape Gooseberry. I have made jam from the Cherry Tomato. The seed was sent me from a friend in America. Women here love the Cape Gooseberry jam. For one thing the taste is heavenly. For another we did a lot of propaganda work on it last year and I think the affection for the jam is because I have grown it so successfully in my yard. People are fond of passing by and remarking: 'Cape Gooseberry' and laughing to show how much they picked up the propaganda … It's not so bad when the children pinch the fruit near the hedge because I have so many bushes. I had to discourage them a bit though because we are sending all the jam to the shop.

Thank you very much indeed for the spinach beet. We have already planted it on one bed in the big garden and it should thrive with all this rain.

Indeed I think my affection for *Lying-In* must be because I can make an emotional identification with the girl there but it is more than that. The writing is a piece of music; it grips the heart: 'the bar was dark and very small. William seemed to know the bartender – he seemed to know all bartenders …' It's singing. You just never forget the lines, the tense, vivid, squeezed out descriptions. Each situation, each involvement has this rhythmic beauty as though life at that time was lived on a plane of heightened emotion. I can follow it well because I depend very much on being captured mentally on such a plane for a piece of writing. It is like something forces the concentration really to a single point and so many other things are explained by the way. I felt it for my second book. For no particular reason a long, dry, thundery, brooding summer wrapped itself around me. It never rained. And the mood of the weather began to explain many other things for me. I think the mind picks on anything to explain the brooding of the heart; sometimes a love affair, sometimes a soul journey to the end of the universe but many other things get explained along the way and that's why I love *Lying-In*. It has the sharpest observations on life. I even began to wonder if you had overcome jealousy at the end of the book. It was thrown in so suddenly and profoundly at John. No it doesn't matter. Nothing matters, after all that's happened.

Yes I do agree that people could be very varied in a place like London. On the surface life appears very much an everyday sameness here but to me it is a very shocking country. Naomi said there is a lot of plot here. You know her most emotional writing was about Botswana. She once wrote to me, after *Maru* and said: 'You are right. There's something about Southern Africans that distinguishes them from other Africans. They have a light in them. I saw it in Linchwe (her adopted son). It used to drive me equally crazy with delight and despair and it isn't sex …' She adored Linchwe. She spent three quarter part of her stays in Botswana bursting into tears. Ah, Naomi was so lucky. She never penetrated the abnormal and most people who have lights in them are happily unaware of it. Her plots too were village life. It has a lot of humour and tragedy. There are subterranean plots which I have come to view with extreme distaste. Naomi felt the tug of the subterranean plot, the strange pull at the heart but that plot has incredibly varied strands. It fills me with dislike for it because it is a horrible nightmare. Some people are consciously directing it and pretending on the surface that nothing's going on and it is some awful secret I no longer care to concentrate on. The first time I thought it was universal and involved mankind, but when most of the nightmares are about a depraved maniac who eventually drives a person crazy then I wonder what's going on here. I like your remark about being watchful and careful.

Rod is indeed a lovely fellow. His lager beer is very bitter to taste. But he's a real sweety. We got a little pally. The other night there was a sudden thunderstorm and he came banging on the front door with a girl. They had been making beer together. At first I didn't hear because I was having a loud argument with Howard. He wanted me to read a bedtime story at the height of the storm and I had to put my hand behind my ear and shout out the words. I kept on saying I can't hear what I'm reading and he kept on saying he could hear quite well then I heard the girl shouting: 'Open the door! Open the door!' I was amazed to see Rod and the girl soaking wet and stared open-mouthed. All he said was: 'Please can we watch the thunderstorm through your window.' He hasn't got a window in his mud hut. I thought: 'Phew, this lets me off the hook with that pest Howard.' We had a tea party and had to shout at each other to get heard above the roar of a magnificent storm.

Yes, I have not been able to hasten the third book. There was depression and you might know how terrible that is for writing. Then there was typescripts one, two, three. Typescript one fed typescript two and typescript two fed typescript three. A friend of mine, Tom, stepped vigorously into the battle, arguing, directing the campaign: 'B. Head,' he said, 'It's time for you to produce a work of genius. Don't produce another Makhaya. He's a simple-minded simpleton at the level of Alan Paton's good hearted priest, Kumalo, in *Cry, the Beloved Country*. Makhaya never sinned. Don't produce another Maru. He's a Frankenstein monster. Don't produce any more men who are crippled sensualists and not real men.'

I waved my hands at this. He's right. Then I am fiddling around with something called, of all things, 'Theophilus' and something called 'Summer Flowers'. He said: 'Agh, it won't do. The title is too fluffy. Has Theophilus got a great brooding weakness and yellow patches like a man?' No, not directly. Theophilus is half my sense of humour and half the anxious eye I am keeping on Satan and he's floating free. It's Satan who has the great brooding weakness and someone half humorous and acute mentally has to keep a permanent eye on him. There's still food and plates and cups and women and children I have to introduce and poor Theophilus at first was trapped with two love affairs through Tom's silly advice, then I cancelled that and made him simply a good man tabbing Satan. There was a war going on and Satan got hit and hit and hit. He's cornered in a room by Theophilus with blood still streaming down his face from a wound in his head. Theophilus smiles humorously at Satan's bewildered appearance The poor fellow had never seen such a fight in his life before. Theophilus says: 'My friend, have you learnt your lesson? Will you leave girls alone? All your troubles have mainly stemmed from girls. We've been teaching you, for centuries about love. Love is like a girl walking down a road on staggering legs with the wind blowing through her hair. Love is like a girl with wonder in her eyes. Love is not your version of contorted passions and vicious desires.'

Satan was still licking his chops. The old game of finding someone as a companion for the unspeakable was hard to kill. He looked out through the window. The world in general was full of happily married people adoring each other. There was one woman standing alone in a furious huff. 'What's wrong with her. Why hasn't she got a husband?' said Satan. Theophilus burst out laughing. 'Do you want real trouble this time my friend. We call that woman Thunderbolt and leave her alone. She's very happily married but cannot help quarrelling with the husband. We don't know what the quarrels are about but every time we try to make a pass at that dame we get hit, we get into awful hell.'

Satan was very distracted mentally. An imbalance between a man and his wife was always meat for a major universal disaster. The world was really a world where every kiss had to be accounted for. 'How long is she going to stand like that in a huff,' Satan asked, his eyes gleaming. 'Oh for one century if she likes,' replied Theophilus. 'And who's occupying the husband in the meantime?' asked Satan, wildly excited. What, here was meat indeed! 'Go and make a pass,' said Theophilus, laughing. Of course Satan ran jubilantly out of the house. He had not time to even say hello to the woman before a hell of a blow hit him, stone unconscious. It was the woman's husband. That's all they did. They quarrelled all the time but they hit anyone who stepped into the quarrel. Even Satan was puzzled. No one could explain a situation like that. It was something new and very fearful …

These themes are supposed to be somewhere amidst work and

housekeeping and things. Theophilus has a nice wife. Satan has a wife too except that he's always wanting to fiddle around with other men's wives and I want to fix him for good with his own blasted business, the damn bugger and damn nuisance. So Theophilus is trying to handle the undying evil in Satan with a sense of humour, keeping in mind a lot of suffering caused by that bastard. Why he can't clean himself up forever, beats me. Why he can't leave other men's wives alone beats me. Why he can't keep his blessed eyes in his own blessed house, beats me. Why he can't stop manufacturing perversion, beats me. Why he can't be normal, ordinary, decent like other men, beats me. And if some woman doesn't temporarily want to be on talking terms with her blessed husband, that's none of his damn business. I am trying to work out that three quarter part of the trouble in the universe has always been men and woman with Satan in between. That he is a real personality is what I'm trying to say. It's a half wild statement but I hope Theophilus can carry the day for me. I make him a little dreamy and absent-minded so people won't think it odd to carry on a tirade against Satan.

That's how the third book progresses with interruptions from Tom, which are very welcome, and gardening work. I was getting worried about the way I was carrying on with the third book, throwing in all kinds of things as the mood took me, when suddenly today I began to relax a little and laugh. *Maru* has been bought by a film man in New York. I sent off the signed contracts and get about three hundred pounds or less for next year. Enough to keep me in food right through. Then by then the third book ought to be complete and some symphony, I hope on many struggles. Love is like a girl walking down a road on staggering legs with the wind blowing through her hair. Love is like a girl with wonder in her eyes ... Love is like ... I have this and that to say. All kinds of things. I have been battling and battling with the characters because I am over-strained emotionally. I am so over-strained that I just couldn't find the usual people of Africa who would be recognisable even as Africans and the struggle goes on and on. Satan is quite alright. They always said he was a black man, anyway. But to deflate emotional tension and strain to an ordinary, even keel is so damn hard. So the film sale of *Maru* is a damn blessing just now as I would have run out of cash soon enough and had to worry about that too. I am very puzzled though about how that film man is going to dramatise *Maru*. It is internally dramatic. But translated to external dramatics I'm afraid someone like Maru would look comic on the screen with those re-bounding phrases ... How universal was the language of oppression! It is one thing to follow a thread of drama, totally inside, and almost everything is inside. The outside bits are so scant they can turn the whole thing into a farce. I felt this right from the time the film contract was mentioned and feel afraid. But so desperate are my circumstances that I knew I'd take the money. But I feel a real terror because I know my work and don't think it suitable film material.

Thank you very much for linking up Howard to the Puffin Club. He's very fond of reading, a story every night and it all began with Pooh and William. It is also the only time I get to talk with him. He can't stand the loneliness of the house and is away straight after meals, wandering, I don't know where, but so many children float around that it seems to be no great worry. He's so fond of other children that there used to be a time when I trailed hordes around with me and fed them too. There was always something and cake when I had my oven. But since I have been ill and there have been some dark days here, I have shooed them all away. I couldn't seem to stand it. I hadn't the energy for one extra gesture. It embarrassed the old man very much, selfishness, chasing the friends away at meal times but all I seemed to want to do was sit down and not think or feel anything. It helps when other people say they have been through the same thing and it takes time to pull out of it.

We are really having a glorious summer with rain on the horizon. And if it really rains what a lot of food, pumpkin, watermelon, cabbage, spinach, green onions, tomatoes. The early rain is a surprise because this time of the year is hell. Hot dry wind storms from the desert. Hot, baking days. First time summer came in so magnificently, since I've been here. First time gardeners get such good luck one can almost feel the rush of growth in the garden.

I shall be posting Naomi's book to Dan by sea mail on Monday. It is really a good picture of everyday life in Botswana. And I like the beginning very much: 'There are hundreds of children in Ditlabeng.' It is so very true of village life. They are all over the place. Ditlabeng means the place of many hills. There is one thing about Naomi I noticed. She's lived to old age because she collects the threads of life together patiently, placidly almost. They are there. There is little of that wild emotional, erratic soaring of the heart but the facts of life get stated. I think she sits in writing. My ticker is giving in. I feel it won't last long. The storms are too fierce and three quarter part of life for me is spent toning down the ticker and a quarter writing. I tried all sorts of mental exercises to get to Naomi's calm of heart and head but I haven't found the formula just yet. I neared it the other day, almost. Something about [being] near the centre of life and putting out one hand to rest on its quiet pulse.

Regards to Dulan.

As ever,
Bessie

41.

P.O. Box 15,
SEROWE,
Botswana.

20 October 1971.

Dear Paddy,

Of course I don't mind you reading from *Rain Clouds*. Talk about being flattered! I am so happy you liked the bag. This year is fabulous for food. I've been shut up for a week in my house because of rain. It's pouring outside and of course gardeners don't have much to do in the rain. I would like to know how far apart you thin your spinach beet. The packet says nine inches apart, but it meant throwing away so much of the stand. Why so far apart? Would the leaves get bigger and lusher if they were thinned so much? I only have beetroot thinned 3 inches apart and you can get very big beets at that distance. The fruit of the Tomato Ground Cherry is not yet ripe but when it is I shall seed it and send you some of the seed. I want to try it out, if possible, for winter because it does not [like] the heat. Most of the crop just gets withered by the sun. It might grow very well in your garden. I have some ginger in the yard, for experiment, and tobacco again. The ginger is supposed to be for ginger beer and the tobacco for cigarettes but no one knows how to make cigarettes. When I was in the loony bin all the ladies there were using snuff. They made it themselves from dried tobacco leaves, so I am going to cure the leaves then persuade Pat van Rensburg, the organiser of Boiteko, to use the leaves for snuff instead of cigarettes. I think he got the idea that I can perform miracles through the strange version of agriculture and progress in *Rain Clouds*!

I was (talking about the loony bin) reading Darwin while there, the origin of the species. He had some argument about English gooseberries being hairy. I failed to grasp the importance of it to plant life because *Origin of the Species* I found terribly tedious half way through. He spans out information over tea with his friend Mr. So-and-So and I kept on losing the thread of the origin of the species. What I memorized thoroughly was his dedication in the beginning ...'But with regard to the material world, we can at least go so far as this – we can perceive that events are brought about not by insulated interpositions of Divine power, exerted in each particular case, but by the <u>establishment of general laws</u> ...' And about evolution he says: ... 'There is grandeur in this view of life, with its several powers, having been originally breathed into a few forms or into one; and that whilst this planet has gone on cycling on according to the fixed law of gravity, from so simple a beginning endless forms most beautiful and most wonderful have been, and are being evolved ...'

I heard over the news about some pictures being taken of Mars. There was a terrible dust storm raging for days. Fancy that! Fancy hearing news about the weather conditions of Mars. I am very out of touch with newspapers here so please could you send me any pictures your paper might carry about the dust storm on Mars. Mars rises just over a small hill near my house about six o'clock each evening, a fiery glow of light in the sky. I used to fight with people so much at one time that I was fond of calling myself, Mars, the God of War and the planet of fire!

Indeed, I am ashamed to trouble you but if there are any books for Howard I would like some more Williams. I must pay the bill, though, as it is a special order. The times William is read are such happy times because the stories are so rich and beautiful, the children so wonderful.

The Williams I have so far are: *Sweet William, William – The Dictator, William – The Outlaw, William in Trouble, William The Conqueror*. Now, as you might have noticed William is very dominant. Second in command is Ginger and poor Henry and Douglas struggle along. They are completely outshone by the genius of William and the author's obvious adoration of him. Girls don't figure at all, so much so that I totally overlooked William's equal among the female species. It is the girl Violet Elizabeth. The first time I took note of her at all was in the story where she prevents her father and mother from making it into the high society of the village. Mr Bott, her father is an illiterate – get-rich-quick man. He made a lot of money on Botts sauce but he and his wife can't make it into the high society of the village because they can't talk English properly. One day a certain Lady Markham condescends to call on Mrs Bott mostly because she wants a donation of money for her charity stall. Poor Mrs Bott is hysterical with excitement and Mr Bott is stammering. Fancy the lady calling on them! At this point, in walks Violet Elizabeth followed by the four Outlaws ...

Violet Elizabeth addressed herself to her father.

'Do you want a thnake to make into thauth?' she said, 'becauth we'll thell you one for three shillingth.'

'What,' bellowed Mr. Bott.

'William thayth,' lisped Violet Elizabeth placidly, 'that you make thauth out of black beetleth. Tho we thought that perhapth you'd like a thnake, too.'

'WHAT!' boomed Mr. Bott.

He looked as if he were going to burst with fury. Mrs. Bott wanted to have hysterics. Lady Markham pinched herself to see whether she was awake, and found, rather to her surprise that she was.

'We thought,' continued Violet Elizabeth unabashed, 'that a thnake might do as well. Ith a nithe thnake. Ith athleep now.'

She took the lid off the box and peeped in. But the snake was apparently no longer asleep. With a strong untwisting of its coils it came out upon the carpet. It was of the grass-snake variety. Mr. Bott leapt upon the grand piano ...'

That woke me up to real genius in a little girl. I just did not notice her before. William simply blots out EVERYONE, his personality is so powerful. I raced through all the books again for the stories with Violet Elizabeth in them and funnily enough she really balances William. She's the only other living being with that incredible genius – it makes up life on the spot. William hates her but she just flings herself at his feet, with feminine cunning. My favourite story is the 'newthpaper'.

William and the Outlaws are in the old barn producing a newspaper.

Violet Elizabeth stood smiling happily in the doorway. 'I made them let me come,' she explained. 'I wanted to find you all an' play with you, tho I thcreamed an' thcreamed an' thcreamed till they let me.'

She beamed around triumphantly.

'What you doing, William?' she said.

'We're writing a newspaper an' we don't want girls,' said William, firmly.

'But I want to write a newthpaper too,' pleaded Violet Elizabeth.

'Well, you're not going to,' he said.

'I can write too, I can,' said Violet Elizabeth plaintively. 'I can write newthpaperth, too, I can. I'm a good writer, I am. I can thpell, too, I can.'

'Well, you're not going to thpell here,' mimicked William heartlessly.

Violet Elizabeth dried her tears. She saw that they were useless and she did not believe in wasting her effects.

'All right,' she said calmly. 'I'll thcream then. I'll thcream and thcream and thcream till I'm thick.'

More than once William had seen the small but redoubtable lady fulfil this threat quite literally. He watched her with fearsome awe. Violet Elizabeth, with a look of fiendish determination on her angelic face, opened her small mouth.

'All right,' said William brokenly. 'Come on, write if you want to.'

For some minutes there was silence broken only by the sighs and groans of the editorial staff. The silence was finally broken by Violet Elizabeth who raised her voice again shrill and unabashed.

'I don't thee what good a newthpaper ith without any crimeth.'

'What do you mean sayin'' that a newspaper isn't any good without crimes?'

'Therth alwayth crimeth in newthpaperth,' said Violet Elizabeth, with that air of superior knowledge which the Outlaws always found so maddening in one of her extreme youth. 'Thereth crimeth and polithe and people going to prithon. If you're going to have a real newthpaper, thomebody ought to do a crime.'

'All right' said William. 'All right. Go and do one then.'

Violet Elizabeth leapt to her feet.

'Yeth I will William,' she said sweetly. 'I don't mind.

The long quotation is really bribery. I mean, a person has to go to the shop for me in England and look for the William books even if I offer to pay the bill. But they are a real need. I can't get the child to bed without a bedtime story these days and I am deeply ashamed to admit that I don't like them unless they entertain me too. The amount of times I've howled my head off at the deeds of the Outlaws and the human beings of that nameless village in England! Richmal Crompton puts in everything, from children to grown up people and every line is precious to me. She couldn't have made it so rich unless her childhood was like that. You just can't invent William. He's too real. It's very good for Howard too as it's his ideal world. I don't know where he gets to like other children so much. I never taught it to him at all.

The story of the neighbour's children is so nice. Does the wife sometimes come in to tea? I am making some cake tomorrow for a tea party with a comrade of mine at the Farmers' Brigade garden. His wife came in yesterday and caught me having a jam session with Miriam Makeba. It was pouring with rain so I put on a calypso of hers called Chove-Chuva, which means it is raining, a rain that will never stop. So she swung into a dance right on the spot. She is a Shona lady from Rhodesia named Nouella and her husband is Tony Hall from England. He met her in Rhodesia and they had to come to Botswana to get married. She told me she was afraid to marry Tony as he was a white man but he pursued her for a year. They are leaving for England in January and I am so sorry because I work with Tony on the equipment side (orders) for Boiteko garden and he's a heavenly person to know. He'll do anything for one and go far out of his way. One day I ordered some seed from him for Boiteko garden. He brought the seed right to the gate. I said: 'Thank you.' So he did not move. So I said: 'Would you like some tea?' So he came and sat down. Suddenly the details of the breakdown all came pouring out. He listened intently. 'Our minds aren't meeting,' he said. 'Your presentation of good and evil is something I've never heard before.' He brought the seed at four. Then sat and sat and sat till about seven listening and listening. So many people did that for me. They kept on pulling and pulling me out of death with a kindness I have never known in my life before. I have lived face to face with death for a whole year.

As ever.
Bessie

42.

> P.O. Box 15,
> SEROWE,
> Botswana, Africa.
>
> 30 December 1971.

Dear Paddy,

Thanks so much for the Christmas cards. A lot of my life is still linked to the life of Tony Hall and his wife Nouannah (I spelt her name wrong). I spent Christmas with them and the house was full of Christmas cards from the family in England to the children – from Auntie Jackie, Auntie Gill and Grandad – people they won't see until they get there in late January. Then they may have to live with Auntie Gill and Grandad etc., for some time unless Tony gets another job in Botswana. It is about the only place that needs volunteers in Africa, so Tony says. He couldn't get a job anywhere else because I asked him why the hell he came to the desert which won't grow crops.

So I picked up your card just after Christmas with the turkey running away from being made into a Christmas dinner and laughed and laughed again because it reminded me of Nouannah and the disaster of her Christmas dinner. First of all we were supposed to eat a duck at lunch time and Tony killed it early in the morning. He said quite a few prayers because I think in one of his previous incarnations he must have been a Jain, those people in India who don't kill things, not even germs. Then he came out with a long story about the duck, a male. This fellow had lived for a year with two female ducks just below his house and failed to make them produce off-spring. He was nice and fat though. Then he and Nouannah sat over a cookery book. (She has piles and piles in her kitchen. She grew up in a tribal reserve and only ate sadza in Rhodesia. That's why her mother tried to dissuade her from marrying a white man – what does he eat? Would he ever eat sadza? Conscious of this one can eat some weird and indigestible food in her house like cheese hamburger pie from the fancy cookery books.) Tony takes part in the cooking. First he said: 'We're following the book with the duck. It says: Use no oil. Prick it all over. Is that alright?' I threw up my hands in wild alarm. I knew nothing. I am just as much an un-cook as they are and as I told you my first acquaintance with food was 1969 when I started the garden. Then he wanted 4 ozs of bread. Ah, from cake making I knew 4 ozs equals one cup. He would have none of that. He went down to the farm and brought back a huge scale and measured out the bread to the last ounce.

The second thing was that on the previous day, Friday, there had been an abrupt interruption to our Christmas dinner plans to eat the duck. Another family had invited Tony and his wife to a picnic Christmas dinner in the bush. We were later to have to put inverted commas in the word 'invited'. First of all the lady of that house had been a pet enemy against whom I had waged a long and bitter war. She, like my other enemy the Danish lady is one of those snotty things from Europe. Well, the appalling breakdown, the radius of scandal and shock so improved my behaviour I even found a place for the snotty thing in the universe. I no longer muttered moron, bugger, first class loony bin and stinker each time her name was mentioned. In the old days I would have found an excuse to not join the picnic but when Tony said: 'We asked her if you could come along too and she said: 'Oh, Bessie, of course, of course.' They're all supposed to say that since the poor dear darling came out of the loony bin. So I smiled quite cheerfully and said of course, of course too. There's nothing like the loony bin to make one love one's enemies. My dear, if I say one more bad thing and add a blow to it, I might go back there, you know. So Nouannah said we'd eat the duck in the evening. And eat the picnic the other lady was supposed to provide. Then Nouannah said, when I arrived there she was packing a basket, I had in my hands a treacle sponge pudding, chocolate cake and a tin of Christmas mince pies. She threw the sponge pudding into the basket with a cake she'd made, some biscuit and a dried up portion of chicken which had been cooked three or four times in the oven over a period of two days. She said: 'I don't want to go to the picnic without something too.' So I said: 'My pudding needs custard sauce. Let me make some quickly and put it into the basket.' So Nouannah shouted: 'Hurry they are coming. I'm going to dress the children. Don't forget to tell me to turn off the oven. I once put three pounds of meat into the oven and forgot it and it got burnt to a small black coal.'

Something went wrong between the sound of the picnic car outside and Nouannah's children. First she dressed the small boy Peter. Then she dressed the small girl Chinisa. Then the small boy Peter took off his clothes and got into the bath again. Then the girl Chinisa threw a sudden tantrum. The girl Chinisa looks African and the spitting image of her mother but she's a foreign body if there ever was one. First of all she's so small and so thin you can't even see her. I can't. My own child is beefy, big, solid. The next thing, from such a speck on the floor comes an ear-splitting volume and such a terrible rage. She is fascinating. I've never seen such beautiful grace and fairy-like movements but when something turns her, and this happens in a split second, she stands and bellows like a bull and flings everything around. I noticed a strange logic in her every gesture. She always ASKS for permission to do something or to eat something with exquisite charm. Then someone fails to fulfill her demands and she gets mad as hell because she ASKED. Like she'd ask to jump into hell fire and you <u>have</u> to be there to see it through to the end. Her parents are absent-minded, I have only one child. I am used to that persistent logic in Howard. I've been drilled to following out his reasoning abilities to avert pitch black sulks. Later in the day I noticed that the Chinisa girl began to throw herself into my arms, because I was the only one concentrating on her next plan and carrying it through. She'd say: 'Can I eat the apple.' And I'd say: 'Of course, go ahead.' Then everyone would start shouting at her: 'Hey where did you get that.' And I say: 'No, no, it's alright, I told her to eat it.' That was enough for her. She'd part gracefully with her food, as long as someone was saying the right thing. She'd not taken it. She'd <u>ASKED</u>.

So Chinisa was having a tantrum. Peter was having a second bath. The picnic car was going hoot, hoot. I was standing somewhere near a window struggling mentally against the din of the household and saying to myself: 'Thank God, I've only had one of them and at that the quiet, solid masculine type who seldom loses his dignity.' I put my custard sauce into the picnic basket. My pet enemy was standing on the stairs. For some reason known only to herself, enemy says in a loud voice: 'Bessie must sit next to my husband in the front, I am sitting at the back.' She had a lot of guests with her. The last thing I wanted to do was sit next to the husband. I suppose that was her Christmas gesture to God because she is insanely jealous of the husband. That added to the din of the children. Why did the moron pick so loudly on me? Out of the blue? I looked around in desperation for Nouannah. She sat next to the husband. She forgot to turn off the oven in which the duck was cooking and immediately began casting appreciative eyes over the moron's husband's physical bare-ness. 'You have a wonderful sunburn,' she said, and other such pleasant remarks about the gentleman, smiling and laughing the whole journey through.

At the picnic spot Nouannah and the Moron unpacked their baskets. I had none and stood at a distance. I could hear the Moron keeping up a stream of small chatter with Nouannah. That's what I hate her for among other things, the meaningless babble, the false smiles, the careful film star poses and tosses of a mane of stringy brown hair, the permanent and stupid equally meaningless endearments to the husband. After a while I began helping to hand out plates of chicken. The Moron cooked it. Nice, juicy, tender. So I said: 'Give me some more chicken.'

Suddenly Nouannah shouted: 'Oh, my duck. I forgot to turn off the oven.' Then she said, accusingly: 'Bessie I told you to remind me.' Then Tony stood up and said abruptly: 'I'm going home to turn off the oven.' And off he went, a two hour journey on foot. He never returned. He went to bed. Nouannah sat in a quiet, thoughtful heap. I've never seen a woman like her for permanent and endless laughter.

When we got home and were washing up the dishes she turned on me: 'Why did you eat so much of that woman's chicken? Do you know what she said to me? She said I ought to have brought my own food as she only brought enough food for her own guests and not mine and there you kept on asking for more chicken. I hate her.'

I looked thoughtfully through the window. So, the Moron was living up to her reputation again. So, in spite of the loony bin I can allow myself the gorgeous, luxurious, intoxicating, delirious joy, joy Oh joy of saying I hate her too. So that's what I said. Then Nouannah said: 'I'm sorry I'm married to Tony. I wanted to run away with her husband from the first day we became friends. She's done so many mean things to me and the only way to set her straight is to run away with her husband.'

I nearly shouted my head off with laughter. It's been going on for years in Botswana – women hating the Moron and making a bid for the husband. The thing is no one dare say it straight like that. I knew quite a few who never succeeded – with the Moron's husband. He's ice. The one thing he hates is marital infidelity. He'll do most other things but he won't take another woman and really pretty women have hit their heads against a stone wall. I think he knows. First they hate the Moron on sight. They always look at the man as a source of revenge against the woman, not as a source of love. No one falls in love with him. They get bitten by the wife and get so wild they want to hurt back. The only way is through the husband. I have never seen such a peculiar set up in my life before. I have never seen the same conclusion in so many women's minds before and Nouannah said it out for the first time. There is something appalling about a mean small, selfish woman. All woman hate her, like that's the kind of thing they don't want around on earth. Whatever a woman is, she's got to be generous, even if she's a bastard. It deepened something I'd known a long time. The feminine world is a powerful, instinctive mental pool of agreement. When there's something wrong with one woman or she's not a real woman <u>they</u> know and they don't care whether they set out to destroy her. I'm sorry for the Moron, she'll never be a normal woman from here to eternity and the picture is so awful, the anguish of that man's married life so terrible that I wonder what he did wrong to go through the excruciating experience of being married to the Moron because he can't push her soul up anywhere, it's a dead, jangling thing and all the women know. That's what they're fighting, death, in something essentially creative, woman-kind.

You don't know how much I look forward to the Odetta record. I pray it arrives in one piece. I have six Makeba's I play over and over. I was surprised to find that Howard knows the songs backwards too.

Ah, the life of a gardener here is a hard one. After the early rain, drought set in. But the early rain awoke a creature from seven leagues under the earth, a ferocious beetle people call vaguely a Sebokolodi. I think it just means general nuisance. It eats everything and travels in swarms. I have a thousand in my garden. They like the flowers of the pumpkin and squash so no food developed. After they'd eaten that, they settled on my gooseberry trees. I just hope they'll go underground again in winter and hibernate for another decade. I have never seen them in my life before and a co-gardener, a Motswana lady says she's not either.

Much love,
Bessie

43.

P.O. Box 15,
SEROWE,
Botswana.

22 January 1972.

Dear Paddy,

There are so many thank you's etc., that I thought I'd start with Chinua Achebe first. Yes, I read *Things Fall Apart* and two of his other books tracing the ancient tribal ways of the Ibo. In one way I agree with you, there's no lift to the heart, there is nothing to make the soul fly away on the surface [of] everyday life in Africa. It is not only with writing, the music too. It is just as flat and unmysterious. The real lift musically I got from Miriam Makeba, but she worked with Belafonte, Bill Salter and together they took the prosaic and made it wonder. I did not know the meaning of some of the Xhosa lyrics so I had to ask some people of her tribe to translate for me. They said: 'Yes, we know the words but that is not our music.' Emotion was changed, highlighted, with the accent placed in the right places, so much so that some of the wails of human suffering in the Xhosa, Zulu lyrics make your hair stand straight up the first time you hear them. I had been working out a certain line of thought about writers in Africa when the links were abruptly broken off, through the end of two magazines I used to receive – *Transition* and *The New African*. What was slowly emerging was the top class scholarship of all the brains of this continent. I feel, basically that the African man is not a romanticist but a scholar along Confucian lines. That I found in Achebe, in portions of his novel but I had been familiar with the style through the writing in *Transition*. They were a bunch of real brain pickers – pages and pages of assessments and critiques of other writers, especially if they were black. I think Achebe was reviewed so often, and so thoroughly he ought to have a king-size ego. I could never make it as a reviewer when compared to what I used to read in those two magazines. There was more too, nothing in life and revolutions and suffering escaped them. I have often cried over the fact of Banda's weird performance in Malawi. Ministers of so-and-so used to write for *Transition* and such deep thought on matters African and economic and philosophical that you'd wonder how such people with brain cells could put up with Banda. They are not heard at all. It is always Banda.

There is something else. The nearest I can come to compare in nations with the present African social structure is the Jews on their early history. They were just the same, flat, prosaic, unmysterious. Their history was made when God began talking to them out of the air – he must have had a tremendous sense of humour because the surprise and alarm recorded was so great and caused so much upheaval and turmoil, right till the time of the birth of Jesus. You will note from his speeches how a particular tradition has built up where he talks in historical terms about Moses, like yesterday. This is still coming here, the same capacity to absorb, the startling, the weird, the surprise and from my side, of course, the massive, the monumental. Achebe must have seen some things in his country with that war! I laughed like hell this morning. General Somebody of Uganda made a coup last year against Obote. Then last month he invited Dr. Busia to the celebrations to celebrate the coup, only to have Dr. Busia couped in Ghana. Then he invites the couper to his coup celebrations, just the same. CAN YOU BEAT IT? This news came over B.B.C. world service, reported in the ordinary, prosaic voice of those fellows.

I mostly hear the news from B.B.C. each morning, with no newspapers at all. I was lost for some time with the Pakistani war till I got a copy of *Newsweek*. I do think *Time Magazine* and *Newsweek* are real abominations of journalism – there's an undertone of ugliness, there's Al Capone there and they certainly give the impression that the American government is usually run by Al Capone. The only exception was the long ago build up they gave to Kennedy when he was unknown.

From the details in *Newsweek*, I was able to fill in some background. This *Newsweek* sort of posed a mock sympathy for the common man in socialist or so-called socialist countries. If what I gathered about the rich '22 Families' of West Pakistan who have all the lolly, is true – and [they] sit on it and use millions of cheap labour – then what the bloody hell was Nixon doing supporting West Pakistan openly against India? That's what came over B.B.C. for a long time but it seems like the politics of Pakistan is a stinking mess of exploitation. In this day and age no sane politician who wanted more place and position would touch a millionaire exploiter with a barge pole. But there was no American criticism of Nixon at all, in spite of the alarming story of pressure, evil and greed in West Pakistan. I suppose this is usual American politics, then the pose of *Newsweek* of doing a great exposure is surely sham.

Then I am not quite sure about what England is doing with this

Rhodesian settlement business, though it is in the news. Some people say this side that they are trying to do a Pontius Pilate act to wash their hands of the whole business but it is not so simple. Smith said: 'The white man in Southern Africa has nothing to fear.' Then he makes open, contemptuous statements about black men. I am sure between he and Vorster, they've got the bomb and they're keeping it top secret. Or they have tremendous reserves of war weapons. The strange and tragic thing about independence is that it was often handed to people who had never suffered and people who live in the grill of it are maddened with hope in world trends of brotherhood and co-operation. I think really of myself. It is an unheard of world, especially where I am at present, where so many people from so many different countries care about people who have not enough to eat. (Just a side line to the Rhodesian business – they will get free, suddenly, perhaps explosively, but I fear much the same sort of situation where the Prison Graduates with no brains or overbloated egos will get to power while some real brains will be ousted. People like to mock when something goes wrong but it's often that people don't vote for ability in the first rush but who cooks up the most emotional stew, then he gets coup-ed when they or the army can't stomach it any more. I heard news that Tanzania is fast heading for a military coup in the near future. As far as I can see, few politicians can live the doctrine of socialism and it's a major source of conflict and political upheaval in Asian and African countries because they are all committed to socialism, of some kind. The natural instinct at the beginning of things is to get rich quick when one has been poor and insecure. And yet, it seems, the whole finances of the world are at a point where some new formula is due. If there were a pool of people with power and goodness to come up with something between Karl Marx and the future ... why, I might be able to put my poverty programme to one side and dream.)

Which brings me to my first thank you. The Odetta record arrived safe and completely whole in a pretty shop packet which I admired for some time. I never get shop packets like that in Botswana and it made me feel briefly that I was back in Cape Town. Next I got quite completely stuck on the side – 'Give A Damn, about your fellow man'. I played this piece so often wishing there were more of it. For one thing it is my early childhood background and has always been my essential life, mingled with my wanderings into all kinds of environments. At 18 I did have a choice of marrying a very poor man who laughed the day long and I wonder now how I would have made out, in his home with about eight children, like the ghettos of New York and abysmal poverty. As it is, I have only the summary of my wanderings and the soliloquies I conduct with myself each night. It is always as though through self-communication, I'd touch on something concrete, as though at the back of my mind the experience of poverty was very necessary. I've kept it there more solidly than any upheavals and breakdowns and to a certain extent music like that helps to solidify vague feelings. There was not much about her development on the cover – you get reams of literature about Makeba but I noted that her accompanants were the Rolling Stones and the Beatles. This took me aback a little because I had never concentrated on their music, though some of the publicity about their searches for eternal truth reached me. Then everything is put over peculiarly with rough almost raucous sound, like her own song – I've Gotta Be Me. Everything is right – 'Here I am, all by myself. Here I was trying to be somebody else. Now I see. I gotta be me …' Her extreme, rough, crude masculinity is like a blow in the face. Her love songs have no tenderness. She's a terrible woman, really three-quarter-part male in feeling and I was so shocked at most of the first notes, they really sound like a man. I just pretend myself to belong to the male world mostly because I get along so well with men but phew! I turned quite pale at the lady's music.

You know one can't have enough of music, so I had to really limit myself to what I have in this way-out backwater and alternate it with the end chapters of Dr Zhivago and his poetry. It is not so much Makeba I am in love with but Bill Salter who wrote the lyrics of 'When I've Passed On' – don't make any marking for my grave. I have lived under terrible stress but I'll be stripped one day and my soul shall be free. Then I'll look back on this life and expect somewhere to find someone who will share the prize I've won, I can't see it now, but someone ought to weep and mourn, when I've passed on (because I am a great lover of my fellow man). For some reason I accept that as my own rigid soul doctrine. It is right. Makeba interprets it beautifully and I can only think he must have been stirred by her own achievements to hand over such gems of soaring magnificence and abysmal humility. I really took it as my theme song for *Maru* and if I were consulted by that film man, I'd say: 'Use that music.' The whole book is permeated by it.

I've heard no more about the film. As I said, I fear it but as you said one never knows what is behind it and how it might turn out.

As I said one can't have enough of music and to a certain extent I am contented with what I have, welcoming as well the shattering fe-male Odetta but if I could have one more addition, I'd be very grateful. It is a girl Nancy Wilson I heard over the radio. In general her love songs are very good full of steam and she has a powerful voice. Most are love in the American style, so sure, so assertive, then she came out with one striking record. It goes something like this:

Black. Is beautiful. Velvet
Black is the colour of the night.
Black is coal.
Black is toil.
Black is soil.
Black is a panther in the jungle.
Black is you and me.
So baby don't you cry. You'll be free before
You die.
Black is beautiful.

That's all I can recall. It is longer but so intensely sung with the haunting shades and undertones of the love songs that that is quite enough by itself to add to my diet of re-played records. My record player takes both 35 r.p.m and 45 r.p.m. Sometimes the smashers come out singly in a small r.p.m, and if the record store has a single cut of 'Black is Beautiful', I'd appreciate it very much.

Which brings me to my third thank you. Giles hastened to send me a copy of the week-end *Scotsman* in which you handed laurels to *Maru* as your choice of book of the year. Thank you very much indeed. Yes, indeed, a lot of the perceptions were vivid, internal dreams so much so that I came to later depend on their accuracy which was eventually my mental undoing because I never took into account that I could be dominated by evil impressions, that someone hated me enough to use them to destroy me. When I made an assessment of the experience I began to understand both Lucifer and Hitler. They <u>know</u> they have no equal for wilful evil, that they can do any damn thing they like. There is a sense of wild revelry and alert planning. It hypnotises one like the rabbit and the hawk. Someone had my lines and hooked me because I was trapped by the apparent display of nobility and equally trapped by the wild evil. There is half of wild, daring courage in nobility so it seemed like my lines could be very easily mixed with Lucifer's. That is a shock and severe learning I hope I'll never recover from. I can't learn enough of it, the narrow dividing line between good and evil and how, in the very beginning I was created totally powerless and how, at crucial points the roads of destiny point two ways – straight to hell ... then straight to hell. I am looking there with severe eyes because I am damned fed up of the paltry game of filth, of personalities who flay their stinking penises in the air because that's all they've got. I compare. The searches for eternal goodness never took in a situation with a total lack of compassion, none of mankind's God-like figure-heads saw what I saw on this nightmare soul journey but mankind saw the workings of Hitler's mind and that's what I really encountered – relentless cruelty and evil.

You said to me, not so long ago, things have to churn over, they cannot be hastened. Why are you hurrying with the fifth book? You have to throw Vanessa and that neurotic Elinor/David relationship away. I so much long to see the novel, in part, of your poem, 'Hyacinth'. I put it at the back of Zhivago because so often I acquired brief loves and barely ventured to take advantage of them, thinking in my mind of ending old links and saying final goodbyes. I've been stuck at Pasternak's lines for a long time ... 'Remember how we said goodbye that day, in all that snow? What a trick you played on me! Would I have ever gone without you? Oh, I know, I know you forced yourself to do it, you thought it was for my good. And after that everything went wrong. What I had to put up with out there. <u>Lord, what I went through</u>! But of course you don't know any of that.' Those lines really belong to a husband I have not yet acquired ... 'Lord, what I went through! But of course you don't know any of that.' One might not say it literally but with a laughing boldness of heart. There was no company for me on my lonely road. Shit-arses one, two, three, four, five have their pretty dolls who know nothing of the perversity of their inner natures. They bow and scrape and smile those men, but they stink.

I have so much news about seeds and here half the night is gone typing this letter:
1. From New Year's Day, the sky darkened and Noah's deluge descended on us in torrential tropical rains. This was too much for the Sebokolodi in my garden. They disappeared overnight. The rain won't stop. Trucks overturn on the slippery clay main road. Houses are washed away in floods. People are killed by lightning. The tragedies mount up and up and the deluge pours. The village is deserted. Half the population ran away to their lands

to plough. That's nearly 22 days of continuous rain. It is pouring outside as I write now and I just don't know how to include this weather in a future novel because it is the exception, not the rule. It can only go with exceptional experiences. Just before Christmas we nearly died in the heat.
2. Would you like to try out some seed which is a failure here due to the extreme heat? I have a spinach here I ordered called Monstrous Viroflay. People say it is really the genuine spinach but it just bolts to seed and the leaves are poor. I do know that bolting is caused by incompatibility with climatic conditions, so I thought it might do well in your garden. On the other hand, the spinach beet thrived. Worms don't like it so much. At one blow we harvested 40 lbs of it from that small bed and are just now due to harvest even more. I am therefore replacing Monstrous Viroflay with its relative Swiss Chard, advertised as spinach beet or perpetual spinach.
3. Another seed failure. Tomato Ponderosa. It is the outsize salad tomato and I really ordered it with our regular Tomato Moneymaker because I thought people would like to make salad, in summer. I had successfully grown another king size variety Tomato Oxheart but the seed firm had no Oxheart in stock and sent me Ponderosa. It grows to full size, then while still green busts open. Then the flies lay eggs there in two minutes and it is rotten right through in two days. Tony examined the crop and said that the skin was too soft to withstand climatic conditions here, so I thought it might be able to grow in the cooler climate of England.

Well, that's all. I have to get busy this side. Giles asked when the other book is coming up. I told him I was feeling like a million dollars. It's from figuring out things, of what a cheap, trashy Al Capone show the things of the spirit can really be, of how near it all is to the jugglers in a circus, of how the cheap and trashy power-mongers dazzle the mind and then saying: 'Why, the bloody bastard is the biggest joke this side of lunacy.' I want to question deeply a line in *Lying-in* about William. You say: 'As though he always knew he was God.' He flings himself around but he hasn't the moral strength to be God. He just goes and pisses with the lady writer from Hampstead Heath. How did the line get in, like that? I am deeply interested. I watched William's parallel with shock. He actually said he was the director of the universe since 1910 or something, with all the phenomena in the sky and the chorus of angels but he was pissing like hell, a small baby with a permanently wet napkin and a shit arse so bad someone had to wipe it up all the time. I must say I laughed at the feminine mind. It took me a whole year to make the summary but I didn't have to marry IT, thank God! It was just there. God knows where it came from but like the things they think will come from outer space with contamination, I wish it out of my sight. I don't know of any psychological laboratory where it can ever be cleaned up, so horrible a sight did I see. You ought to meet up with William one day and tell him right to his face that he is a shit arse. I did it to the Moleka of my book and you could see some kind of rainbow there. What! Didn't I blow him up! Bastards aren't that necessary if mankind has died so often. We don't need another Hitler who hypnotises.

As ever,

Bessie

44.

> P.O. Box 15,
> SEROWE.
> Botswana.
>
> 17 March 1972.

Dear Paddy,

I have a cat who also once shit indoors. She's there to catch or chase away snakes and if she has babies they are to stay and chase the snakes too. At the beginning of summer a terrible amount of snakes crawl about when it is very hot. The most ghastly thing is to meet up with a cobra – the blessed thing is ferocious, he charges at one, spitting fierce jets straight towards the eyes; they say he wants to blind his victim, then kill. I lost my nerve after three encounters with them. Every time I see a snake I throw the cat out of the window and sit indoors with Howard. Well, the blessed cat looks awfully pretty with her dainty ways but the shit was so awful that I threw up. It took me quite unawares. I had no idea of the stench. Then we took in Tony's dog, Nut, and he likes to pee and deposit dollops of hell around the house when I don't wake up in time to let him out at night. I'm sure all shit smells bad but animal shit is very upsetting.

I still don't agree with the instructions on the back of the packet of spinach beet you sent me. They said to thin out nine inches apart. Well, I was forced to upturn the spinach bed to clear an area for a new variety of tomato we are trying out. The stunning thing was the gigantic tuberous roots of the spinach beet, enormous things like monstrous roots of molar teeth. I could see they want us to make way for those roots underground but I still said to myself I get quite big beets thinned three inches apart. The variety we are trying out is called 'Indian River.' Isn't the name gorgeous? A seed catalogue is really a wonderland of fantastic titles some of which could be used for novels like Indian River. Indian River is supposed to grow to a height of 5ft and bear tomatoes all up the vine. I have a good idea of what five foot could be as I am 5 ft 2". We had so much hell and loss with tomatoes busting that Indian River is having a trial run in my yard before I order the one ounce packet of seed. The Italian Jam tomato and a variety called Moneymaker sprawl with food in our garden but we are always trying out something new. If Ponderosa does well that side I'll send you the remaining seed. I thought you might like some more Leraka so I'm enclosing some seed.

Giles sent me *The Umbrella Man*. I had just time to peep at parts of it but it is so intensely exciting, the style is very male and tense. I had to put it to one side because I am working like hell towards the end of my third book and struggling to keep the arguments strung high, and somewhat hysterical. Just right now the pitch of hysteria has to be maintained for something like 21,000 words to balance the conclusion which is a big puff of peaceful white cloud. I want to attempt a total summary of the experiences recorded because it gives weight to what the book is all about – it was lessons for the soul. So I have had to put aside all other material till about April when at least the first draft will be through. The title I finally settled for is – *A Question of Power* and I throw the title line in at the end ... 'If the things of the soul are really a question of power then anyone in possession of power of the spirit could be called, Lucifer ...'

How well then your own explanation of love and power blend with what I am doing just now! I shall put the letter among the notes I have for the conclusion, except that strength pure and simple felt by a particular individual deludes him with a sense of supremacy at the expense of other human lives – people then are highly expendable commodities; he has no love except for himself and his own importance. I try to say that the gods were originally like that at a time when they had an insight into their powers. It was abolished by the monastic forms of religion and sacrifice established by personalities like Jesus and a softness and tenderness entered mankind's history. These questions are examined in the book in an African setting, in a village in Botswana. I kept on working at isolated, unrelated typescripts and gathered all the material together into my present work. For one thing the title started me on the journey but whether the book would see publication day is doubtful. I'd like to test your reaction to something I worked on. It is so brief and nearly irrelevant to the story but it could be the cause of the book being rejected.

First of all the proposition is that of a God forced by African circumstances to divest himself of his vesture garments and be ordinary like everyone else. The process of this spiritual striptease makes him uncover horrors within. That's bad enough as in general his job was religion itself. He is not clearly outlined in historical terms except to say that wherever religion was, there he was. The snag comes in with another personality, a portion of whose previous lives create[s] a tangle of evil. The tangle of evil is unfolded by inner perception back to the point where this personality lived a life as Buddha. Here starts the evil. Buddha made no joke of his

Nirvana. He actually stopped the propulsion of his soul into the cycle of birth and re-birth. It was really: 'Stop the world, I wanna get off.' He is pulled back to life through association with the first personality because a plan was unfolding to introduce this softer, tender approach to human affairs. The relationship between the two is like the mental complement you get in Jesus and Paul. The first personality introduces a planned evil into the life of what was Buddha. Buddha had a wife he took as a soul companion over a number of lives and trained her in the disciplines of the soul. Unfortunately, spiritual associations aroused a fanatical type of love so violent that under adverse circumstances, the monk becomes a brutal murderer. The first personality joins the soul of Buddha's wife to that of a prostitute. The Buddha is pulled down into the life of David of the Jews. David meets Bathsheba. He sees in her eyes the tender blue glow of a great love. The dominant passion is ownership and he commits a hideous murder such as only Al Capone could dream of, contradicting the brilliant nobility of the man's soul. Then there are the confused contradictions and orders of the prophets. They tell David it had to happen like that. It was planned murder, ordered by God. So there you have it. The Nirvana of Buddha is cancelled. He is propelled into birth after birth, by the chain of passion he had not really overcome. It is things like that, very briefly explained which may get the book rejected. But the apparently mad story of the Jews takes on a strange coherence in the light of this examination. I had to put it like that because once a cycle of evil is there, ghouls trade on the soul and the central character in the book, a girl, is hacked to pieces by awful bastards – there is nothing left of her in the end but huge gaping holes where the jackals of hells snapped out their pound of flesh. The sensation of being held down and eaten slowly to death is a part of the hysteria of the book but someone quite new takes on a disaster and crime that created a long chain of evil circumstances. So powerful are the forces of hell that they do not concede that immense suffering is enough; they want total doom; they want the total destruction of the soul of the Buddha – after all he could be Al Capone too.

I put down these things almost matter of factly as they appeared in a sort of stream of consciousness way, a kind of under-current life that proceeds side by side with real life. The terrible mental-confusion at the end was a life and death struggle with the 'brains' of hell itself. He'd been ordered to do the soul assassination of someone basically innocent of crime. The real murderer of Uriah was the first personality who had planned the evil. This first personality had also introduced to Buddha, the road to Nirvana and a new idea of goodness which opposed power. As I first saw it as an expression on the face of Buddha, it was inward concentration. He moved slowly towards me, with his eyelids covering his eyes; his whole life had been turned <u>inwards</u>; it was not that of the prancing ghoul concentrating on earthly thrones and prestige, and a holiness of soul he had was indifferent to prayers or anything; he heard nothing; he cared about nothing; he saw nothing; he had become nothing but his inward simplicity. To face that and at the same time work out the questions here, in Africa, was like signing one's death warrant in advance. God knows how I am still alive. The brutality of my experience was so terrible, the things done to me so degrading, the viciousness of the 'big brains' from downstairs so extreme, he wasn't human – he was power at its most ultimate. Power does not attack something its own size, it attacks the powerless. One might pull through to a sense of peace but my terror is so extreme it's like living from day to day with the barest chance of survival.

These things come up in the book. The major part is the African contribution to the argument but the way things are put creates many snags and I have already written to Giles expressing anxiety about the work, like I know in advance it can be rejected. I know it does not matter eventually. In the main it is so personal that it might only be useful for my own record of inner growth. It might help to know your personal reactions to the above-mentioned. They are incidental but they link the present to the past and the first half of the book has some of my best lines – flat proposals are made – they appear to be lost in mental confusion and breakdown and are picked up at the end again.

If Giles had to accept the book I'd very much like to dedicate it to you for so many reasons – the garden comes in, the Cape Gooseberry, and I have much to thank you for during this time of correspondence. So let me know if you'd like that and I can tell Giles. He might like things like that passage on Buddha cancelled or put down without any direct reference in case people say Gollancz publishes the writing of loony bins.

Indeed the opening passage of Naomi's book is majestic: 'There are hundreds of children in Ditlabeng'.

Let me enclose a little piece that appeared in our daily paper here with a picture of her and I.

Do you have a copy of the piece you did on Achebe? I now vaguely remember *Things Fall Apart* – but often throughout the narrative, he'd pause and reflect on his European education with deep analysis and balance this against his African background. I remember liking these passages best, the stillness of one sitting back and reflecting, often with amusement, on life. A lot of that sort of thing appeared in African writing – that's where the soul really soars, a type of philosopher so prosaic, he keeps his finger right on the pulse of life ...

As ever,

Bessie

45.

P.O. Box 15,
SEROWE,
Botswana, Africa.

16 April 1972

Dear Paddy,

Well, *A Question of Power* has gone off to Giles about a week ago. I have to wait to hear from him but he would surely mention something to you at some stage. I'm also dedicating it, if accepted to my friend, Randolph Vigne and someone else around here. Thank you very much for agreeing to have your name in the dedication. I read in Darwin's book that Karl Marx wanted to dedicate *Das Capital* to him and he refused. How did Darwin sense that Marxism did not really stand for the evolution of the human soul, least of all human society? People can't bloody well evolve and feel happy under the constant threat of the secret police and Siberia.

Well, of course I said all I wanted to say on damnation in *A Question of Power* (damn it, I can't shorten the title) but two of my most treasured lines were left out:

a. Bathsheba's speech: 'Guys and dolls, his company is no play time, if you want to have a nice time.'
b. Satan: 'The white racialists would like that. They always said he was a black man anyway.'

I could not get them in somehow and I like them very much. I suspect one day that I'll get onto that Bathsheba story and put line a. in. Bastards and prostitutes hate exposure and the shuddering horror the girl went through after seducing David must have been a scream. Every time I think about it, I howl.

There is something causing me considerable discomfort though. Two of the Satanic personalities in the book, Dan and Medusa are pitch black in colour. Unfortunately, that was how they appeared in my nightmare. I tended to write things down straight from mental photographic recollection and lines like this – Medusa's soul was a black, shapeless mass with wings – are going to be awfully misread. The other mad thing was that they were terribly anti me on the grounds that I wasn't a genuine African but a half breed. They were after the soul, they wanted to kill my soul but used this hatred of my appearance as a front. Then the depths of racial hatreds, class and arrogance were in them. I kept on trying to balance all the arguments at a soul level but it is extremely difficult to say that you are digging out all the horrors of mankind at their roots. The word 'people' recurs often – they are briefly introduced as black and white then the switch is totally on their worth as people. For *Maru*, I had a terrific cast. For *Power* (that sound nice?) I do it again. Like you said of *Maru*, I feel in my bones, this is another masterpiece. God knows this author is bloody vain but then I went through hell.

I have gone stark raving mad here. The Nancy Wilson record arrived. I've almost played it into extinction – every blessed morning I wake up it's first Nancy Wilson. After a time I got a very funny feeling about her – she sounds just like Billy Holliday. I thought she might be the re-incarnation of Billy Holliday, that is Billy Holliday's soul just moved into her. The voices are identical, I know because in South Africa I was mad about Holliday and the way Nancy says 'my man' and wails is just the way Holliday used to. Some of her tunes are very difficult to sing over while watering the garden. I can't get the style.

[*ends*]

46.

P.O. Box 15,
SEROWE,
Botswana, Africa.

19 May 1972.

Dear Paddy,

Could you help me? Could you arrange to receive the carbon of my novel – *A Question of Power* – from my agent Hilary Rubinstein, A.P. Watt & Son, 26/28 Bedford Row, London W.C.1? I asked him to please transfer it to you.

For one thing both he and Giles are agreed that the novel is meaningless and something they can't understand at all. For reasons of his own Giles wrote in such a way as to squash any further comment on the book but the attitude of my agent is very suspect. He is so anxious to label the book unprintable that he refuses to send it on to McCalls, who could give me a second opinion. They are so much in haste to say that the book needs no opinion at all that I am left stunned and open mouthed at the sorts of letters I have received from Hilary and Giles. Giles practically told me I needn't reply to his letter. God knows my relationship with them has been entirely impersonal and I wish to leave matters like that. I sent Giles a postcard, something about our paths likely to cross again. I had an uneasy feeling that he was a friend and one of the banes of my life is keeping eternal friendships with people. Anyway I was mighty confused when I sent the postcard and fear I might have written: 'You damn bugger,' by mistake.

The first need is to get an unalarmed opinion on the book, the development of a small dialogue about it. I am sorry but it stops my life just now. There is a new song behind it but the pain of that book is so terrible, someone will hook out the obstacles and fears it created in my mind. I would value an opinion from both you and Dulan. As you know I have had no communication with Dulan but he wrote the sort of review for *Maru* that caught at all the essentials. It would be different if I had set myself up as a creator of James Hadley Chase. Ian Fleming did not have to cry about anything. He just had to churn the stuff out and go and sip a cocktail in a posh lounge. It is quite something else to meditate, to return each day to a solitude that grows deeper and deeper each day. It is quite something else writing down the hard work of one's inner life. It is not just that easily dismissed. Things I concentrated on, what I call the doctrine of the ordinary are developed to a conclusion there, things I learnt about good and evil are rounded out such as I was not able to in my other books. Could you and Dulan please send me separate opinions, then I could see what I ought to do with the typescripts after that? Please tell Dulan that although I've never written to him I did very deeply appreciate his review of *Maru*. The third book almost spills out from *Maru*. It has no love theme such as *Maru* had, no belief in love at all but there is a terrible battle with two men on a level that makes everything said wisely more than personal. I just feel terribly frantic. This is the first thing I thought of doing.

As ever,
Bessie

47.

P.O. Box 15,
SEROWE,
Botswana.

24 May 1972.

Dear Paddy,

Our letters must have crossed in the post because I'd just written asking you to take one of my typescripts from Hilary Rubinstein, my agent. Then you tell me Giles had already let you read the typescript. That's quite all right.

Hilary isn't doing the right thing. McCalls also published *Maru* and they wrote to me asking if I was working on another book. I said yes. Hilary wrote saying that he wasn't sending *Power* on to them till Giles had read the book and he set Giles up over my head like the sword of Damocles. The next thing Giles brought the sword down with such a vengeance, I stood rooted to my P.O. Box for well on an hour, totally incapable of movement. In some way I was stone dead, temporarily, with a terrible roar in my head. I remember posting a postcard off to Giles but I have no idea what I wrote because what I was saying when I came to was: 'Oh the damn bugger.' I thought I might have written that on the postcard.

I am not unsettled about anything said about the book but by Hilary's behaviour. Why won't he send the typescript on to McCalls? There's a 50–50 chance that someone there might catch hold of my hand. That's how I usually work, with someone holding my hand. I don't care a damn about rejections but I do care about the hand holding. It is just that much more difficult to re-work certain parts alone or to throw the book away and move on to the next song. To a certain extent I had half started a hum; I was off on another track and now those buggers suddenly made me turn around and re-examine *Power*.

Hilary's letter came first. It was the height of patronage and very annoying, between the lines it said: 'Poor dear darling just came out of the loony bin and is not responsible for what she is saying. There's half a chance that Sello is the President of Botswana. Shudder, shudder, shudder. And as for the portrait of Satan! Shudder, shudder, shudder ...' His letter was hysterical, scared and patronising all at once. I alternated swear words with howls of laughter, then I thought that I might need the kind of agent who leaves his home and forgets to put his tie on because the sorts of things I have in mind are – the riddle of life, the riddle of death, and the beauty of loving. He bloody well thinks that that wild and beautiful song can be made staid, conventional, pretty, with a public guaranteed in advance. Do you know of any agent who forgets to put his tie on, is fairly absent-minded and might have read Plato and Pasternak with his whole heart?

From my end it is difficult to sort out just how impersonal this whole business is. You'd think you have a buddy and get a terrible slap in the face. Bob Gottlieb one of my American editors rejected *Maru* on the grounds that it would upset the American public. Quite the opposite happened when *Maru* came out. I permanently despised Gottlieb after that letter. He was reduced to his proper size, a small-minded, liberal Jew one ought not to take seriously. I only moved over to Giles because I had not picked up any meaningful correspondence with the McCalls people. Giles could have simply said he was buzzing off somewhere and did not want any new work. As it is he wrote the sort of letter, so confused and contradictory, the only thing apparent was an anxiety to shove me off the scene. His sizing up of the book was just words that added up to nothing. It isn't 'prose poetry bordering on the meaningless,' as he says. I produced a very poor first draft of *Rain Clouds* and no one shoved me off the scene. They were anxious to give guid[ance] out of the stage fright I suffered from.

I don't quite agree with you about the build up of the South African background. It was just to say that I had no authority in my life and always formed my own moral code. I am not a small-minded-petty little goody-goody and yet at the same time intensely moral. It is like finding a morality in the free air. I'll do anything that comes to hand, walk into any den or hovel or brothel and yet find no need to become a prostitute or Al Capone. But my buddies were prostitutes and Al Capone. It is unavoidable in South Africa, nearly all black people are criminals of some kind because they starve. In the story I used the word 'slum background' to explain how easy it was to adapt myself to the tormented hell of the two men, Dan and Sello. The torment was heightened because they are actually creative forces who can generate these currents outward and affect mankind. It was terribly painful because it was the source, evil and secretive.

The Sello story is part public property and part private. In the story I clung to the private side but the public side led to my son being assaulted in 1968 and finally a journey to the loony bin in 1971. The last episode was intended by me either to throw off Sello and Dan or to invite death. I was driven with my back to the wall and let fly with the hatchets.

The main thing is I moved on dead sure ground till 1971, that is why I packed the whole of the Sello story into Part One and really closed it. He produced two themes, the majestic monk and his lower self which appeared as Sello in the brown suit. In me there was and still is both a terror and respect for the austere heights because I know what it cost to travel up there, the discipline, the sacrifice and the unswerving meditation on what we called God. This God was a vast and generous theory but the captivating imagination behind it, was Sello. He produced the theories and he could not expound the disciplines unless he had been through the fire first.

I am sorry but I laughed from the start. It was the pattern of the monastic life. Contrary to what the priests expound, the mournful serious morality, the friendship between Sello and I rebounded with laughter. He was fond of under-cutting me because I have a vast blind spot for detail. He has the kind of perverse mind that likes to spring the big surprise and a kind of sense of humour, so deep it takes you hours to figure out the joke. His mind works like this: I'll put my buddy into this predicament and my buddy will start to say: 'Hey what the bloody hell is going on here. Look here all you bloody people, I'll tell you I'll stand no nonsense from you.' That's the sort of situation he likes, a clownish performer to use as a front for the latest joke, the latest theory on soul development and he knows I'll always come in on cue – and perform.

It took me some time to realise that there was considerable torture under the joke this time, a continuous reversal and confusion of decisions. There were certain things he made public to Batswana people that set them rearing against me in wild alarm, the possibility of some kind of love relationship. Some pictures were issued in mid-1968 (a woman told me they were religious pictures) which resulted in my son being assaulted. People took it into their heads to spit on me and call me Bushman and bastard. At each point of alarm and hysteria, he quickly produced that picture of "his future wife." 'She's a good housekeeper isn't she,' he'd say to me. 'That's what I need most of all. I don't see (those details).'

He kept on deflecting the attention from the real issue at hand which was actually the evolution of our own relationship. He had a terrible domination as the super monk, a sway and control over my soul from centuries of spontaneous co-operation. Love has a thousand faces but most intense is the love of the heights. It is split-second timing and co-ordination of thought and feeling. It was always a case of – if you jump into the fire, I'll jump in straight after you. The anguish of the Botswana episode was to break those old links. They were no longer needed. I found that if old links could not be snapped perversion of terrible kinds developed and there is a soul explanation for the deviate – someone would not let go.

Here sets in complication number one. The first thing I did on sensing any kind of man/woman love between Sello and I, was to roar with laughter until people began hitting my son. It wasn't love like that. It has always been male laughter and the big surprise of the burning bush and things like that. My position suddenly began to seem vulnerable to me. I thought: 'The man is socially powerful and he's told people something. I'll most probably decide to marry him in a pinch, simply because I'm blocked in, can't get out and it might be the most reasonable thing to do.' Ah, once I had figured that out – out came the loud shout of *Maru*. 'Hey Maru, look here, I'll marry you simply because this situation is a bit too much for me but here are my terms: I'm not going to have anything to do with cattle thieves or people who live on other people's blood money or stolen goods. Give up all that blood money.'

To my surprise everything was reversed. He got hold of Maru and the monk quietly admitted that this was time for good-bye, that he wasn't at all like Maru, that he was full of bad intentions like James Hadley Chase and awfully sorry about this and here was the picture of his future wife.

Then moan, moan, moan. 'Oh, what will become of me, I cannot say goodbye to the comrade. Oh, oh, oh.' All during this time I was supposed to have a head of steel and not be bothered by anything. It was all right at that time because my sense of humour kept me going.

In stepped Medusa. I began to lose the humour. In stepped Dan and I lost my sense of humour altogether. All Dan had was that red fire of hell and his penis. Now why did Sello give him free entry into the world of the monks?

Both Sello and I had <u>great</u> loves. None of Sello's loves became evident except for Medusa alias Mary Magdalene. But the face of Jesus was copied by a thousand men and the face of Buddha was copied by a thousand men because vast numbers of souls happened to like that version of goodness.

The back references to Buddha and the complications that arose out of his Nirvana were one of Sello's repetitive themes. First of all Sello expounded the basic theory, that of reducing form, sensation, movement feeling to no form, no movement, no sensation, no feeling. Then as was his practice, he produced Nirvana but he had a control over the disciplines which Buddha the pupil had not. He pushed the theory to its extremes, succeeded in extinguishing his soul while seven of his followers repeated the feat after him.

Sello let Dan into this heaven, maybe some time ago. He said he had to use evil to get those men back to the cycle of birth and death. He said '<u>to use evil</u>.'

So from that time my soul destiny is extremely dubious. The Dan man was one. There was Moleka. He was the complete re-run here of the David story of the bible and from what I gathered from Sello, that David story followed the life of Buddha.

The Moleka story started as soon as I arrived here. The man had a sort of yellow glow in his eyes, it came over as worship, he had a love of depth, something you could hold on to for an eternity. It's not my style but I took one look at him and keeled over so hard, I started to shake from end to end. I was absolutely convinced that this was love, the end. Then the clamour arose. Each detail that led to the murder of Uriah was re-lived. He turned up as a woman and the sister of Sello, a woman named Naledi. Sello forcefully married Moleka to his sister. I nearly died absolutely convinced, as David was, that that was my possession. I never questioned that that love was feminine, soft, debilitating. It was a flame, like that eternal light and not put out. The Naledi woman rose up: 'You killed me,' and her face was streaming with blood. A whole force rose up: 'Don't go near that man. He is the death of your soul.'

I figured out later that that love was Buddha's one weak link. He admitted into his heart the worship of his wife. Sello mixed it up with something like shit from hell and that caused the murder. I know half because the people who have been through the disciplines of sacrifice, GIVE WAY. They generally NEVER take something over someone else's dead body. They say: 'I'll do without,' or 'I'll die.'

We closed that door, we killed the love and he said the woman would one day be his.

Much, much more dangerous and terrible was the Dan story. He was allowed to meddle with the Nirvana men. Sello let him in. He, Dan, saw the height of their austerity and power. He pinched. For my benefit and destruction he stole some of the love themes:

a. The Bothwell song – 'My darling if I lose you I have nothing else.' The record was so terrible, it was agonised high tension pain. I recognised the anguish of a man who had never been allowed by society to love. Dan put his face in front of the record.
b. Someone in that Nirvana heaven doubled the relationship I had with Sello, if-you-jump-into-the-fire-I-jump in after you. That man had the river coming down in full flood, signalling a love so precariously balanced that it caused the death of two people at the same time. Dan looked at that, pinched it and turned on the storm. I kept on hearing the Bothwell record and the wild rush of the river. How was I supposed to survive? Everything was smeared over with shit of a small piddling bastard, so cunning he seemed to think that by stealing the light of those Nirvana men he could be God. They were white men in their present lives. The seven of them, with Sello and I made up the bulk of the work we called God. I met three of them.

The writing of *Power* was an attempt to partially blow open the story. I thought Sello was ready, and all those men who reached the heights of austerity can wake up and see the whole pattern of destiny and God/goodness, its power and explain it to mankind without the mumbo-jumbo the priests subject people to. We formed the base of all mankind has now of goodness but when there is so much killing and hate it is obvious that there is a crossroad just now – an abrupt swing to complete darkness or an abrupt swing to complete light for all men.

Sincerely,

Bessie

48.

P.O. Box 15,
SEROWE,
Botswana.

7 June 1972.

My dear Comrade,
I had kept on meaning to write and thank you for the seeds but you were silent for a long time, so I was not sure where you were. The Swiss Chard you sent is definitely a different variety from the one we are using. I planted it the same day and it has already germinated and I am eager to compare it against the variety I have planted. I told Bosele to be careful not to pick it too early as I want to see how big it is. People are mad about spinach and denude the beds before the leaves are fully grown.

Thanks too for your letter on my book. I have received many such powerful letters forcing me to suppress it and not to even dream it is printable. The storm has centred around the Gollancz people and my agent as though Gollancz is the only publishing house in the world. I am just looking for a little more than having my insanity flung in my face. Admittedly I went through hell but it was a learning even if an erratic one most people do not usually encounter and there is enough boxing material in me to see where I am going.

The typescript has been read by the whole of Swaneng. Liz read it. She said the parts on Pat are very beautiful.

As ever,
Bessie

P.S. I am very grateful to Gollancz for letting you have the typescript. At least you could see what prompted the wild letter I wrote you. Evil had gained a complete control of my mind. It took me a whole year to untangle it, slowly, bit by bit. It was so cunningly done that I do not think I was meant to survive. People do not believe in the forces of evil or hell least of all that they could be personified in living people. I laughed so much when you came out with the names of Seretse and Masire.

Seretse is a very good man. He is not the devil. I hope I gave you the right impression this time. I have been rather confused about him and deeply sorry about that post office business.

But people who read the book here told me that the personalities take second place to the arguments on power and evil. You, Giles Gordon, Hilary Rubinstein are only thinking about who is who.
[*ends*]

49. [*handwritten on air letter*]

[*no address*]
6 July 1972.

Dear Paddy,
I'm 35 today and so is my waistline. Thank you for your letter of [June] 17th. I'd asked James Currey to take over the carbon typescript from you. He most probably could not do much with it and I knew he had contact with Randolph so I asked him to finally hand it to Randolph Vigne as a gift from me. K sent the top copy to McCalls. I just want them (McCalls) to see I did do work. Hilary would not post it on for me; that's why I was mad like that.

I am just extremely depressed at present and not capable of writing much. I have just received Dulan's letter on his reactions to *Power*. I do appreciate it and enclose a short note to him below:

Dear Joby Dean,
Thank you for your long letter. First, I like your story about the ravens for children but never created the occasion to say so. Secondly, about *Power*, I acknowledge that Sello is both the strength and weakness of the book. He's been my stock idea of a male and long acquaintance makes one tend to over-write. I never really cared a damn what I said about the devil, alias Dan. He is the abyss of horror. I simply depended on contrast and implication. Really insane people like Dan never get to the loony bin because they have control of horrific powers. People without those powers are killed or driven insane. Therefore, *Power* was a discussion over Good and Evil. Then more. The ancient and somewhat exclusive road of the mystic or monk who says: 'I know humility. I know love. I know goodness.' It never helps much.

Yours sincerely,
Bessie.

50.

P.O. Box 15,
SEROWE,
Botswana.

8 July 1972.

Dear Paddy,
Your letter and Giles offer are certainly a surprise. Yes, I do accept Giles offer to take over my work from A.P. Watt and Hilary. For one thing I just pulled the roof down on my head and when I do that I become quite indifferent as to what happens next because it has usually happened so often in my life that losses are a natural part of living for me.

The gentleman, that is, Giles Gordon, has an odd way of turning up but this is rather soon. I always say that I make permanent friendships with people and link this to a subconscious activity – that friendships of all kinds started long ago in many past lives. It is often so strong and yet accompanied by a strange feeling of non-possession. Maxim Gorky once explained this in mathematical terms to a friend. They were sitting on a bench in the afternoon sun in a park. They were deeply absorbed in a philosophical discussion and Gorky said that at some point, one hundred years later he and his friend would find themselves on a park bench, in the afternoon sun, engaged in this same conversation. I can't remember Gorky's formula but I think he got it from Tolstoy and Tolstoy got it from Gandhi but I agree with the general statement that people always meet again and again.

The main thing is that for a writer the publishing business is a terrible hurly burly and very upsetting. On the one hand a person may view his times and his life earnestly and write from that standpoint. On the other, unfamiliar people keep on dashing in and out and it is difficult to explain things to someone you don't know, that this particular piece of work bears such importance to one's development. Are you interested, so to speak? The pull and tug with Hilary and the final explosion was simply this issue, not the unprintabability of *Power* but the feeling that I had [to have] contact with someone I could explain something to. I told him I had two hands but I had not pulled on the hand of Susan Stanwood. She kept on shooting out friendly advances, particularly after I came back from hospital and I kept on failing to write to her. Once I only sent in a filled-in questionnaire.

I was terribly depressed at the time and said of *Maru*: 'It is about the soul, but it is vague material. The soul is a complicated area and needs a stronger argument.' She wrote back right away and said that she was interested in my changed attitude to the book as this would surely affect my future writing. I did not reply. She kept on sending eager little notes to which I barely replied, or left unanswered. Suddenly I had nothing and thought of her. Hilary blocked me and then I simply cared about those eager little notes I had ignored. It happens like that. I just could not confide in her in any way. She was unknown; Hilary could have said he did not like the book but would forward it anyway as I had mentioned again and again the letters of the Stanwood woman. It's always like that about a book, until someone loves it and a rejection with affection and such words as 'I'd hate to lose touch with you,' simply help a person get on with another book because the next time one might produce something that meets needs both ways. You would agree with me that one couldn't be a damn guy fawkes and go on parade over eager to please. Norman Mailer once wrote that all they told him, as a writer, was that he had to study the market. God where do you end up? Someone telling you what you ought to write. Thank you very much. I enclose with this letter, a letter to Giles. Could you hand it on for me?

Sincerely,
Bessie

49.

P.O. Box 15,
SEROWE,
Botswana.

22 July 1972

Dear Paddy,

First of all I had sent some return notes to Dulan, just to more or less acknowledge his and towards the end made a miscalculation in time ... I meant to write two <u>thousand</u> decades and left out the thousand.

Next to the pottery. The pottery is a part of our Boiteko project. It is run by a man and his wife, Peter and Christine Hawes. I have just talked to the wife and she suggested that it would be better for you to get in touch with them yourself and she could give you some idea of what they are doing. They will be having some nice things in about a month's time when they do final firing for glaze. She said she would also have to talk to Peter about packing and see whether he could come up with a more secure way of packing the things so that they are not broken on the journey. Their address is:

Peter and Christine Hawes,
Swaneng Hill School,
P.O. Box 101,
Serowe, Botswana.

In the meanwhile, I have quite a large collection of the pottery and the instructor of the Builders' Brigade, RICHARD JAQUES, will be arriving in England in a month's time, with his wife, Eileen. I am sending with him three of the pottery plates and when he arrives in London he will make some arrangements to hand it over to you. I have left the price label on one so you get an idea of the cost of the plates. The price label says 70c, that is about 7/- . There are two plates then and a sort of small dish for Dan. The plate with the label 70c is very fancy and has BOTSWANA glazed on it, so you and Dulan can argue about who is to eat out of it. Richard is a rather gorgeous fellow and a very dear friend of mine. You often can't hear what he is saying and he is dreadfully shy so I hope he finds your house.

Summer has just arrived, you say. I wonder. This morning as I turned on the radio for B.B.C. world service, I heard the following: 'Good-morning. It is 0.6 hours Greenwich Mean Time and a Saturday morning – a rather horrible Saturday morning, in London, raining, wet damp, warm and muggy ...' English weather is so terrible that the B.B.C. announcers often begin the news with it through sheer misery. I was so tickled by the weather report that I found myself quoting Shelley in a mixed up way: 'If summer comes in England, can spring be far behind?' I looked out of my window at a brilliantly blue sky and thick white dew on the cauliflowers in my garden.

We haven't any more of the Monstrous Viroflay left which has grown so well your side but I still have a half packet of the tomato Ponderosa to send if it can grow there. We are more or less getting into our stride this side with gardening work. My partner and I, the 'Kenosi' of my book, drew up a planting programme to defeat the insects and the summer sun. Then all the women lost their inhibitions about the fancier types of vegetables and began to state their preferences. They told 'Kenosi' to tell me they liked the Italian Jam Tomato. At first they did not like its strange bell shape but suddenly it became very popular. It is good for us because we can grow it easily. Anyway I enclose a copy of the garden report we have just drawn up.

Yes, people here have been telling me that my third book is just like the Doris Lessing books. I have only read *The Golden Notebook*, a very depressed love affair with a man she despises, an American. You may send it and please a packet of Marjoram.

Sincerely,

Bessie

[*handwritten*] P.S. Just received a letter from Giles.

52. [*handwritten on air letter*]

[*no address*]
23 August 1972.

Dear Paddy,
Richard and Eileen Ja<u>c</u>ques (I left out the <u>c</u> last time) will be in London on about August 28th. They left about 2 weeks ago. I gave them your phone number from the top of one of your letters so they might phone you first. The items I sent with them were the first crude products. The pottery improves as time goes by.

Oh, I get along with Giles alright. I am more or less used to him.

A state of affairs has developed here in Southern Africa where, to a certain extent B.B.C. world service is the only reliable source of news. There's a lot of jamming from South Africa and Rhodesia. They deliberately jam Radio Tanzania. The most awful racket comes through and Zambia is very dubious, so many personal wars. Another thing, they have a mania about experts – one programme after another of an expert talking on this and that till in the end it gets you down – you get to dislike those patient explanatory voices. Voice of America I once contacted for the moon expedition but I disliked it, and finally settled for B.B.C. It's good and has the review of the British press. The British seem to enjoy involvement in world affairs – so much is a hang over of their Empire days and they argue vehemently in a broad way. I'm on China just now. Something nice came over about Mao's China.

Bessie.

53.

P.O. Box 15,
SEROWE,
Botswana.

9 September 1972.

Dear Paddy,

Thank you for the Marjoram seeds. I am enclosing some Coriander seed in exchange for them. The Coriander grows like weed in my yard and I have masses of the seed but I can't grow Thyme and other herbs. Also, the Marjoram will grow well but last time I tried to seed it and failed so I shall propagate this new lot of Marjoram you have sent me from its shoots. Botswana is, at times, a depressing country for vegetable gardeners. I am still moping about the winter months when the outdoors was tolerable but these days it's like a broiler outside and I have to count a hundred before I can get myself out of the house. I really like gardening from six to seven in the evening but it means rushing all the work at once. So, this afternoon, I simply gave up counting and sat indoors.

God, the way I dither. It's taken me weeks to decide to change my typewriter ribbon and I can't make up my mind yet. I think my life is getting very inefficient.

The Chinua Achebe book arrived and I enjoyed it, on the whole. He is particularly strong at depicting the ordinary Nigerian and particularly weak at portraying an elite he obviously identifies himself with. Some of the stories of the African privileged are so revolting and his weakness is that at some stage he came to accept this as the status quo. He does not condemn it strongly enough and I get a feeling he half shoved himself in, that it is important to be 'in'. I noticed this particularly in 'Vengeful Creditor' and 'Girls at War.' Funnily enough, I hear from many people that the Nigerian elite can be found here too, in the government capital in Gaborone. People coming back say that parties are 'income bracket' there. The upper income set only go to the upper income parties and so on and that there is rigid segregation there along income lines. The African is a sham I think but a comic one. He gravitates immediately to privilege but behaves in it like a gawk.

And yet, I wish Chinua Achebe was a Nigerian politician, of influence. The man has a glow in his mind. It runs with you through every line of his writing and it is a version of humour with a twinkle in the eye, so needed for politics at all times. I might laugh, but not as superbly as he; his laughter is more generous. His only equal in the literary world is the American magazine *ATLAS: A Window On The World* — the same twinkle-in-the-eye humour that arouses a glow in the heart and actually makes you the buddy of Mao Tse-Tung. I took note of this because I have been doing a lot of reading on China recently. On my birthday I was given a book by Han Suyin,[38] a supposedly objective presentation of China today. If that is so, it left me ashen with shock. Mao's China refers to other nations as dogs and the out-going propaganda is so virulent you read on and on with dread and dismay. Only *Red Star Over China* by Edgar Snow[39] restored my balance. *Time Magazine* and its like and obviously the government too, take the Chinese hysteria in dead earnest, hence Vietnam and that whole mess. As soon as I read Snow, I lost my sudden hysteria too. The Chinese level of communication, in the ordinary way is swear words and abuse. You cannot swear unless you can also be a very human sort. As soon as I read *Atlas Magazine* I started to laugh. The bulk of it is taken up with observing every detail of Chinese propaganda and replying to it, with humour. At one time Lui somebody was to be Mao's successor. They came out with a front page picture of Mao and Lui with the caption: MAO IS LUI IS MAO IS LUI IS MAO ...

Then on one issue they re-printed a picture of Chou-En-Lai <u>wearily</u> waving the 'little Red Book,' containing the thoughts of Mao. They had an article inside about the guesses about Chou being tired to death of the thoughts of Mao. Both these issues were seized by the customs officials at Singapore and it seems that Asian fear of communist China is the excuse for the British and American presence there. I think Asians are money grabbers and capitalists of the worst degree and they really are incompatible with the Chinese revolution. Supposedly they are caught up in the socialist revolution, it's the God of this age they must bow to but they are not, not one bit. I have lived with more socialism here among my project companions than I'll ever find in Asia, both in the social structure of the tribe and in volunteers from England and America. A great longing overcomes me now to go to China and live in one of the communes and

---

38 The pen name of Rosalie Matilda Kuanghu Chou (1916–2012) whose best known work is the novel *A Many Splendoured Thing* (1952). Head probably read *The Morning Deluge: Mao Tsetung and the Chinese Revolution 1893–1954* (1972).

39 This history of Chairman Mao and the Chinese communist revolution, published in 1937 by Edgar Snow (1905–1972), was credited with introducing Mao to the West.

write a book there. I'll have to see, maybe in old age when I can travel a bit.

The Middle East situation has also this unconscious humour in all the tragedy and I again blame the Arabs. So much of the trouble is black people and what they do to power, in a world where eyes see too clearly and it is hard for a man to lie. So many people I talk to these days are increasingly hostile towards Israel over the Palestinian refugees but what about Arab oil millionaires? Why isn't that wealth diverted to the poor? They enjoy the suffering of those refugees, and as soon as you ask: 'Where are the Jews to live then?' no one wants to hear. Seems like years can be spent weeping over the Palestinian refugees. They are there to keep the pot boiling. The Arabs don't want any kind of settlement. I have seen evil. It can go on for years and years and years. It has an inexhaustible power. Rarely, if ever, is there a goodness to counter it.

Yours sincerely,
Bessie

54. [*handwritten*]

P.O. Box 15,
SEROWE,
Botswana.

17 March 1973.

Dear Paddy,
I'm glad Eileen brought the pottery.

I prefer not to write for the present. My writing life is okay but I am in the middle of one of my usual last ditch battles with the devil. What happens towards the end of a war? Someone is going to die. That's how bad it is. In any case a family are helping me; and Howard.

Bessie.

55. [*handwritten on air letter*]

[*no address*]
11 June 1973.

Dear Paddy,
Would you please thank Dulan for his kind appreciation of the article I sent on one-parent families.

If you have any of my letters left would you please destroy them all. All the reasoning was inaccurate as at that time I lived under a terrible pressure of evil – the magnitude of which only becomes clear to me now. All my book clearly stated was that pride was the greatest sin and it is only the surface of the problem. There is another aspect – that mankind has no sin but is the victim from a single source of evil. Dostoyevsky noted this. He said: 'Even the most evil people are naïve.' When you see an evil that is not naïve or without the slightest pretence to humanity – you say – that's the source.

There is such a horror in me – I cannot believe my situation. I would be grateful if you have destroyed all my letters. Not that I do not wish to tell the truth, except that it be told accurately.

Yours sincerely,
Bessie.

56. [*handwritten*]

[*no address*]
7 July 1973

Dear Dulan,
Enclosed please find the signed copy of the Davis-Poynter letter. Howard and I are quite well thank you. In the same post I also received a letter from Paddy so I thought I'd write both in this one to save a stamp!

Dear Paddy,
Yes you may certainly keep the gardening letters and thank you for destroying the others. Nothing I said was accurate for a long time because I could not pin point what was hitting me. I kept on thinking it was persons other than what it really was. There is little left of that particular battle, except the evil itself.

Stripped, it was all that tortured me. Covered it had a wide radius of harm.

Sincerely,
Bessie.
Yes, your new book sounds very beautiful. I imagine that it will be very useful.

57. *[handwritten]*

P.O. Box 15,
SEROWE,
Botswana.

8 November 1973.

Dear Paddy,
I've just read your review of *A Question of Power* in the *New Statesman*. I am so humbly grateful to you – more important still that you took Elizabeth and called her Everywoman. I wondered who would see that humility that never rose above life itself. Thank you so much!

Much love,
Bessie.

58. [*handwritten on air letter*]

[*no address*]
6 July 1974.

Hi-ya Paddy,

I'm 37 today and so is my waistline! Giles said he had discussed the idea of the *Serowe* book with you. And it so happened at that time that I had just fallen in love with a great man – KHAMA, THE GREAT, who died in 1923. I'd been looking up something for the Mackenzie family then when Giles proposed the *Serowe* book, I fell in with the idea, because due to probing into the missionary writings, I soon saw that Khama had reversed the tragedy of Southern Africa – in this area, so I was able, to my great joy, to build the story of Serowe against a <u>big</u> landscape.

It was the *Serowe* book that made me stay here. One does not have a very long life and I put so much effort in my stay here that I thought I might as well die here. One can be terrified of death until you face it.

Glad you like the book dedicated to you and Giles. It's everyday stuff.

Regards to Dulan and Dan,

Bessie.

59. [*handwritten*]

P.O. Box 15,
SEROWE,
Botswana.

28 December 1980.

Dear Paddy and Dulan,
How great was my joy at meeting you in London! How happy I was to see you! How happy I was to see that ancient bag! It survived the breakdown of our project in Serowe. How happy I was about everything!

I'd been away from my home in Serowe for a year and decided to return and revert to my old address – P.O. Box 15, Serowe, Botswana.

One feels sorrow at the way friends become innocently involved in the tragedies of one's life and there is a period of my life that I cannot undo or re-live in a different way but I've longed not to have lived it. That was the cause of my long silence.

Much love,
Bessie.

60.

Bessie Head,
P.O. Box 15,
SEROWE,
Botswana.

20 January 1981.

Dear Paddy,

Thank you for your letter of 9th Jan.

I had been away from my Serowe home for a year and my own garden here reverted to a wild wilderness that I am terrified to enter in case it harbours gigantic cobras. Strangely though, when I had the garden going I had snakes all around the house. I think they loved the cool and damp of the vegetable and flower beds. But since I have not kept the garden for a year, not one snake do I see. I want to leave the garden wild like that while I try to complete an historical novel as the garden takes up too much of my time. I had been living in the government capital, supported rather fabulously by a grant from a volunteer organisation and working at some of the research centres there to patch my novel together.

I never worked on the weaving side of our project but only in the garden so that when I returned to Serowe I talked to one of the women who had woven the bags. I informed her in great astonishment that a gift of a bag from our project that I had sent to a friend in London was so strong, it looked as new as it was nine years ago when I sent it. She was not so surprised. She said the bag had been woven from the twine that is used to thatch huts. But I have noticed something about these almost home-made goods we produced on projects. They were very strong indeed and the workmanship was often very beautiful and of a high quality. Sandals I bought on the project always lasted two years. A very pretty pair of sandals I bought in Berlin in 1979 lasted me three months and had to be thrown away.

The book *Serowe: Village of The Rain Wind* comes out at a time when one project after another has closed down. The project I worked on, Boiteko, has only a small group of about ten women, spinning wool and, I think, knitting jerseys. The buildings of the pottery, tannery, kitchen and sewing room stand desolate and deserted with white ants busy chewing away at the wood-work. This goes for all the project plants in Serowe. They stand desolate and idle yet once Serowe was the show piece of development with a new project starting almost every day. My book was written at this peak. My book took eight years to get to the galley proof stage but it explains why Serowe pioneered a completely new educational system. The area I live in, Bamangwato country, had for some time had the original and unexpected imposed on it so that a deeply absorbing story emerges from this history. I am always sorry as the author to admire my own books but I enjoyed correcting the galleys of *Serowe* so much, the feeling that a genial and expansive world has been depicted. The book is divided into three parts tracing a history of social reform and educational progress over a period of one hundred years. It is in part three of the book, dealing with completely new and untried educational experiments, that the present breakdown of those pioneer efforts has occurred. The major breakdown has occurred in what you will read of as the brigade system of education, a combination of technical and academic education which Serowe was the first to pioneer in the country. All throughout part three of my book, the young people receiving this training and experiencing its hazards, talk of it with furrowed brows; failures are reported, even at that early stage and the difficulty of the experimentation is already outlined, in my book. But no one expected the complete collapse that has occurred in Serowe. Two things are happening. Serowe was possessed by international aid donors who funded the innumerable projects. Two years ago the rumbles of collapse were heard and they started sending in their researchers to draw up reports on Serowe brigades. They deeply resent a government take-over of the brigades as they regard the village by now as their possession and I talked to one of the researchers from Holland and listened in amazement as he claimed a village so far away from his own land and his vehement dislike of the fact that all that could save this system of education in the country was that it should become a formal government concern. He said to me: 'We are doing our best to see that the government does not take over the brigades.' Towards the end of last year the government bestirred itself and called a commission of enquiry into the brigade system of education. The enquiry still proceeds and will result in some decision, either that the brigade system of education is not a valid one or that brigades should become a formal government concern.

It was like a village making decisions to get along with its own affairs, to the extent of becoming an international family. I doubt such vigour of achievement can ever be found anywhere else in the world, and the *Serowe* book remains valid on that account. Due to lack of modesty on my part, here I say I have never enjoyed reading one of my own books as much as I have *Serowe: Village of the Rain Wind*. I am sure you will love it.

I have a mess and muddle here in my house, an accumulation of papers having outgrown my small living space. I struggle through files trying to decide what to burn so that I have space for new material. I haven't yet had time to read *Poets' London*, but will send a note on it once I get some order again into my life.

Howard looks forward to the music Dan promises to send him.

Much love,
Bessie

61.

>Bessie Head,
>P. O. Box 15,
>SEROWE,
>Botswana.

>29 January 1981.

Dear Paddy,

This is just a short note. It would seem as if old friends link up again.

Giles Gordon wrote to me. We quarrelled some years ago and were out of touch. He may have mentioned this to you. He wrote saying that he very much wanted a copy of *Serowe: Village of the Rain Wind*. I wonder if you could help.

The following discussion took place between James Currey and I. I asked James Currey if he would send you a complimentary copy of the book as it was dedicated to you. He said: 'No, no, we could not only send Paddy one copy. I suggest some review copies as well.' I wrote this down on a piece of paper, one copy plus some review copies and handed this note to James Currey's secretary. Could you phone James Currey's secretary and confirm this? It is possible that since the book is dedicated to you that you could not review it personally but you could say to her: 'Well how many copies do I get for review? I could perhaps hand them around to one or two friends who could do the reviews in my stead.' I thought you could hand one of these on to Giles.

Publication date is roughly set for April.

Much love,
Bessie
[*handwritten*] Heinemann phone number is 637 3311.

62.

Bessie Head,
P. O. Box 15,
SEROWE,
Botswana.

12 February 1981.

Dear Paddy,

Thank you for your letter of 5th February. We received Dan's tape and enjoyed listening to it. I am hoping Howard will write down some comments to include in this letter. The instrumental side, as produced by Dan is very aggressive and assertive, the girl's voice – very passive and unassertive. But she comes through with a pretty sound. Those two must be a perfect complement to each other, like Jack Spratt and his wife. The one ate fat, the other stayed lean.

I am hoping to send you a more recent picture of Howard. We still have no photographic services in Serowe so what pictures we do have are those taken by visitors who sometimes send us a print. One such rare print I sent to a fan of mine who died recently. Her sister wrote to me asking if there were any loose ends that ought to be tied up and I asked for the return of the photo of Howard and one of me. She hasn't replied yet.

Poets' London was unexpectedly read amidst high household drama. I was still busy sorting out manuscripts, book reviews and other precious junk into careful piles when I was suddenly thrown flat on to my back for a few days. Water is about the most precious commodity you can have in Serowe and to have a tap or water supply in your home is the height of luxury. When I set up my home some years ago I was given a pipe-line of water from the secondary school on the understanding that a seedling nursery attached to the cooperative garden would be built up in my yard. I broke with the project in 1976 but the principal of the school who knew the background of my work on the project said: 'You have made sacrifices to help others. Continue to use the water.' In late 1979 some government officials came nosing around, found my pipe-line and cut it without warning, charging me a high fee for using the water illegally. In the meanwhile the government had given Serowe a water supply, with village taps at key points. I'd done it before so I began hauling water on my head from the village tap. My beautiful garden and all my trees died before my eyes. (The garden is still beautiful, a waving savannah land of tall grass and wild flowers). The problem of getting linked to the government water supply is formidable. So many people are clamouring for taps in their yards that bribery and corruption is now the order of the day. When I heard this I just counted myself out. I'd never have the bribe fee and I certainly don't have the official government fee, so I thought and decided not to join the queue. Life was made easeful for me a few weeks ago. A friend loaned me a 25 litre plastic drum. Set on a wheel barrow, a few trips to the village tap bring in the day's supply of water, whereas from eight until eleven in the morning I'd often be drawing buckets of water to get the house tidy. I noted that the plastic drum made my back stiff and sore but I thought I was building up new muscle strength.

One evening I lifted the plastic drum to prepare water for a bath, I felt a sudden rending pain at the base of my spine. I straightened and turned to walk and a second ball of pain exploded, snaked around my right thigh into the groin and paralysed my right leg. Just then a warm stream of blood began to flow down my leg. It occurred to me that I had bust an internal organ. I thought: 'No one survives internal bleeding. I am going to die.' (I must say I laughed when I came upon Keats's death calm. I felt like that, not at all frightened of meeting my sudden and unexpected ending.) I stood for a while waiting to die and when I didn't die rather abruptly, it suddenly dawned on me that I was not bleeding to death from a bust organ but that the violence of the pain had made me start menstruating rather violently too. The pain was so fearful that I was forced to go to hospital. The doctor thought I had either stretched or slightly split the cartilage that joins the vertebra together. There was nothing to do but take pain killers and stay in bed. I said: 'I don't employ servants, I do all my own work and I'll have to use that plastic drum again when my back heals.' So he said: 'I'm afraid you won't be able to lift heavy weights again.' He wrote a letter to the water people requesting an immediate installation of water in my yard. The letter worked like magic. A tap is to be installed immediately. From not being in the queue at all I suddenly jumped to the head of the queue with perhaps a tap in my yard by next week. It takes months, years, bribery and tears to get near that precious state!

But days of imprisonment in bed finally enabled me to read *Poet's London*. I enjoyed it so much that I was only sorry when I came to its ending. It took me back to my high school days and the mission and the library filled with the England of daffodils and skylarks. It now astonishes me that all the best or most well-known poets were compressed into those anthologies. All the poets were quite well known to me, often the poems learnt by rote for exams.

I once read of D.H. Lawrence: 'He not only perceived the glittering surfaces of the Zeitgeist. Lawrence's intelligence rose above the Zeitgeist and plunged beneath it ...'

Your book skips lightly and happily over what in my youth I used to find very depressing terrain. Perhaps I only excuse my love for Lawrence. His heights and depths were captivating. I had the kind of library facilities then where more could be known about the poets or their work. Often the poem captured in an anthology also captured some inner glitter. There was not one of those though who did not depress me on further reading. Maybe I read a very bad biography of Shelley but he seemed to have small, murky depths. He lived in some permanent dream world where beautiful women were always walking up to him and kissing him. Either the women were real or not real. I could not tell but this caused Mary Godwin agonies of jealousy and the nit wit Shelley apparently wrote a poem to celebrate the misery of his married life: 'I fall upon the thorns of life. I bleed.' The whole lot of them, even Robert Burns were depressing to pursue beyond the high school anthology. Something small and murky would turn up.

Now, when I look at your book and the portrait gallery I am shocked by the endless parade of men with tender, vulnerable, feminine faces. It might have been this that repelled me, something soft and sappy at the centre. I like the more rugged, masculine outlines of modern poetry. The short quote from Maureen Duffy's *Taking Down the Runners* is vigorous, tough and masculine.

But I enjoyed the anecdotes about personalities so well known to me. Often the names of poets and writers live in time and beyond their times. It would seem some compensation to have all those plaques over London remembering treasured names. One is very seldom treasured in one's actual life time, not as a writer, not as a poet. There is a sense of living tragedy associated with the writing world, rather than fame or glamour. There is so much tragedy recorded in your book.

Much love.
Bessie

63.

> Bessie Head,
> P.O. Box 15,
> SEROWE,
> Botswana.
>
> 7 March 1981.

Dear Paddy,

My back seems fine but I do agree with you that it was certainly an unusual way of getting a water tap in my yard. The water tap was put in within three days of handing over the letter from the doctor and I am absolutely flabbergasted by the sequence of events that brought that precious commodity into my yard. None of my friends believed a doctor's letter would have effect like that.

Your harmless letter to me of the 22nd Feb. went through the censor's mill. I received two letters from London, both posted on the 23rd of February. One was from you and one from the John Johnson literary agency. John Johnson had given me a faulty cheque and messed up my bank account and caused a terrible muddle for me between banks here and in London. I hastily whipped open their letter and horror of horror YOUR letter was inside their envelope. Their letter to me adjusting the muddle was inside your envelope. This has happened time and time again, a lot of times with Heinemann mail to me. I find the Heinemann letter in another envelope and communication I don't expect in the Heinemann envelope. I keep on standing at the post office with a mild nervous breakdown, unable to move for some time. This time I approached the post master and confronted him with the mixed up mail. He asked me to write a letter of complaint which he will forward to head office. I enclose a copy of the letter I addressed to him. I'd be interested to know if the dastards let this copy letter through to you. I am certainly not engaged in subversive activities so I can't explain the censor and this treatment of being a major criminal whose mail, to and fro, has to be examined.

Howard chooses. Howard chooses and then announces his choice in a violent and aggressive way. He has two sets of friends here, quiet brilliant boys who will one day take care of the world and many of whom I have loved deeply. He has another set whose every word is a swear word. He failed his O Levels because of the latter – drink parties and lost weekends.

He works two nights at a disco playing records. Otherwise he sleeps almost 24 hours for the rest of the week. We have a nightmare, I fear. When I approach his room about normal everyday chores he ought to perform he shouts at me: 'Shut up, you fucking shit!' He has twice fisted me on the head. You get a job here by personal pull. The manager of my bank said: 'You want a job for your son? Bring him.' I got him as far as the interview. A string of bank managers have liked me. I am dead poor and live on their overdrafts. They are dazzled by my reputation. The bank manager talked with that dazzle in his eye. Howard had the job. He wouldn't take it. There's nothing of me in Howard. He's a total stranger and has been all his life. He knows we aren't the peas of the same pod and he hates me. He is like his father. I worry about my next life because this one has been so traumatic for me. In sheer anguish I often pray: 'God, God, God, don't let this child put me off children forever.' I have a dread of women who say they made a decision not to have children, not to do this or that and who have weird, twisted-up attitudes towards men and life. One dreads to be near that brink, a sort of condemned freak lost in a whirlpool of psychological muck. I've seen too many women like that – stark raving mad because of some great trauma in their lives.

One gets to a point where one knows one's limitations as a parent. I've always kept a sense of order, no matter how bad life was for me. It's been a quiet, intellectual household. I've always been surrounded by a vast international circle of friends, in deep earnest about helping the world and he's been aware of that world. The conversations that have taken place in this house have been of a very high order. The struggle the young man goes through is with his own coarse, brutal inner spirit. I would have preferred another child, more in my image but life does not always give one gifts. I'd rather stare unpleasant facts in the face and perhaps, here and there, there would be a glimmer of light eventually. The boy does have some strength of character. He won't drink or smoke if he's decided that it's bad for him. But then he finds another horror he wants to try out. This time it is a stream of swear words which are most trying to live with.

Marie Antoinette could be a challenge, especially in novel form. The backdrop, the French Revolution is BIG, the lady small. I have here the horoscope of Marie Antoinette which I copied for you from a book of astrology. In between the strange mumbo-jumbo of the language of astrology, the author, Joan Rodgers, has some interesting observations I think, on Marie Antoinette and I send it to you in case you might like it. You can't read it if disturbed by Moon signs and Sun signs but if you just ignore the mumbo-jumbo a fascinating picture of Marie Antoinette emerges, sympathetically written.

As ever,
Bessie

64. [*handwritten*]

> Bessie Head,
> P.O. Box 15,
> SEROWE,
> Botswana.
>
> 13 April 1981.

Dear Paddy

I [am] glad you liked the Marie Antoinette horoscope. I received a reply from the director of postal services who wrote that the mail passed through many intermediate administrations so they were unable to investigate my complaint.

Thank you for your kind and helpful comments about youth in general. Sometimes when one struggles alone with problems they often seem beyond endurance.

The sister of my dead fan returned Howard's photo which I enclose. Much to my surprise Howard suddenly bestirred himself and decided to write to you. It's such a nice letter he wrote that I thought that my own letter writing talents could take a bow this time so that you could enjoy his letter.

Much love,
Bessie.

65.

P.O. Box 15,
SEROWE,
Botswana.

31 December 1982.

Dear Paddy,

Thank you for your card. You know you owed me a letter since 1981. Aha, may I speculate on the silence??? My censors scared you when they put your letter into the John Johnson envelope. One night you woke up screaming: 'The letter bomb! The letter bomb!' So Dulan said: 'I'm putting my foot down. You are not to correspond with Bessie Head anymore. Not only does she have strange nervous breakdowns but she has strange censors too.'

Paddy Kitchen, I am surprised. A student, Jane Bryce, is doing her MA thesis on the work of the black American writer, Alice Walker, and my own. She writes: 'I went to talk to Paddy Kitchen, who told me you wouldn't call yourself a feminist and in many ways you relate intellectually to men better than to women ...' I could not understand how you had come to this conclusion, that I relate intellectually to men better than to women. Did I not write to you for some years and NOT your husband? Did I not essentially live in a pleasant and balanced world where know-how about the care of humans, children, plants and animals dominated? In that world men and women share this knowledge equally and there's no question of relating to one or the other. Not so long ago I had to look at back-files of letters and extract book contracts and business letters so that I could place them in a separate file to hand to a lawyer. I read with great astonishment a letter I had written to you in late 1970. It was written a few days before the police arrived to throw me into the loony bin. It was full of information about plants and my garden and only one line indicated my extreme distress. I wrote: 'But my inner anguish is so high at present that it is about all I can do to stay alive ...'

I know women who relate to men better than to women. In 1977 I was a part of the International Writing Programme at the University of Iowa and shared an apartment with a woman from the Philippines. From the beginning she looked at me with open hate and hostility. We were 26 men to three women. She slept with all the men on the programme, except an Israeli Jew, who rejected her. She served men and cooked for them because she had huge ego/vaginal needs. She said to me: 'I like a man to eat well.' I would never talk like that because I know about the nutritional needs of all mankind. I might have a vagina like all women but it is subject to my spiritual needs. I ignore it because the things of the spirit come first, so I had generally only had beautiful relationships with men and women and people have come to accept me as I am, a somewhat solitary and lonely person but one who would not hurt them in any way. So you are wrong, Paddy Kitchen and <u>you have to eat your words</u>. I told the student so.

There have been some changes, in my household. After 17 years of silence my husband wrote, in October 1981. The letter was mainly addressed to Howard whom he longed to see. We parted when Howard was two years old. I wrote back explaining that Howard had been at home all this while due to a low pass for O Levels. Eventually, it was agreed that he would care for the last part of Howard's education whereby he acquired a skill or a trade. I had mentioned some difficulties to you that I was having with Howard but everything was made secure for him to enter Canada where his father lives. He had landed immigrant status before he entered Canada and I did all the work here.

Howard left for Canada on the 26th May, this year. They are so alike in every way that I thought they would accommodate each other but this is not so. I only received unhappy letters so I asked that he be returned home again rather than that some catastrophe occur. I still await some news.

My waistline continues to keep pace with my age. I am 45. My waistline is 44 inches. I gave up smoking in February this year and generally drank beer to distract from the craving for a smoke, hence the huge expanse of waistline.

Best wishes for the new year to you, Dulan and Dan.

Bessie

66.

> Bessie Head,
> P. O. Box 15,
> SEROWE,
> Botswana.
>
> 21 January 1983.

Dear Paddy,

Thank you for your letter of 14th Jan. After your postcard of 26th May 1981 in which you promised to write, I never received anything more from you. It beats me why my mail should be seized and censored because no one makes clearer and more sensible choices than I. I examined everything in those early years and, while being well aware of the suffering of black people in southern Africa, I knew I could not cope with the underground intrigues of the liberatory struggle, so I stayed out of it. I also stayed out of the fatal story of independent Africa but kept myself busy with so many other things – subsistence agriculture, love and racialism, good and evil, rural women, traditional oral history – hardly a list to disturb the Boers or an independent black power structure.

I am relieved that the student must have made a mistake about what she thought you said. I thought myself that it was impossible that you could have said that I relate to men better than to women because all those years we wrote, not once had such a matter come up, but there had been exchanges of marjoram seed, gardening news and our cooperative here. What you must not have understood was the undertone of terrible disturbance in my life. Feminists do claim *A Question Of Power* as a feminist novel but I wrote to Jane Bryce that, except for the nervous breakdown, it would never have been written, that the nervous breakdown had been inevitable because no one could cope with a situation like that. But feminists are so excited about discovering WOMAN! I stay out of it. There were things that worried me about my attitude to love and men. I need to light a lamp, a glow and keep it going all my life, I need to worship someone and I don't want to change because it means I have set high standards that I expect from a man too.

I was not very strong-minded when I gave up smoking but very, very sick. I had got to a stage when any strong odours would set off a violent spasm of coughing – the exhaust fumes of a car, underarm perfume, etc.

and I began to drag my way through life. I was walking with my nose near the ground. Just then a journalist for the B.B.C. came to visit me. She listened to the coughing and described how smoking had killed her husband. In order to dissuade him from smoking, doctors had given him a breakdown of the damage inside him – you light a little fire and then inhale it; what happens to the tissues inside? Everything is thrown off balance. Her husband died but the sermon/lecture came at the right time. The next day I gave up smoking. I felt so much better immediately and the sense of having regained a buoyancy and swift light step was so good to me that I put the perisher out of my life forever. I am afraid I was like Dulan – a new thought needed a cigarette. To take away the fearful craving I kept a small can of beer near the typewriter. Ah! you should see the size of my tum! But I will lick it yet!
[*ends*]

67.

> Bessie Head
> P.O. Box15,
> SEROWE,
> Botswana.
>
> 21 March 1983.

Dear Paddy,
Thank you for your letter of 21st March. Let me begin first with Howard as everything has reached crisis point. The whole of last year nothing worked out since he arrived in Toronto and in November my so-called husband and his precious girlfriend wrote to say they were asking Howard to leave the house. There had been a daily clash of wills and the poor little man had his nerves shot. He had asked for love from his son and never got it, so now Howard had to leave the house, just like that. They couldn't care anymore. There is no way in which he can survive in Toronto because he has no money and no job so I sent an express letter asking that he return Howard to Botswana. My husband has done two things in Toronto. He has posed as the representative of the ANC and a liberator of black people in South Africa and he has lived off the resources of a white Canadian girl whose parents are wealthy. Refugees traffic to and from Botswana to the whole world and the following story was told to me by a South African refugee: 'I met your husband in Toronto and I had to address a meeting. He introduced me to the audience and he went on and on and I thought he would never stop. Eventually he allowed me to talk, then he took me out on the town.' That's what all black South Africans are doing abroad. The biggest thing you can sell and shit on is the suffering of black people in South Africa – that's why early on I would have NOTHING to do with it. That's why *When Rain Clouds Gather* is so a-political. Why did I send the child to a man like that? First, the man wanted to make trouble. He said he wanted his son and I would be a barrier and if so he had the means to do something about it. Howard was not making an effort to plan his life so I showed him the letter from his father and he wanted to go. They took one look at each other and began to rip each other to pieces. They wanted Howard to leave the house end of February but he sorted it out in an unexpected way. He had a small job baby sitting for someone and he went to her house. She was out so he stood outside waiting for her.

An old Italian woman in a house opposite called the police. As the police car stopped near him Howard took fright and ran down the road so the police caught him and now he is in police care. I wrote to an aid agency, Canadian Universities Service Overseas for help for him. They know me. They send volunteers to Botswana and the volunteers are asked to read my books. I enclose a copy of the letter I wrote which explains everything.

We have had a bad summer of drought, but last summer was just as bad. About mid-summer the birds of *Serowe: Village Of The Rain Wind*, fled the village so I don't wake up to the first hesitant peep-peep, followed by a chorus of bird song. The insects of *A Question Of Power* just turned back into the earth again to hibernate until next summer because there is no food above the ground. So there is an eerie silence and desolation everywhere.

I am trying to economise a bit on the weight of the letter. I do thank you for your kind enquiries about Howard. I wanted to enclose the carbon of the letter I had written for help.

Nothing will make me go back to smoking. The advantages are too great – a new lease on life and one bill off the household expenses. For years a packet of 30 cigarettes cost 6 shillings and now the same packet costs 10 shillings. One always looks around for things to give up but I haven't given up beer yet. A small drink now costs 6 shillings.

I think one should get away from writing after a book is done. The concentration is too intense. I have an historical novel almost complete but the way it was written, not my usual way, but in fits and starts. I have valued learning the history but nothing is more difficult than bringing history alive. Once I am done with it I am going to dig out every weed in my garden just to run away from the agony of what I have been through. All through winter I will dig in the garden and just sweep my yard. I am sure mental fatigue is at the bottom of Dulan's depression because you told me he wrote four books one after the other.

I wonder if the man, George Thomas is fun to work with or whether he is a pompous bore.[40] You haven't complained but I do agree with you that one can write and then really feel run down.

Howard's last letter sounded more mature than all his other letters so that I am hoping that this will be a turning point for him. I'll let you know. [ends]

---

40 The reference is to a biography of the MP and Speaker of the House of Commons that Paddy was working on at the time.

68.

>Bessie Head,
>P.O.Box15,
>SEROWE,
>Botswana.

>15 June 1983.

Dear Paddy,
Thank you for your letters of 2nd May and 15th April. I did not write as I was waiting to hear from Howard. He is a bit more settled. He writes that he rents a room with a Jamaican family and lives on social welfare of about $80 a week. The University of Toronto has a transitional year programme and he has applied to enter that and for a study grant. I would hope he were successful as life in Botswana is tough indeed if you cannot make it on your own. There is so much competition that people first provide jobs for their relatives and friends.

I am not so well off just now and have not yet finished the historical novel so I would not mind taking up your offer of a gift of £100 for Howard. Could you send it directly to him in a form he would be able to cash, such as an international money order? He was 21 years old on the 15th May and I would hope that it would be a symbolic gift to him of coming of age. I think it would also make him feel a bit more secure in his present situation. His address is:

229 Wychwood Ave,
Toronto M6C 2T5,
Ontario, Canada.

The student, Jane Bryce, wrote to me again and I told her she had mis-heard you. We had never discussed feminism or men in the long correspondence we had had but much water had flowed under the bridge about vegetable gardening! Indeed, I am taken aback when women walk up to me and say *Question Of Power* is pure women's lib as I had stepped so fully into the personality of Sello. The towering males of my books are usually me. I am a very masculine type of woman with a soft feminine voice. I had fun when I went to Nigeria, last year. They had started teaching *Question* at a University. The book is full of swear words I invented myself. They expected a towering, violent, loud-spoken woman. They also shout at each other and they could not hear what I was saying and kept complaining that I was whispering. A gentleman said: 'I am stunned to find that the author of *A Question Of Power* is such a softly-spoken woman.'

I also asked Jane Bryce to phone you a message about motherhood. I was deeply touched by your concern for Howard.

I think I spelt '<u>eerie</u> silence' wrong in my last letter.

Much love,
Bessie

69.

>Bessie Head,
>P.O. Box 15,
>SEROWE,
>Botswana.
>
>27 July 1983.

Dearest Paddy,

Thank you for your letter of 20th July, which I have just received. I am so happy that the student, Jane Bryce, talked to you and Dulan about the letter I wrote to her. My feeling towards the student is a bit illogical. I have a view of her work and some letters and I just love and trust her completely. She is a stranger to me; we are not really thinking together but the student arouses this deep love and trust. I was frightened and asked her to talk to you and Dulan about the letter to reassure myself that I had not done something wrong. I told her I trust you and Dulan, absolutely. I cannot send a copy of this letter to the student because I have a laugh on her but I am sending you a copy of the letter I have written to the student. The student is a mad, wild feminist; she is <u>femaleness</u> in its <u>ultimate</u> form. In her thesis she scolds all women who do not take their femaleness and female responsibilities seriously. All the mad, wild feminists of the world passionately love *A Question Of Power* and Elizabeth but they make a mistake. Elizabeth is brutally assaulted but she remains in close intellectual communication with the two men, particularly Sello, and heeds their communication because it is important. Elizabeth is a hugely integrated personality absorbing all her past lives, many of which could have been male, celibate and monk. They make a mistake. Elizabeth is not <u>women</u>. The student, Jane Bryce, is WOMAN. But she arouses trust and respect, in me. I needed a kind of supervisor for my papers other than my son, someone to help him. Everything is explained in the letter I have written to the student.

Thank you also for the gift you sent to Howard for his 21st birthday. It is something very big for him.

I could not be so brave as to try to learn to drive a car, like you. I am absent-minded and could not concentrate on the niceties of driving lessons. I'd always be absent-minded and just bang into another driver so that even if my ship came in one day I would never buy a car.

When we wrote then you had a strange feeling towards Barnwell. You also expressed a strange feeling towards Dulan. Something could take both away from you. That was 1969 when we first wrote to each other. You said you loved Barnwell and Dulan. If you told people about this someone would take Barnwell and Dulan from you. You could never tell people how much you loved them both. This is what you wrote to me then. I was puzzled but decided not to query it. Since you mention writing about the village now, I would assume that fear had left you? You may not remember it but this is what you wrote to me then. (Sorry life is so painful but when I broke off the correspondence with you after the nervous breakdown, I had done so with many other people. I could not cope and needed to shut myself into myself in order to put myself together again.)

I wish I could finish the damned difficult historical novel. The damn thing isn't finished yet. Damn and blast.

Much love to you and Dulan.
Bessie

70. [*handwritten*]

Bessie Head,
P.O. Box 15,
SEROWE,
Botswana.

20 September 1983.

Dear Paddy,

This is just a note to say Howard safely received the £100 you sent him as a gift. It translated to a gigantic $180 Canadian dollars. He complained that I had not given him your address so he had not been able to write to thank you. I'll give him your address but just now he left his last address and has gone to Montreal to live with Tom of *A Question of Power*. Tom married a Canadian girl and has just settled in Montreal. I don't have an address but I know my son will be safe and well with Tom.

Love,
Bessie.

71.

Bessie Head,
P.O. Box 15,
SEROWE,
Botswana.

9 October 1983.

Dear Paddy,

Thank you for your letter of 29th Sept. The wretched British government must make people so unhappy about poverty. Why close a library on a Wednesday just to depress people so badly about inflation? I am afraid I would break down and weep.

I don't think the young swallows would like our parts this year. We have had two years of bad drought, last year was so bad, we went through a silent summer because the birds had to go away and the insects could not come out of hibernation. It is even deathly silent as I type now, unlike good years and continuous bird calls. In good years we walk through a perfumed village because the Makoba tree blooms at this time but this year the Makoba tree stands black and stark against the horizon. A sort of dead weight of despair settles on one's mind but when I worked in my garden the other day I felt a lift in spirit. My guava trees had buds on them. Normally guava, tomato and gooseberry bushes won't bud and fruit when the atmosphere is bone dry. I kept watering the bushes just to see something green but it is good to know I will have a little harvest of fruit too.

The way we live in Botswana must be paradise, surely. In Johannesburg alone 30 people are brutally murdered every day and I would imagine something similar in England, London. In Serowe we may have one murder a year, in the government capital about two or three. So people get absolutely hysterical when the murder of the year takes place. We have one going just now but I pause over it because I think people have not examined the trauma behind it. A woman, getting well on to sixty years of age, went to bed with a young man aged 29. The woman's husband had held many important positions in government. On the 30th Sept. (Independence Day) they left home together to attend the President's cocktail party. It runs from 5 p.m. till 8 p.m. I have been told, with a huge milling of people. The woman suddenly disappeared from the party with a young man. Her husband followed soon after and found her in bed with the young man. The woman was an agile sort. She ran out of the house like ten devils were after her but her husband beat the young man to death with a stick. Then he calmly called the police. The young man was married with three children. The storm this has unleashed! It turns out that this is standard practice in Gaborone. The wives of men in important positions, many of them well on in years, seduce young men. As soon as the husband is away on state business, the young man is in his bed. The young man is bought for lost week-ends at hotels.

I have had a little experience of the charm of the new generation that was born at Independence. We are like suppressed dreams – the young are confident, self-assured and fluent. I have known a young man talk to me with the assertiveness of a mature man. It is this that the elderly wives of the important men are purchasing at a high cost and it has raised a high storm of disgust simply because it has been exposed. There is a trauma behind the death of that young man. I know my generation of black people and they had silent, dead marriages. I worked inadequately at it in *Rain Clouds* where Makhaya complains repeatedly at man/woman relationships, as black people experience it, where a marriage is like a death, where a man and a woman have no communication, physically and spiritually. A close relationship with another human being can be so stressful that it is only worth the venture if each moment together is precious, treasured. The women would not buy the charm of the young men if there were not this lack in their marriage, that most black people have no sense of love, they have no sense of their worth as men and women. This disaster is both in African custom and tradition as well as the stress of the colonial era.

Love to you and Dulan,
Bessie

72. [*handwritten*]

Bessie Head,
P.O. Box 15,
SEROWE,
Botswana.

5 January 1984.

Dear Paddy,

Thank you for your letter of 20th Dec. Indeed, I heard of the bomb explosion at Harrods on a news bulletin. Mrs Thatcher's subsequent statement: 'The British are not intimidated by bombs ...' I feel is not going to solve the situation. Surely the British are intruders in northern Ireland and that kind of colonial history and colonial mentality won't help? I have understood that most people in England keep a closed mind about Ireland but the bomb at Harrods shows how determined the IRA are to get rid of Britain. There is no dialogue, only this bloodiness, so a lot more people are going to be killed. I fear one always thinks of personal friends in London on such occasions and the car bomb turns my backbone into a column of ice. The British govt. will have to give way in northern Ireland, oh, the sooner, the better.

I am pleased that your book on Barnwell goes well and that *Serowe: Village of the Rain Wind* serves as a talisman. I myself am at the tail-end of an historical novel and my Christmas and New Year have been grim slog work. I really felt lonely, stuck grimly to the typewriter day after day. On other days there's a break for shopping and checking the mail and a few chats with people. To make matters even harder to endure we have moved into another summer of drought and eerie silence again. We had a summer like that when I typed out *When Rain Clouds Gather*. The heat was so terrific that I was forced to sit at the typewriter in my pantie and bra. I have typed out the historical novel the same way from dawn to dusk only in a pantie and bra with a fearful eye on the window in case someone should call. It's good for my writing though because I had to describe the drought and rinderpest epidemic[41] of 1895–1896 so lines read dismally: 'The whole earth died that year ...' I look outdoors and it is so.

Your mother is wonderful. The new typewriter must be a Christmas

---

[41] An infectious viral disease affecting cattle; it has a high mortality rate. In June 2011 the United Nations FAO announced that the disease had been eliminated worldwide.

present. I got one like that, Japanese make too (Silver Reed 500), from a wealthy American fan in Gaborone. Mine cost about £150. How much did yours? For years I typed out 5 books on a light, tinny Remington. You know how long a book journey is so ones fingers get entirely adapted to the little tin things one works on. I suffered agonies with the new typewriter. It was heavy and almost immovable and I could not swing the line-space lever back to the margin. For weeks my wrist and fingers ached until they built up muscle for the new typewriter.

I am not so surprised to learn that *Poets' London* was translated into Japanese. The Japanese are great travellers in a rather ghastly way, like the Americans. I read an article on it some years ago in the *New Statesman*. They work like mad the whole year then take the packaged tours around the world, with cameras and binoculars. A bus picks them up off the plane and disgorges them out at a big hotel, and so on. I can see earnest Japanese tourists, a copy of *Poets' London* in hand, looking up all those plaques! I saw a bus disgorge an American package tour in Amsterdam. The din and racket in the hotel were <u>fearful</u>.

I fear I cannot quite sort out what Howard is doing in Canada because he does not supply a consistent story. He has changed addresses three or four times [in] 1983. The last did not seem like a fixed abode but he lived with Tom in Montreal for a week then was back to Toronto but with Tom phoning him every day. Tom writes that he is too disorganised to work or study properly; but he has taken up music in earnest. He was very grateful for the £100 you sent and twice wrote for your address to write a letter of thanks. I hope he did. People in Serowe also gave me gifts for him but no letter did he want to write.

Things will pan out a little better for me [in] 1984 and I'll be able to send him some money, especially to buy new clothes if he isn't coming home again. I hope for something from the historical novel and some lectures in Australia. I leave end of Feb for a writers' festival there.

Best wishes to you and Dulan, mother, Dan and girl Barbara, for the New Year.

Love,
Bessie.

73. [*handwritten on air letter*]

> Bessie Head,
> P.O. Box 15,
> SEROWE,
> Botswana.
>
> 15 November 1984.

Dear Paddy,

Thank you for your letter of 6th Nov. I understand that shut-in world and works. The last time you wrote was the time of the IRA bombing of Harrods. Howard is back home again. He had never thanked you, he said, for the birthday gift you sent him last year, so with your letter he made haste to rectify this error. He had been very unhappy in Canada as he is a boy with a very strong sense of belonging, so he is happy to be home again. He came home [on] 25th Oct.

The new book is due just right now. It has a Johannesburg, South African publisher. Heinemann African Writers Series are closing down and not accepting new material but keeping old numbers in print. I'll send you a gift copy of the South African edition once I am able to place a few orders with the Johannesburg publisher. I'll have to move into a new area of publishing with the closure of Heinemann AWS and this is being arranged.

The drought continues. Indeed, here, it is a seven year cycle; and we are into the 4th year. We have not even had the teasing rain that carpets the earth with a thin, fine greenery.

I loved my Australian trip. The Australian audience loved me in a way such as I have never experienced before. I also learned much about the history of the land. Let me know if you would like a blow by blow account. I have some pressure on me just now.

Love,
Bessie.

74. [*handwritten*]

Bessie Head,
P. O. Box 15,
SEROWE,
Botswana.

18 June 1985.

Dear Paddy,

Thank you for your letter of 18th May. *Barnwell* arrived three weeks ago and is being read amidst household tragedy again! On Sunday I polished and shined my house. Last night, around mid-night, I padded to the toilet in bed socks. I slipped on the shiny floor and crashed to the ground on one knee. It took my 89 kg weight and is so painful that here I am in bed, unable to do anything, but read. Before that I was up to my ears in cooking loads and loads of Cape Gooseberry jam. I prepared some holes for lemon trees as I have a good recipe for lemon marmalade jam. The gooseberry sprang up wild on this rich soil preparation, and waves and waves of golden fruit fall to the ground. *Barnwell* was to wait, partly because I wanted to post my new book to you. I am expecting £375 from my agency for a Danish translation of *Maru*. I had no money for postage. So I worked at the jam until I was thrown into bed today. It is heaven sitting in bed in a spotlessly clean house.

Heinemann AWS was sold to a rubber and tyre company. It took them a year almost to inform everyone. They held up all new developments for me and made 1984 a hell of a survival for me. I am having a new set of publishing arrangements.

My Australian trip was the most richly educational trip I have taken so far. That white-dominated world is closed and narrow. It is as though many small villages in Europe and England transposed themselves onto the Australian soil. Life in the United States hinterland is like that too. They kept that village mentality. I find the U.S. and Australia akin. But with the Adelaide Festival they open up. I talked to the most receptive audiences in the world. When I arrived I was the dark horse. No one knew where Botswana was and I look representative of nothing myself. I said I come from a village in Southern Africa. You should have seen that village mentality! My books were on a stand with 36 best-selling writers of the world. They would touch no one but me. I was sold out. I managed to get out of Adelaide before those best-selling writers put arsenic in my breakfast coffee.

Love,
Bessie.
[*at the top of page 1*: P.S. Howard is away from home at the moment, still arranging his musical career. He pops in and out all the time. He's okay.]

Some Notes on <u>Barnwell</u>
23 June 1985 (I had planned to put these notes, plus the letter and other odds and ends into the new book but I became worried. Half-way through *Barnwell* I read that the whole family exits London for No. 22 in the summer. You had also sent me this address. I decided to send the notes, etc. to No. 22. I will post the book 2nd class air mail once I get a cheque from London. The book is precious. Is it safe for me to post it to No. 22 Barnwell?)

I am pleased indeed that I fell down and hurt my knee so badly, it stopped the busy daily round. It's quite better now but in the meanwhile I have spent some happy hours <u>in</u> Barnwell. It's a village I would not mind visiting. The illustrations are exquisite and your descriptions of the country-side, breath-takingly beautiful. A book is always good when a writer's feelings soar and soar like that.

There are times one seems to ponder on the ultimate in human goodness and trust. I quote Row, the shop-keeper, on his delivery round: 'People trust you. Some houses, you go in, and they're out, so what you do, you put the fats in the fridge, the frozen things in the freezer, and then leave the rest …' Oh, I have never heard this before!

The other story on this level of the sublime was the one of Eric and Agnes Garratt and the gift of the Sunday dinner of roast beef and Yorkshire pudding – not only to you but to any strange guests you may have dwelling there. No, I haven't heard it before, not every Sunday, accompanied by such fore-thought and care and rich entertainment that included a demonstration of a dance. You made the right decision to live part of your life in Barnwell.

We still have much in common, not only the roll of toilet paper that is used to blow the nose and quickly wipe up spots on the floor, but also a kind of heathenism. I was reared from the ages 13 to 18 by British missionaries. Once I left the mission orphanage, that was the end

of church for me, except the occasional need to be there for a wedding or funeral. So I laughed and laughed at your references to Christianity. But to quote Dulan's grandmother: 'I feel it in me waters that the people of Barnwell love this book.'
[*ends*]

75. [*handwritten on air letter*]

Bessie Head,
P.O. Box 15,
SEROWE,
Botswana.

20 July 1985.

Dear Paddy,

Thank you for your letter of 10th July. The postage on the hardcover of the new novel was pretty steep P8.25 (£4.25). Then I had some luck. A friend, a British Volunteer, Jo Mcmahon, is coming to England for the school holidays. She leaves Botswana on 14th August. About the 16th or 15th, on her arrival at Heathrow airport, she will try to phone you. She said she would post your copy at the airport. She then takes a plane to Yorkshire. So the book, *A Bewitched Crossroad*, will soon arrive. Will you let me know if you receive it safely?

Howard has popped in again and read your greeting with great pleasure. I am pleased indeed that the son of the shopkeeper, Ron Rutterford, heard those extracts from my letter to you.

I made the lemon marmalade jam together with some lady friends, hence the explicit instructions about the Motoga Cloth, at Woodford's No 1 store.

Love to all,
Bessie.

[*at top of page:* P.S. The book is addressed to Holyport Rd [ie. the London address].]

76. [*handwritten*]

> Bessie Head,
> P.O. Box 15,
> SEROWE,
> Botswana.
>
> 28 August 1985.

Dear Paddy,
I am so pleased that my postman delivered the book safely. She told me she would be rushed as she was taking a plane straight to Yorkshire.

I cannot resist your offer of a book. What I am short on is a good cookery book. Years have gone by with poverty and struggle and plain stews. I have never been able to invite friends to dinner. Things may improve. Do you have a good cook book in mind that you use and admire, one that is easy to use and yet imaginative at the same time? I use a gas fahrenheit stove and prefer the old measurements of lbs, ounces, pints and cups.

Love to you and the family.
Bessie.

77. [*handwritten*]

>Bessie Head,
>P.O. Box 15,
>SEROWE,
>Botswana.
>
>3 October 1985.

Dear Paddy,

Thank you for your letter of 22nd Sept. I look forward eagerly to the cookery books. I always believe that two is better than one (when I shop I have a compulsion to buy two of the same items in case one breaks down), but by the time I came to *Traditional Jamaican Cookery*, my mouth began to water uncontrollably. Three is better than one.

I am friendly with a family from Yorkshire and am also trying to master Yorkshire pudding and roast beef. They complain though that the flour is too heavy and the pudding is not crispy enough.

The *New Statesman* article explained that I did not attend the Zimbabwe Book Fair. Some things have happened to me to make me want to stay home. There is a great focus on Africa for the same old reason – exploitation, so I am cautious about invitations. I also find a lot of university people and journalists too rapacious so I cleared a lot of horror out of my life. But I committed myself to the Zimbabwe trip. I wanted to clear up a mistake. In 1983 I was invited to the first Zimbabwe Book Fair. I sent a false telegram that I was dying of lung cancer. I simply did not want to go to Harare with the South African poet, Mongane Serote, because he is evil. I am also absent-minded about death simply because my life has been too lonely. No one would care if I died. But this telegram was a bad, bad mistake. James Currey, the Heinemann man, stood at the Heinemann stall and excitedly announced to anyone who came up that I was dying of lung cancer. A German Volunteer friend walked up to the stall. She said for a split second she thought the Heinemann man had a gun in his hand and was shooting her. She nearly collapsed.

James Currey also wrote to all the Heinemann departments that I was dying but not he or any of the Heinemann people wrote a letter of sympathy.[42] So, absent-mindedly, I tried to transit through Harare, in good health, to Sydney, Australia, in 1984. I learned something about

---

42 Currey gives his version of events in *Africa Writes Back* (2008).

Zimbabwe security. It is pretty tight and alert. The immigration people roughed me up at the airport. On my return from Australia I was detained briefly. I had a Botswana passport but I was reduced to refugee status and issued with a refugee visa. Then I knew I was in trouble. The man shouted: 'I don't care. We'll hand you over to the Botswana government. The Botswana government will have to sort you out.' Then I knew I was in trouble. On my return home I wrote a letter of apology to the Zimbabwe Publishing House, who run the show. There was no reply.

So, I was invited to the 1985 third Zimbabwe Book Fair, so I accepted, anxious about the refugee visa, anxious about the exit through Harare, anxious to clear up the muddle. Someone in the Zimbabwe Publishing House planned for my <u>non-appearance</u>. My astonished German Volunteer friend first wrote to me that my name was a big spread in all the papers in Harare. Then I was instructed to pick up my air ticket in Gaborone. On arrival in Gaborone the air-line company said there was no ticket. They caught my anxiety. The whole of Friday and Saturday morning they telexed Air Zimbabwe, Harare. Air Zimbabwe phoned and phoned. I saw all the telexes. No, the ticket was stuck between the Wade Travel Agency and the Zimbabwe Book Fair. Air Botswana said I should go home. I refused and hung on grimly. They sent instructions for the ticket to be sent to the airport. It arrived early Monday morning just as the plane was about to leave, was underpaid with instructions that I pay the balance. I said I was going home. There's a cat in the Zimbabwe Publishing House, grinning from ear to ear. This was the pay-back.

Love to you and Dulan,
Bessie.

78. [*handwritten*]

>Bessie Head,
>P. O. Box 15,
>SEROWE,
>Botswana.
>
>9 October 1985.

Dear Paddy,

This just a note to say that the three books arrived safely and much sooner than I expected. I like them all and I think I will be able to cope with the recipes, my oven, etc. They have a very honorary place beside my bed. I suffer from insomnia and for years now I have lost the ability to sleep at night so I often hunt for the book that is compulsive reading. It astonishes me how much one can learn from rather out of the way books about living – the murder-mystery writers are in a class all their own with very high writing standards and they teach deeply about the dark side of human nature. Nutritionists teach about the survival of the species. Bee Nilson strikes just the right note with me as well as the Jamaican book which is rich with historical items. Sleep will not be a problem to me for nights and nights and I shall emerge from this session eager to try out new diets to knock off those extra kgs, eager to impress friends with that sumptuous dinner! <u>Oh, Benghiat's recipe for marmalade jam is poor, poor</u>. I'm sure mine is superior! Jane Grigson is deep, deep, right from the beginning from that R.L. Stevenson quote: 'Every book is, in an intimate sense, a circular letter to the friends of him who writes it. They alone take his meaning; they find private messages, assurances of love and expressions of gratitude, dropped for them in every corner …' It is the most beautiful and ultimate definition of a book and reading that I have ever read. I will quote it and quote it myself. Thank you for the gifts.
Love to you and Dulan.
Bessie.

79.

Bessie Head,
P.O. Box 15,
SEROWE,
Botswana.

6 November 1985.

Dear Paddy,

Thank you for your letter of 24th October, and also for your generous appreciation of *A Bewitched Crossroad*. It is still much so here: 'Each day the sun rose on a hallowed land ...' except that in June the Boers moved into the government capital and killed 12 people.[43] Those filthy Boers are not likely to try it again. The major part of the world did not approve. I am deeply touched by your report of what you see on television. The writing's on the wall for the Boers. They are a people of such deep cruelty and cunning that I really fear them. I read an interview with the ANC leader Oliver Tambo. He said: 'People can endure their pain no more ...' I cut it out and put it into my treasure box.

I borrowed the Alfred Hitchcock volumes from the library. He produced volumes of murder mysteries so I have a good idea of the writing standards too. I liked what I had read of Dulan's writing so I would receive his murder mysteries, with pleasure.

It is enchanting, the struggle with your old mother. I am sorry but I laughed and adored it. I have an old lady opposite as a neighbour. She was the most perfect woman, busy and upright. She suddenly became impossible. She stands in her yard and swears and swears at everyone. She makes a long speech about my yard: Why did the land board give me such a big yard when I can put nothing in it?

Please hold this down as tight as possible. I have a German volunteer friend in Harare. She worked here in Serowe. She was so happy to know that I was coming to the Zimbabwe Book Fair. She teaches 200 miles outside Harare. The elections had disrupted school work so teachers had to teach on Saturday, but she had planned to meet me so she gave her classes to another teacher. She went to the Zimbabwe Book Fair and noted

---

43 A reference to the 1985 dawn raid on houses in Gaborone conducted by the South African National Defence Force in which many Botswana citizens as well as civilians of other nationalities were killed.

that the Zimbabwe Publishing House had a new imprint of *Maru*. Then I sent her letters about the ticket drama in Gaborone. She sent me their imprint. They contracted this imprint with Heinemann AWS. Neither Heinemann AWS nor the Zimbabwe PH had informed me of it. I argue, Paddy. Why did the Zimbabwe Publishing House keep silent about *Maru*? When you print a writer's work and you invite the writer there is a joyous welcome from the publisher. The writer alive is an asset. Three times I got my books sold out or huge quantities of them – Holland, Nigeria, Australia. The Dutch publisher sent me a huge cheque for over $1,000. Heinemann AWS (Nigeria, Australia) sent me still the same royalty of £50 or so. They distribute me world-wide but they still send me £50 or so. I am stark, raving mad but God I am scared. Heinemann last year was sold to British Rubber and Tyre. In the turmoil of South Africa this company was demonstrated against for ruthless exploitation of black people in South Africa. I am an asset to them, dead. Please shut up tight about this until I send you some more information. Please tell no one. I am trying a lever on my literary agency.

[*ends*]

80. [*handwritten on air letter*]

Bessie Head,
P. O. Box 15,
SEROWE,
Botswana.

28 November 1985.

Dear Paddy,
This is just a note to say that I have received the two murder mysteries of Dulan. I was so thrilled with the autographs. Oh insomnia, where are you now? I want to send Dulan a little note after I have read the books.

A storm continues here. When *Maru* was first published Dulan hailed it as a masterpiece. The Zimbabwe Publishing House has produced it illegally in collaboration with Heinemann AWS. Do you know how they reproduced it? The story sequence reads thus: Pages 112, 115, 116, 113, 114, 119, 117, 123, 121, 127, one completely blank page, 125, 126. My foreign Volunteer friend saw it on display at the book fair. She sent it to me.

The mess is so terrible that for some days I had a complete nervous breakdown. I found it impossible to get out of bed. The glimmer of hope is that my literary agency is demanding the withdrawal of the Zimbabwe Publishing House imprint of *Maru*.

Love to you and Dulan.
Bessie.

81. [*handwritten*]

Bessie Head,
P. O. Box 15,
SEROWE,
Botswana.

10 December 1985.

Dear Paddy,

This note is really to send an appreciation to Dulan on 'Only Children'[44] but I thought I would also report on the Zimbabwe affair. The storm in me has subsided a bit. My literary agency forced Heinemann AWS to telex Zimbabwe Publishing House about the jumbled pages. They produced 5,000 copies of *Maru* with the pages flung about anyhow. My agency has demanded the withdrawal of their imprint from the market.

Secondly, Heinemann do not have world rights to *Maru*. Some time ago the rights to *Maru* reverted to me from Victor Gollancz. They only have a sub-lease from Victor Gollancz to distribute their edition of *Maru*. They went ahead and signed an illegal contract with the Zimbabwe Publishing House claiming world rights to *Maru*. My agency has demanded that the contract be cancelled. I have the rights to *Maru*. I do not like this crooks and robber story. The Zimbabwe Publishing House spent a lot of money advertising my appearance at the Book Fair. A friend here was in Harare at the time. She sat bolt upright when my name appeared in bold lettering on a television screen. But there was no me there. This contract was for Heinemann AWS and the Zimbabwe Publishing House only. They never intended paying me any royalty. What is diabolical is that they spent money trying to attract the attention of the authorities in order that they ban me from entry into Zimbabwe. I gave them the excuse to do so.

Love,
Bessie.

---

44 The note to Dulan is not in the file in the archive.

82.

Bessie Head,
P.O. Box 15,
SEROWE,
Botswana.

13 January 1986.

Dear Paddy,

I hope my other letter reached you and that you have not yet left 4 Holyport Road. Enclosed is a note for Dulan about *Accomplices*.

About the Zimbabwe Publishing house edition of *Maru*. My agency extracted from Heinemann AWS the contract they had signed with the Zimbabwe Publishing House. It was a contract entirely for the benefit of the two publishing houses with no royalty payment to me. Heinemann marked up a fee of 15% for themselves. They stated on the contract that they have world rights on *Maru*. It is one book they do not have world rights on. Victor Gollancz reverted the rights to me some years ago. My agency next extracted from Heinemann AWS that the contract was illegal but that we should go ahead and cancel it and draw up a new contract, with the Zimbabwe Publishing House. I wrote to my agency that this is what I will never do. I will have no dealings with that publishing house. The lever on my literary agency worked. Seldom do you get a literary agency operating with integrity.

Happy new year as is said at this time.

Love to you and Dulan.
Bessie

83.

>Bessie Head,
>P.O. Box 15,
>SEROWE,
>Botswana.

>20 February 1986.

Dear Paddy,

Thank you for your kind letter of 12th Feb. That uncontrollable weeping has subsided but I sat up many nights before I brought peace to myself. I am not having my son in the house any more. There are a few of his possessions here and I feel I owe him money. Should he contact me I will give him these things. His cruelty was terrifying. I felt I had to take care of him. I tried in every way to bring peace to the situation. When he started to shout and shout that he could not stand my voice, I wrote notes. I asked him not to talk to me. His idea of living was to sleep every day in bed until midday, eat two huge plates of meat and rice, and then take a huge bath for four hours. The toilet was in the bathroom. If I indicated that I needed to use the toilet, it would only make him stay longer in the bath. People say he is in Gaborone. He wanted a Mercedes. There are a lot of boys in Gaborone smuggling Mandrax, diamonds and getting a Mercedes overnight. I sent him to his comrades.

I am no failure. For three years I took care of the education of a young girl who lives near me. I was working on a Peace Corp training programme. At tea break they told me they wanted to pay school fees of children from poor families. The young girl had passed her primary school education and sat weeping in her yard because her family could not pay secondary school fees. I told the Peace Corp people. For three years they sent me cheques. The young girl and I would plan and talk things over. Peace Corp often sent the cheques late. I would say: 'Peace Corp hasn't sent the cheque yet but when it comes, I will pay the school.' She would say: 'I know'. I arouse that kind of trust. I am an efficient person and a good planner. She failed her Junior Certificate. I quickly got her into a typing and book-keeping class for one year. Next year she goes to Teacher Training College. She turned out to be one of the great joys of my life. She is ever so pretty in an ordinary kind of way. Suddenly she says lovely things when you least expect it. I don't know where she acquired a grasp of english but her english is superb. She used to smell horrible but now she perfumes herself and touches up her hair with straightening creams. I do work like that for other women's children but I cannot help my own child. I am not a failure. He is. A human must give something back for care and love.

The story about Heinemann AWS and the Zimbabwe Publishing House and me and *Maru* is bad. Heinemann AWS admit that they signed an illegal contract with the Zimbabwe Publishing House but they now demand that I sign a contract with ZPH. The story about ZPH is horrifically bad. They are not only doing illegal things with me, they are doing it with a whole lot of writers. I told you about my foreign volunteer friend. She is German. Her director of the German Volunteer Service arrived in Harare just last year. He quickly picked up stories about the double-dealing and cheating of the Zimbabwe Publishing House. It's not only me. They are stealing and cheating from a whole lot of writers. They run their business that way. A lot of writers are involved. When my friend took my letter to her director she wrote to me that he was not surprised. He knew. I was just on the list of authors they would steal from. Things like this and my son brought on that spell of uncontrollable weeping. The agency is good. They agree with me that no contract will be signed with the Zimbabwe Publishing House. They [must] withdraw *Maru* and destroy it.

Love to you and Dulan. I have a harvest of guavas. I am making Guava Jelly Jam with the Jamaican recipe.

Bessie

Lilian Ngoyi
(1911–1980)

Lilian Ngoyi's life and letters

In the 1950s, Lilian Ngoyi was 'the most talked-of woman in politics' (Mphahlele 1989: 105). By the 1970s however, when these letters were written, she had disappeared from public life to become a lonely and sometimes forgotten figure. More recently, as the heroes of the struggle against apartheid in South Africa are being re-established in the national memory, Lilian Ngoyi is being restored to her rightful status. She is remembered in books and newspapers and at events such as the annual celebration of the 1956 women's march against the Pass Laws, a march which she led with three other women, Helen Joseph, Rahima Moosa and Sophia Williams. Streets and public buildings have also been named after her.

The letters published here begin in 1971, almost ten years after Lilian Ngoyi was first banned in 1962, and so they reflect a period in her life which has not entered the public record. What amounted to internal exile was imposed on the banned person; as Lilian puts it, 'No church, no funerals, no cinemas' (letter 107).[45] She was first banned under the Suppression of Communism Act, following her imprisonment during the crackdown on dissidents after the Sharpeville massacre. The order was renewed after five years. When the second order expired at the end of 1972 (letter 94), she was once again able to meet friends and colleagues, and, during the following year, to travel to Durban and Cape Town (letters 97

---

45 Banning orders were framed to curtail activities considered a threat by the apartheid government and could be imposed on persons or organisations. Banishment was sometimes also used against individual people, but more usually a form of house arrest was imposed. Banning meant that the person could not make speeches or be quoted, could not meet with more than one person at a time, could not have contact with another banned person, could not attend gatherings of any kind, could not enter certain buildings, had to report regularly to a local police station, could be restricted to a certain area, and to a curfew.

and 99). The banning was re-imposed in 1975 (letter 107) but this time its conditions allowed Lilian some communication with friends (Joseph 1986: 198).

Being banned meant that Lilian's Orlando house became her prison, no longer her home. There she lived with her daughter and mother, forbidden to receive friends or other family members and unable to earn a living. Consequently, although she was extremely house-proud (Mphahlele 1989: 107), she could not afford the maintenance of her home and its fabric deteriorated rapidly. There must have been many days when she felt lonely and forgotten, so that the letters from abroad from friends and admirers, like Belinda Allan, were not only a source of material succour if they contained money, but were also an emotional lifeline. In her letters, however, Lilian seldom complains about loneliness or poverty. Distress over her daughter's drinking and mentioning her broken spectacles is the nearest she gets, and then she uses it as an opportunity to say, by way of thanks, that now that she has a little extra money she hopes to pay for their repair. Rather than dwelling on her own sorrows, her letters are notable for the interest she continued to take in the lives of others as well as in national and international affairs.

Unlike Bessie Head and Dora Taylor, Lilian Ngoyi was not a published writer. But she was a powerful orator, celebrated in her day for being able to 'toss an audience on her little finger, get men grunting with shame and a feeling of smallness and infuse everyone with renewed courage' (Mphahlele 1989: 107). Her letters reflect her aptitude with words, but, interestingly, it was not a skill about which she felt confident. She had not had much formal education, meaning that a command of written English had not been taught to her. Therefore, in her letters she often excuses her poor spelling and punctuation – she tended to write the words phonetically, as she had heard them. On the other hand she was a keen reader and her range was wide. Her skills with English had developed as a result of her reading, and her letters reveal someone adept at conveying her thoughts and feelings in pithy terms, as when she reports asking herself how she could serve on the Peace Council when she had 'peace in my head and war in my stomach' (letter 93). She had a good ear for English idiom and a capacity to create her own when the occasion required, as when she said of the imposition of an inferior Bantu Education: 'We women are like hens who lay eggs for someone else to take away and do what they like with' (Stewart 1996: 16).

Lilian's life

Lilian Madediba Matabane was born near Pretoria in 1911, the only girl in a family of five boys. She has recorded in her autobiographical letter (number 93) that her father was a mine-worker and that through her maternal grandfather she was descended from the 'Royal family of the Mphahlele in Pietersburg', now Polokwane, in the Northern Province. Her mother, a teacher, used to hold night classes and met her future husband when he came to them. Lilian's mother gave up teaching as her growing family needed her and she took in washing to make ends meet. When Lilian had completed the first six years of school and because the family could no longer afford school fees, she enrolled as a probationer nurse at City Deep Hospital in Johannesburg, completing three years' training in general nursing. Then she married and, following her mother's advice that sewing would enable her to take in work at home while caring for her children, she became a seamstress.

Lilian records (letter 93) that her husband, Ngoyi, had trained as a teacher but worked in industry because teachers were so poorly paid. It seems that he died young, leaving Lilian to care for her child, Edith, for her parents and for the distant brother who is mentioned only in the report by Beyers Naudé (letter 127). The family moved to Johannesburg and then had to relocate from the city centre to Orlando (about 20 kms away, in what would become Soweto) where they lived in 'The Shelters' in the 1950s. 'The little one-room shacks had tin roofs which were held down by large stones. The rooms had no windows, no chimneys and no lights. One tap at the end of a row of shacks served thirty families. The narrow tracks between the rows of shacks stank with sewage and rotting rubbish' (Stewart 1996: 6). Later the family was able to move to one of the small and uniformly drab houses in Soweto, newly built by the municipality for the workers. It still stands in the part of Orlando called Mzimhlope. It was from the same 'matchbox house', 9870B Orlando (there were no street names in the township), that Lilian would write to Belinda Allan some 25 years later.

Lilian was drawn into political life through her work in the trade unions. Because she decided to concentrate in her autobiographical letter on the details of her life that were not on record, a brief account of her political career in South Africa is included here. In 1945 she took employment as a machinist in a clothing factory where she remained for over a decade; there she joined the Garment Workers' Union under Solly Sachs. When he was banned she took part in a protest march which ended at the City Hall in Johannesburg and there her young daughter was injured when the police tried to control the crowd with batons (Stewart 1996: 10). In 1952, she went to an ANC meeting in Orlando in support of the Defiance Campaign which was directed at the segregation of public buildings such as post offices and railway stations. She was arrested for trying to send a telegram to Dr Malan, the then prime minister, from the section of a city post office reserved for whites. At this time too she joined the ANC Women's League; she was a commanding orator and had a meteoric rise in the organisation of which she was soon elected president. She helped to found FSAW (Federation of South African Women, later known as FEDSAW) in 1954 and two years later was elected its president. She was then elected to the national executive of the ANC, and was also treasurer of the Council of Non-European Trade Unions. Ngoyi was the first woman ever elected to national office in the ANC. It had once excluded women from full membership, but in 1943 when the Women's League was established, a campaign for universal adult franchise was begun within the organisation. This meant that for the first time in ANC policy 'the word adult was advanced in a way that included women' (Ngcobo 2012: 3).

In 1955 Lilian was also chosen to attend The World Congress of Mothers in Lausanne, organised by the Women's International Democratic Federation, and she tells the story of her clandestine travels with Dora Tamana (letter 93).⁴⁶ Lilian dwells particularly on the warm welcome she received in Britain, Germany, China and Russia, before and after the Congress, which suggests that being accepted everywhere as an ordinary person gave her confirmation of her political beliefs. Her friend Helen Joseph has described her at that time: 'Lilian was beautiful then, beautiful and black; in her forties, but looking only thirty, head often tilted a little to one side on her slim neck, laughing eyes and a flashing smile to show an enchanting little gap in her front teeth' (1986: 4).⁴⁷ Joseph also writes that after experiencing a 'world in which she walked free and equal with others' and after witnessing the worldwide struggles of women, Lilian returned to South Africa, 'enriched and inspired' (1963: 166–67).

Because her travels abroad lasted for eight months, Lilian Ngoyi did not participate in the 1955 Kliptown Congress at which the Freedom Charter was drawn up. As a manifesto, this statement of human rights became a cornerstone of ANC policy and would, half a century later, become a basis of the principles of the new South African Constitution. Although she missed the Congress, Lilian acted promptly on her return to further the Charter's principles of freedom and equality by helping to organise the Transvaal protests against the extension of the Pass Laws to women. South African women had been resisting attempts to make them carry the 'dompas'⁴⁸ since 1913. Through this hated document the government had long controlled the freedom of men; now it determined to apply the same restrictions to women. Men had to carry their pass at all times because permission to live, or even to seek work, in the cities was recorded in the pass and the police could demand to see it at any

---

46 Dora Tamana lived with her family on the sandy acres between Table Mountain and False Bay, in an area called Blaauwvlei. She was active in organising self-help feeding and gardening schemes for women and worked in the Cape Flats Distress Association. She joined the ANC in 1943 and was a founder member of FSAW.
47 Helen Joseph and Lilian were colleagues and comrades from the late 1940s and their lives took comparable courses. Like Lilian, Helen entered politics through her work with Solly Sachs of the Garment Workers' Union, and she was a Treason Trialist and placed under house arrest in the aftermath of the Soweto massacre. Helen died in 1992 and was, at her request, buried by Lilian's side in the Avalon Cemetery in Soweto.
48 'Dom' is explained as meaning both 'damned' and 'stupid' in Afrikaans.

moment. The pass could be used to prevent husband and wife living together and to endorse out of the cities anyone whose political or trade union activities were considered threatening. The cruel results of an extension of the Pass Laws to women were evident to all – the impossibility of holding family life together in either the cities or the rural areas, the impossibility of women finding work in the cities, the impossibility of visiting a migrant-labourer husband and of caring adequately for children.

The following year, 1956, Lilian and other FSAW women decided to organise a second country-wide protest by women. This time their networking was so successful that, despite the authorities' attempts to prevent them, 20,000 women came from all over South Africa and assembled at the Union Buildings in Pretoria (the administrative seat of government) in order to present their petition. Lilian Ngoyi, Helen Joseph, Rahima Moosa and Sophia Williams de Bruyn were chosen to lead the march and they carried the huge petition which the women had prepared to present to Prime Minister J G Strijdom. Although he had been informed that the women were coming, he was not in his office when they arrived, and it was left to an aide to receive it. At Ngoyi's suggestion the women then stood for 30 minutes in utter silence and with fists raised in the ANC salute. They ended their action by singing '*Nkosi Sikilel' iAfrica*', while the Natal women sang '*Strijdom! Wathint' abafazi,/ Wathint' imbokodo!/ Uzokufa*' (Strijdom! You have struck the women/ You have struck a rock/ You will be destroyed).

In December that year, the Security Branch came at dawn to 9870B Orlando to arrest Lilian. She, with 155 others, was charged with High Treason. Two years later, charges were withdrawn against many of the defendants so that, after four years of proceedings, only 30 people, among them Lilian, remained on trial. Finally, they were all found not guilty. Like many of the other trialists, Lilian had in the meantime lost her livelihood and her family had endured great hardship. During the trial it had been possible for her to supplement her income by sewing (mostly the distinctive green, yellow and black blouses worn by ANC women) and by renting a room to one of her fellow-trialists, Dr Alfred Letele from Kimberley. He conducted his medical practice from this room while Lilian and his waiting patients shared her front room where she worked at her sewing machine.[49] The house became 'one of the best known houses in Orlando. On the wall there was a copy of the large group photograph of the 156 treason trialists with Lilian standing proudly among them' (Stewart 1996: 41).

Even these resources were, however, denied her once the trial was over. Following the shootings at Sharpeville in 1960, the first national State of Emergency was declared and Lilian, like most of the Treason Trialists and hundreds of others, was arrested and detained. She was not brought to trial but spent nearly five months in detention, much of the time in solitary confinement. All of the organisations to which she belonged, except FSAW, were banned, making membership a punishable offence. A few months later she was banned for the first time in her personal capacity. (It was soon after this that Lilian Ngoyi came to the attention of Amnesty International as a prisoner of conscience.) At a stroke, her public, political life was ended: she was listed as a communist, she could not attend public gatherings, make speeches or be quoted, and at home she could not be with more than one person at a time. Imprisoned in her home, her company was limited to that of her mother and daughter, and, with terrible practical consequences, it meant that she could no longer earn a living, not even by sewing from home. The report by Dr Beyers Naudé (letter 127) indicates the extent of the deterioration of her home which was a consequence of this banning. Except for a few months in 1973 when she was between banning orders, Lilian was forbidden to leave the immediate vicinity of her house. Lilian's mother died in 1971 and it is in this same year, the tenth year of her banning, that her correspondence with Belinda Allan began.

Letters
The letters to Belinda Allan came about when Lilian was chosen to receive a small monthly donation from the Riverside, New York

---

[49] On the wall outside Lilian's house in Orlando there is now a colourful commemorative sculpture by Stephen Maqashela which represents this machine.

City group of Amnesty International. As with assistance from the Defence and Aid Fund, it was customary that a recipient would write a personal letter to the individual sender (not the organisation) in order to acknowledge the arrival of 'the parcel'. When she moved to Europe with her husband, Belinda Allan (more about her below) continued assisting Lilian out of her own pocket.

The earliest letters that Lilian wrote to Belinda have disappeared. There are some other gaps too, either because of surveillance from within the South African postal system which Lilian distrusted and refers to as 'some Monster ... devouring our letters' (letter 87), or because letters were lost in one of Belinda's moves, or, towards the end, because of Lilian's ill health. From the first surviving letter in 1971, it is evident that Lilian would not be content with a merely formal note acknowledging the money. The full person is present in what she writes. As the months passed, the friendship grew until Lilian felt able to entrust Belinda with some of her most private family matters. Despite declining health, Lilian wrote as regularly as she could to Belinda until the month before her death in March 1980, at the age of 68. She was unfailingly interested in her friend's family life, especially her daughter Diana, and, although she could be reticent about her own family, was always ready to recount what she could of her own limited activities, such as gardening, and to comment on national developments.[50]

Everything that has survived from this correspondence is reproduced here, with a few minor editorial excisions. The long autobiographical letter (number 93), composed in two parts and dated simply '1972' was written at Belinda's suggestion. She says 'I knew that she was desperately short of money and thought we [the Amnesty group] might be able to publish some part of it. In the event we decided that we couldn't do so as it would be likely to boomerang back on her situation, but I am glad we asked her as it is a remarkable document' (Personal correspondence, May 2012). Also

---

50 Lilian does not mention Memory, who became her adopted daughter and, after the deaths of Edith and her son Neo, has made Lilian's Orlando house her home. Neo is not mentioned by name except in Beyers Naudé's report, but appears in letter 124 in response to Belinda's inquiry, and regularly after that.

included in these letters is the report written by Dr Beyers Naudé (letter 127) written after his visit to Lilian and sent to the Amnesty members in Kiel, West Germany who had asked him to inquire into her circumstances. They had also been helping to support Lilian since 1975. His report gives a clear picture of her immediate needs as well as indicating a sick brother who is not mentioned in her letters. Her account of his visit in letter 125 indicates their immediate rapport.

As Lilian's letters show, her home had never been a haven set apart from political life, and nor could it be a place of peace and security. On the one hand, her own political activities would impact severely on her home and family life,[51] and on the other, the homes of African people had never afforded them protection against the State's intrusions, for the security police or other branches of the force could enter at will. The political centrality and the vulnerability of her home is graphically present in Lilian's writing. One crisis, for example (letter 126), reflects an imposed collision between domestic and national life that is all too typical of her peoples' circumstances. First she rejoices over the visit paid by Beyers Naudé and the subsequent arrival of a stove in good working order and furniture to replace what was broken in her home. Joy is, however, followed immediately by horror as she recounts seeing the attack in the school grounds (opposite her garden) that was made on fleeing primary-school children by policemen and their dogs. Just as her own tattered life reaches crisis point, an intervention by sympathetic friends is made which renders her, as she says, 'a new woman'. At the same time, as the nation's crisis rumbles on, she is made to feel afresh her helplessness when she witnesses the ruthless violence of the police attacking schoolchildren who were protesting with stones.

Other personal high and low points are recorded in the letters too. There is the misery caused by her daughter's drinking and her inability 'to get off the high liquor horse' (letter 105) which brings Lilian as near to self-pity as she ever gets, and there is her furious

---

[51] Jean Stewart tells a story in this regard: when Lilian first decided to participate in the Defiance Campaign, her young daughter was seriously ill in hospital. When her mother reminded Lilian that she might land in jail and be unable to care for her daughter, Lilian replied after some thought, pointing at the stars in the night sky, that she felt obliged to make a choice that would serve all the children of the land (Stewart 1996: 13).

outburst against the State's brutality that killed Steve Biko (letter 130) and its power to ensure that no one was found responsible when an inquest was held. Counterbalancing these sorrows is constant pleasure in growing flowers in her garden from seeds sent by friends, and her brief delight in 1973 when she is able to travel to Durban and Cape Town because her banning order has not been renewed. Her freedom lasted for three months and she reports that she 'enjoyed every inch of my holiday' (letter 100). It is fitting that as a loyal member of the ANC she should have used it to visit Chief Albert Luthuli's grave outside Durban, and, a couple of weeks later, Nelson Mandela, then in his ninth year of captivity on Robben Island after the Rivonia Trial (letter 98).

Lilian did not try to follow a single formula in the greetings she used in her letters, either at their beginning or end. The opening salutations vary from the affectionate 'My dearest Belinda' to a formal 'Dear Mr and Mrs Allan'; sometimes he is included by his first name, sometimes 'Donald' comes before 'Belinda', sometimes Diana is included, and sometimes they are collectively addressed as 'My dearest Children'. Early on, Belinda is called 'Brenda' and even 'Brinda' because, as Lilian explained, she could not easily check on such things as names and addresses because she had to keep her letters hidden in case of a police raid. The closing salutation also varies: sometimes it is 'Lilian', sometimes 'Lily' and sometimes 'L. Ngoyi'. All of these variants indicate Lilian's circumstances, her mood, and her ways of placing herself in relation to her friends while creating the bond she needed with them. The plenitude of her self-styling and forms of address also suggests the vivacity with which she had once spoken on the public platform.

Throughout her letters there are other signs of how Lilian used her creative energy once she had been banned. One resource was the small garden that she created across the front of her house and which she liked to fill with colourful flowers so as to counter the drabness of her surroundings and to indicate to herself and passers-by that she tried to remain undaunted. It is probably because her garden was closely tied to her emotional well-being that when her daughter's problems overwhelmed her she reports that she has been unable to care properly for it: 'every body is asking why your garden such a flop? Inwardly my first garden which is peace and family love has deteriorated because of trials' (letter 106). For Bessie Head, the joy of gardening was accompanied by the dignity of communal productivity and her wish to help people to eat nourishing food; for Dora Taylor her garden became a solitary place of beauty where she could find relief from the oppression surrounding her; for Lilian Ngoyi, a colourful display of flowers in front of her little house carried a message to neighbours and to friends abroad that her spirit remained undefeated. She reports 'My match box garden is in bloom it is the centre of admiration. One woman just said, "one must just turn and look". I am happy about such remarks' (letter 128). The tangible, personal connection created by growing flowers from the seeds she had been sent from abroad gave her correspondents a place in her world, and her garden represented her wish to communicate and hold them in her imagination.

In her autobiographical letter, Lilian confesses that because of what she calls 'poor geography' she is sometimes unable to imagine peoples' lives in other countries. Her travels and her discovery that women faced similar challenges in other cultures helped to change this, but later in the correspondence she raises the old difficulty when she speaks of her anxiety for Belinda and family during the fighting in Israel and Lebanon in the 1970s. She knows that Belinda's home in Beirut is somewhere in the war-torn region but she cannot pinpoint exactly where things are happening: 'geographically I'm lost, I just pray' (letter 100). Thus her garden and receiving seeds from her friends must have helped her to establish a sense of the reality of the foreign parts from which they came: it was one of the few ways available to her through which she could sustain the relations of equality and creation of mutual knowledge that are a striking feature of her letters. Another is in the exchange of news about children, a third is the requesting of books. Her genuinely personal interest in the development of Belinda's child, Diana, is not simply a mundane aspect of letter-writing, but a vital form of reciprocity.

Towards the end of her life, friends, family and well-wishers managed to buy a car for Lilian and she obtained a driving licence on her fourth attempt (letter 133). By then she was 67 years old and no longer in perfect health, so it was a great achievement which 'made all the world difference' (letter 134) by restoring her to usefulness in her community. Her car (Lilian refers both to a Datsun and to a Ford Cortina) was not an item of personal luxury but was valued because it enabled her to enjoy driving 'a sick woman to hospital, or any Human being, then [their] saying thanks Lily. I feel great' (letter 134). But with the car came practical problems – 'If ones car is left outside it is stolen and some valuable parts stripped' (letter 134) – which necessitated Lilian's sacrificing part of her other treasured resource, her garden, for 'a sort of a garage' (letter 136).

Belinda Allan: the letters' recipient

Belinda Keown was born in England to Irish parents. Her great-grandfather was Rector of Dundonald parish near Belfast; her father worked for *Punch* magazine, becoming its drama critic in London. During the Second World War the family moved away from London to Surrey where her mother later became a magistrate in Guildford.

From 1967–1969, Belinda lived in Greece where she first became involved with the work of Amnesty International and its first official report on conditions in Greece under the Colonels' Junta.[52] From Greece, Belinda moved to New York where she worked as assistant to the publisher of the *New York Review of Books*, Whitney Ellsworth. He and his wife introduced Belinda to the Riverside branch of Amnesty, run by Professor Ivan Morris and his Japanese wife, Nabuko, both of whom are mentioned in Lilian's letters.

Amnesty had only recently been set up in the US and so there were not many groups in operation. Therefore, members of the Riverside group were each responsible for more than one prisoner of conscience. Two were allocated to Belinda – a Greek political prisoner and Lilian Ngoyi in South Africa. She was responsible for writing to these prisoners each month, sending them a small amount of money, and trying to raise awareness about their situation. At the same time, she says, Amnesty members had to be careful not to

---

52 Following a coup d'état in April 1967, Greece was ruled by a series of right-wing military juntas which lasted until 1974.

make the publicity too specific as it might involve the prisoners in reprisals. The group also regularly sent books to Lilian, knowing how much she enjoyed reading.

Soon after her correspondence with Lilian began, Belinda married Donald Allan, an American journalist who had worked for *Time*, *Newsweek*, and *The Reporter* among other papers. Shortly after their marriage, he joined UNICEF (United Nations Children's Fund) and was posted to Beirut to run its Middle East Information Bureau. He and Belinda were based in Beirut from 1972–75 where she worked for the publishers Harper & Row, managing their local sales office. This meant that Belinda was able to travel with her husband to countries such as Iran, Egypt, Syria and Jordan. Their daughter, Diana, was born in Beirut in 1974.

Donald's work was a mixture of public relations, providing information about UNICEF's work, writing and commissioning articles, and travelling to oversee several projects in the region. Many of these involved refugees and displaced people, particularly the Palestinians who had been displaced since 1948 and had to live in camps in Lebanon, Jordan, Syria, the West Bank and the Gaza strip. Some months before the Civil War broke out in earnest in Lebanon in September 1975, Donald had been posted to Switzerland to take responsibility for UNICEF's European Information Office. After the sunshine and their acute interest in people in the Middle East, the family was reluctant to leave for Geneva, but once their many friends had to flee Beirut because of the war, they counted themselves lucky. Once settled in a pleasing house in Crassier, near Nyon, Belinda began a degree in Education and Child Development at the University of Geneva. Although she was no longer part of an Amnesty group, Belinda and her husband continued to send Lilian books and modest amounts of money, and, as Lilian's letters suggest, their gifts arrived more regularly than others.

Donald, who died in 2008, had five children by previous marriages and they came regularly to holiday with the family in Beirut and later in Europe. From Switzerland, the family went to Africa, to Nairobi in 1980, but a visit to Lilian in South Africa could not be contemplated. A couple of years later, Belinda and Donald separated and she and Diana returned to England. In Oxford, Belinda met the American anthropologist, Barbara Harrell-Bond, who asked her to assist in the Refugee Studies Programme that she was setting up at Queen Elizabeth House. At first there was some opposition to the multi-disciplinary approach of the programme and to the involvement of refugees in teaching and research, but gradually, as the programme gained international recognition and financial independence (much of the fund-raising done by Belinda), the University's appreciation grew to the extent that it recently nominated the centre for the Queen's Prize for Excellence, which it won. In Oxford, Belinda remained active in Palestinian matters, working with a Community Mental Health Programme in Gaza and her daughter wrote her doctoral dissertation at Harvard on the Shatila refugee camp in Beirut. Belinda died in July 2013.

Lilian Ngoyi's death
Pasted on one of the letters in the Lilian Ngoyi file in the archive is this clipping:

> MRS LILIAN NGOYI
> Mrs Lilian Ngoyi, a leading black African nationalist known as the "Mother of the Black Resistance", died at her home in Soweto, South Africa, on March 12. She was 68.
>
> She had been a "banned person" for the past 16 years which meant that her movements and personal contacts were restricted and she could not be quoted by newspapers. She was also one of the first people to be held under the 90-day detention law, and spent 71 days in prison without charge or trial in 1963.
>
> Mrs Ngoyi was President of the Women's League of the African National Congress before it was banned twenty years ago. On August 9, 1956, she led 20,000 women to the Pretoria office of the then Prime Minister, J. G. Strijdom, to protest against the extension to women of the "pass laws" which control the movement of blacks. [*handwritten*: *Times*: March 12, 1980].

It must have been from this notice that Belinda Allan, in Switzerland, learnt of her friend's death.

Helen Joseph reports that Lilian's death was sudden and 'a great shock' (1986: 198) to her and their circle of friends in South Africa. Lilian had been in and out of hospital with heart problems – her letters indicate that she had had high blood pressure for some time – but seemed to be recovering. The community's farewell to Lilian was, as described by Helen Joseph, memorable:

> The large church was packed with people and bright with Congress colours. Six women of the Federation and the African National Congress Women's League maintained a guard of honour in their green blouses and black skirts, standing still and silent on each side of the coffin where she lay under the Congress flag.
>
> It was a gathering of old members of the ANC and the Federation and the Women's League, but they were joined by the young [...] all differences disappeared and young and old, black consciousness and Congress, joined together in tribute.[...] A moving announcement had been made: "Lilian Ngoyi lived a life of great simplicity and we shall bury her in simplicity. The coffin will be borne on a cart drawn by two horses."
>
> A thousand people walked behind her, five miles to the cemetery. All the way, the people of Soweto came out of their houses to wave their farewell to her as she passed, giving her the Amandla salute, the clenched fist of strength and struggle (Joseph 1986: 198–99).

84. [*sent to Belinda's New York address*]

9870 B Nkungu St
Orlando West 2
P.O. Phirima
20 June 1971

My Dearest Belinda

In reply to your letter of June 7th 71. I'm grateful to you for raising the matter of what books interest me? I'm only sorry that at the moment, I'm trying to find out if my interests were not in the banned list, and this will not be too long. I need hardly say how delighted I was to receive this book, [it] is most interesting and painful. You know it is a wonderful feeling to know that we are not alone. I have, however had a serious blow, of losing my mother. She passed away in March 71 on the 26th at daybreak, and was buried on April the 4th 71. Despite my troubles, funeral arrangements were splendid. I must express my very sincere appreciation of the work of the people. I wish I could write a book about all what has been taking place. I have a lot of friends in New York, who send me regular parcels, which I think you will understand. We are in a country in which one cannot express herself freely. I wish we were nearer each other as it might help you to talk with me freely. But there is Another Source of strength open to all of us. And this is it. Our Souls can never be imprisoned. I'll write again soon.

Thanks a million.
Sincerely yours
Lily

85.

> 9870B Nkungu St
> Orlando West 2
> P.O. Phirima
> 20 September 1971

My Dearest Belinda,
On the 7th of June 71, you had written to me, and also sent me a very touching Book in a paper back about Mary Queen of Scots. I wrote back to say I'll check on the banned list of books, which is just a mass. Now since [then] you have not written to me. How come? I think your choice of Books will suit me. You have been very wonderful, the book made me feel self pity of my position was not necessary as there are women in this Globe who were tortured to a bitter end. Please do write My Dear, I feel your letters most soothing. With Spring here, all is beautiful. Flowers are the order of the day, beautiful varieties. Of course I have a very small garden, it's hardly a garden but a passage, but I squeeze as many flowers, as long as they have bloomed. It would be nice to hear from you sometimes, but soon. Thanks a million for what you have done in the past.
Yours Sincerely
L. Ngoyi

86.

9870 B Nkungu St
Orlando West 2
P. O. Phirima
12 November 1971

My Dearest Brinda,
I am delighted to inform you that I received your letter and a very sweet letter. I'm rather too disappointed to learn that my letter to you written in Nov just immediately after your letter asking if you could send me some flower seeds [did not arrive]. I was so thrilled to know that you enjoy my letters. I shall not write a long letter to you until I hear from you. I have enclosed my picture – not a very nice one, but I wanted you to see what my garden looks. I received parcels regularly from Professor. You will notice I addressed your letter to him because I'm sure the other one is lost. I had hidden your letters, because sometimes we are being raided and other letters are usually confiscated. I then forgot your surname. So please forgive me for addressing your letter to Professor. I hope when you answer do give me your Surname. I have received the books all thanks, and I have been trying to check this end the list of banned books, and if you have the following in your care I would love to have them.
1) *Heavenly Discourse* by Mark Twain
2) *Treasury of the Worlds Great Letters*.
3) *Treasury of the Worlds Great Speeches* (published by Simon Schuster).
4) *Their Morals and Ours* by Leon Trotsky.

Please, do not think I'm asking too much, but if you find them, send one by one. I will write a longer letter though my writing is bad, I would have taken typing I was given a wonderful machine I mean a typing one in Germany, but by now it would be gone to the other side. Please Answer and tell me what you think of my garden and send the seeds I'm anxious to see [what] U.S.A. seeds will look like. You will notice I have all assorted plants, my main pleasure is when they have bloomed. Also I have a very small lawn. Thanks love, what happened to Nabuko. She is silent. Tell her I miss her letters. Greetings to all. I'm starting my 800 words letter to you [ie. letter 93].
Yours Sincerely
Lilian Ngoyi

87.

9870 B Nkungu St,
Orlando West 2,
P.O. Phirima,
31 December 1971

My Dearest Child,

Thank you for your charming letter and the very special news of your on-coming wedding. I'll send you a card. I'm also delighted to learn you admired my garden, that is my little Friend, and my Dear Thanks a million for the seeds. You are really wonderful. What really worries me is if letters some do not reach you, it's a real disturbance of mind. No my love the Treasury of the Worlds great speeches has not arrived. The letter and enclosure arrived on the 30thDec. I was already worried thinking that some Monster is devouring our letters. I'm very much excited about the seeds. I only hope your Husband-to-be is as nice as you are. I could have long started my long letter, but I was disorganized by your silence. I'm happy you think my writing is good. I'm unable to type. Why do you say Sadly Nabuko has left? What happened Dear? There are those things do happen when not needed, but we must be Above them. Do you mind giving me her address in Japan, I had it, but misplaced it. If my ban is not renewed it will expire in Nov 1972. Can you imagine how I would feel? I shall write again, I'm having so many Christmas cards around me, Oh what a wonderful feeling, that I'm not alone. Friends sending cards, seeds, isn't it wonderful? Next time, I'll expect your picture. I'll write soon my love. Best wishes for the New Year to all our friends.
Sincerely yours
L. Ngoyi

[*at the top*] PS. I'll write as soon as the book arrives. Thanks in advance

88.

                                            9870 B Nkungu St,
                                                    Orlando West 2
                                                           P.O. Phirima
                                                 10 February 1972

My Dearest Belinda,
Thank you for your letter and its kind invitation. I need not even try to get a passport, because it shall never be given me. But Darling the 6th of March will ring in my ears, and I'll attend your Wedding spiritually. The thought of seeing you is just what I need to cheer me up. I did not want my card to arrive late, thus it is there. No your friend has not sent the January parcel yet. Perhaps it will arrive one of these days, and it is anxiously waited for. I hope you have recovered from your cold. I shall never forget to remind you to send me your wedding picture. I have also started on my long letter. Will you be going for your Honey Moon? I wish I could join your Mother
Thanks love
Yours Sincerely
L. Ngoyi

89.

[*no address*]
18 February 1972

Dearest Brinda

This is to thank Mr Peter for his letter and contents. I'm posting my letter on Monday, and Perhaps I'll have to post in separate packages. I do not want to interrupt as I know how busy you are these days preparing for the Day. Another letter following
Yrs Sincerely
Lily

Thanks a million

90.

9870 B Nkungu St
Orlando West 2
P.O. Phirima
21 April 1972

My Dearest Mrs Allan,

I'm herein answering your letter of the 12th April. I must thank you very much for the 10 dollars which amounted to the sum of R7.34. A great help. What a lovely picture of you and your Husband. I have received the last two cheques. Thanks a Million. The address is very much correct, some times our letters are being tampered, and this really had put me out of form. The one sent on the 3rd April has arrived. I'm very happy you received part one, and surely you will receive part 2. I will get my bible and read 1 Corinthians 13. Oh! I wish you a happy marriage. I wish I was there to see you in your gown, and enjoy the jazz bands. Oh well that is just life, I hope Professor will find some one to make him happy. Does it mean when you go to Beirut, Lebanon I'll be forgotten? I envy you truly. I wish I could be somewhere where I could not be followed by the S.B. Yes Dear lucky you. No, my love you did not send Treasury. I would be happy to receive one. You are from a well educated family, I envy you very [much]. I notice your mother is a Magistrate in London. Wonderful and you and your husband are holding key positions in your Countries. I'll write again, I'm too excited. The post will soon leave. Remember me to your husband. I'm very much impressed by your picture, and wish I could be reborn and enjoy the life of youth, full of love and fun. Thanks once more Dear. Love to all our friends.

Yrs Lily

91.

9870 B Nkungu St
Orlando West 2
P.O. Phirima
21 April 1972

My Dearest Brinda,

I'm here answering your letter of the 14th – 4 – 72. Could you imagine how excited I was to learn that at last you have received my first half of my long letter. I'm surprised it had to be sent by <u>sea</u>, because it was weighed in my presence, I was asked to give them the amount on the envelope. I mean stamps. Anyhow [better] late than never. Let me start by thanking you ever so much for the 10 dollars how wonderful of you. In any case our friend <u>Mr Peter</u> had already sent me two cheques each $25 let me say they were R16 and some cents each. What a relief, but the £20 which he had last said was following was never received. I'm better off. I wonder what I would have been without your wonderful assistance. A great feeling to know I'm not alone. May I therefore thank you a million. I'm very much thrilled to learn you are impressed by the letter. I wonder if you can write it in a form of a book using my way of writing and english, but put it in order according to its stages. How do you think Dear? Any how let us wait until you get the other half. If all goes well my ban will expire in Nov. I'm now 61 years, and have no security. I'm no longer as strong as I was physically, but my spirit is strong as a rock. I love life, and would be pleased to see a change in the Country I love and its people before I close my eyes in death. How is your Husband? I wish you a happy life. In marriage one has to give and take, to understand each other, and discuss your problems, that is very important. How is professor Ivan Morris? I miss his letters. You see we now are Members of one family. It is getting winter, we find ourselves shrinking, because our climate is very hot. I wish I could come there for a holiday. I need one, stay in a hotel like the Peking Hotel in China, have a good rest, go out sight seeing some historical places. I'll write again. My love to all of you, and your Dear Husband.
Yrs Sincerely
Lily
[*at the top of page*] P.S. Mr Peter's letter was written the 1st April

92.

[*no address*]
5 June 1972

My Dearest Belinda,

How wonderful to read once more one from you. Thanks very much. Yes our friend Peter has written me a very nice letter, June, and enclosed my parcel as well. I'm very happy you got the two long letters. I thought you would say this is no good, but it is factual my Dear. If I was telling verbally of my experiences you would laugh and cry. Life has been tough, but I think I was lucky to go abroad, and see for myself the struggles in other countries which were bloody, but still men and women looked forward for their victory. I'm also hoping with confidence that before I die I will see a change in this country. As it is now the students are putting protests against Apartheid – African students against Bantu Education, Bus Drivers against lower Salaries. There is no peace and some 400 Bus Drivers in jail, white students also some beaten by Police and are in jail. Every thing seems to be very wrong. Months are becoming shorter to bring Nov nearer me. I ask myself this question. Will my banning order be lifted or will it be forgotten? Since 1961 I have lived with it. May be it will be renewed. If so, God give me the courage not to weaken. How do you find married life? I hope you will not be a nagging wife, but discuss your problems at the right place, right time. My warmest greetings to your Husband. I only hope you will not give up writing to me. Your letters are of great comfort and give me courage to face day to day problems. This year, I think my soil is [a] bit tired. It's a very small garden, and has never rested, as when it is in bloom gives me very much pleasure and keeps me busy weeding. Greetings to Professor and our other friends. One day I'll come there to see you, and speak verbally to you all. Thanks once more for all.
Yours Sincerely
Lilian

93.

This is the two-part autobiographical letter which Lilian wrote at the suggestion of the Amnesty International group in New York. It begins in an autobiographical mode and then, gradually, direct addresses to a particular reader enter the writing so that it approaches more and more the mode of a letter. Only a typescript copy of the original has been seen.

[1972]

Lilian Ngoyi
Born in Pretoria, Blood St 191, I was the only girl in a family of five boys. Why I was born in Blood St, was of the fact that my Grand Father was one of the Royal family of the Mphahlele in Pietersburg [Polokwane], Transvaal, who because of the missionaries turned away from his own customs of being primitive. [He] attended night school, and was a minister of religion. So whenever my mother gave Birth she had to go to her home, so that my Grand Mother could help her with the other kids. My family was very poor, but most struggling. My mother used to hold night schools, and she taught my father, who in turn married her. He was then working in the mines earning £3 in six weeks, and my mother would do washing, bundles upon bundles, and in the evening hold a night school.

Some times I would be absent from school to attend to my younger brother, and my mother would take me with to her place of employment. We would never be allowed in to the house of her employers, we would remain under a tree, whilst my mother was ironing in the beautiful house, and she was not allowed to breast feed her child in that house. She would come to us outside under the tree. At the same time I could see a big cat roaming in the house, even their big dog would roam up and down the house. If mother is given lunch she would be given a slice of jam bread, enough for her, then she would cut it in halves to give us, and a lot of tea with very little sugar. Though so poor my parents were very religious and lived an honest life. Every evening there was a Bible on the table, and we were taught to recite the Lords Prayer. 'Give us this day our Daily bread and forgive us our trespasses as we forgive those who trespass against us.'

As I grew up I noticed hatred in the missionaries, for though they preached the Gospel, but when it came to a black man they too saw black. And love thy neighbour as you love your self did not exist. Oh! well I thought to myself perhaps the black man was made second by God just as there is brown and white sugar. The whites were whites, it did not matter how [old] our black fathers [were] or [if they had] education more than a white boy of five years. Because of our skin we remained 'boys' and 'girls'. I too then became very religious [and] prayed very sincerely that God should have mercy on us, that though we have suffered so much and [were] being segregated, when we die we shall be with God. As a child I started getting fed up as I sincerely prayed, but no answer. Things went worse. Also I started thinking, how can this white God, who will not look and answer our prayers be with him in his Glorious heaven? I followed the struggle of Moses [and] the children of Israel.

By this time we were out in the farms, no school. My mother asked my Father if I could be sent to a boarding school. There was a bitter argument as my Dad said he can never educate a girl because she would get married, but my mother won him over and I was sent to a boarding school. Mother [continued] doing washing also sewing until I was in my Std 6. All this time I'm studying the way we suffering, but my mother firmly believed our tears shall be wiped away in the next world. I believed we should start enjoying life here. Funny enough, when the African population was full in churches, most of the whites were in cinemas, some to tennis courts, they seemed most relaxed, and had the best food. We were eating mealie meal porridge daily, no sweets, no salads, except sometimes we get wild spinach. But at the boarding school we got stamped mealies with white beans, coffee and bread twice a day, but never rice or cheese, not even milk with our morning porridge.

After my Std 6 I asked my mother if I could not take up nursing, because it was too straineous watching my mother working so hard. Then I applied for nursing. During those days, when you have passed your Std 6 you were allowed to take up nursing. For three years I did my General Nursing, but my mother really did not approve of nursing. She thought I should take up dress making. I use to imitate her, and sew little dresses, and these were sold, then our neighbours use to bring material for me to sew for their children. I then fell in love with a teacher, who because of the salaries in teaching worked for a paint firm, [and] because of his qualifications was earning a better wage. We then got married and a burden from my mother's shoulders was eased. We had two girls and a boy, and at their early age my husband was involved in a car accident, and died after suffering for a fortnight. I was now back where I started. My mother-in-law felt I should go back to Hospital, but my mother said I should improve my sewing, as when I do sewing, I'll be able to look after my children, before school, and after school. So this I did. I was able to take my first girl to do her J.C.[53] And she got married and the other two were big when I started my struggle, this time Politically.

I always felt within me that these whites should be approached to register our disapproval of the wage we were earning. This time I was working in a garment factory. I was immediately elected a shop steward. During 1952 there was a Defiance Campaign where white and black people of South Africa would just get in a place reserved for whites only and voluntarily get to jail. This impressed me a great deal. I followed the organization behind all these good ideas and was shown the African National Congress offices. Membership card two shilling & sixpence. Good. Then I also registered to go and defy, but before my turn, there was an Amendment in our Parliament that any body who defies during January 1953 would be sent to jail for 3 years with out an option of a fine.[54] I asked the Congress officials if I could be called upon to defy [and] they showed me the [Amendment in the] *Rand Daily Mail*. I said I was aware of its contents and its implications. So they said [not] unless you organise five other people, and they seemed to be at my finger tips. So we choose to defy in the white section of the General Post Office. As soon as we got in I went to grab a paper and send a telegram to the then Prime Minister, Malan. As I was writing next to a white man he politely said to me 'Excuse me Annie. You are in the wrong department.' You see, without asking for my name he calls me Annie. I said to him 'Excuse me sir, my name is Lilian. And I am not in the wrong department. I'm sending a telegram to the Minister of Justice and because of apartheid I feel I should write this just here.' The telegram read 'Please stop your ruthless laws, other wise the black man is rising.' Just as I signed my name I felt a strong arm on my shoulders. When I looked up, a Police. He said 'Come with me, you a[re] under arrest.' Good God! I then thought, I'm now gone three years without my family, and this was the very first time for me to be in a jail. We were pushed to the cells, the five

---

53 Junior Certificate, written after ten years of formal schooling.
54 The Defiance Campaign began on 6 April, 'the date set aside by the government for countrywide celebrations to mark the tercentenary of Jan van Riebeeck's arrival at the Cape in 1965' (*Readers Digest* 1993: 383) and strikes were planned for June that year. The government took a range of steps to crush the defiance movement, among them bannings and new legislation.

of us. We were given stale porridge but within hours some Indian women had cooked lovely supper for us. Then we had to sleep on some mats on the floor. Early in the morning we got up to have just our faces washed, no soap, no face cloths, but [we] used our handkerchiefs. It was time to go to Court, escorted by a police man. The court was filled to its capacity and shouts of 'Africa' were like a big thunder. To our greatest surprise we were allowed out [on] bail on our [own] recognisance. The Court adjourned and the case was called three times, and in the end we were not found guilty as there was no law specifically [... stopping] the non whites from the white section.

I then joined the ANC Women's League before it was out lawed. I became very active and I was, after [a few] months, elected its President in the Transvaal. I was also co-opted in the male section as a treasurer. Then we decided to co-ordinate all sections of the Congresses to form the Federation of South African Women. At this conference, I was elected its President and Helen Joseph as the Secretary. And at the same [time] I was in the executive of the ANC. You see my hands were very full. At work I was a member of the Garment Workers' Union Executive. This was difficult, because workers in this country were [racially] divided. Ours was [the] Garment Workers African section. It was where I learned to protest. We protested the dismissal of Solly Sacks, who said a worker is a worker despite his or her colour. All the same he was sent out of South Africa.

When ever we had meetings in this Executive, I used to put up my views strongly. Then they, the members, said I was putting Congress ideas and our next elections were by [secret] ballot, and suddenly I was dropped. I was also asked to serve in the Peace Council of South Africa. I was not very happy because I thought, how could I have peace in my head and war in my stomach. But my colleagues said I should [stand]. Peace, I thought to myself, this is really a bluff. No African, meaning a black man, has peace what so ever. I did not know the value of the Peace Council, until I went to Germany, to one of the worst concentration camps. Yes, now I was really for peace. I saw the gas chambers [in Buchenwald] (see letter 108). I was shown some lamp shades made of human skin, which were pulled whilst these unfortunate human beings were not given any chloroform.[...] I asked myself, if such horrible things have happened to whites by whites, how much more when it came to white to black. I'm also among those mothers who say no to war. (I did not mean to come [so quickly] to this part of my letter. You will note, it is my serving in the Peace Council. Yes, let us get at this.)

I was then elected as a delegate to the World Conference of mothers in Lausanne, Switzerland.[55] I declined because of the little knowledge of the world, and my poor English and education. But the women said under all costs you must go. So I accepted. Because of poor geography I thought abroad was no soil and people there were supernatural. Then came the question of [a] Passport. It was just ruled out for me to apply for one, and my anxiety of getting abroad was kindled.

In parliament there was this Bill that our children should be taught Bantu Education. An education to prepare them to know that they are nothing less than a servant. The whole Congress was opposed to this type of education. To me it seemed as if we were treated like fowls, in this respect that a fowl has no decision what so ever over its own eggs. The owner of the poultry decides whether to give a neighbour the eggs, or put them through an incubator. We demanded universal and compulsory education. Despite our protests, the Bill is now law. I remember when the first man [went] to the moon, when he set his foot on the moon, he said 'This [is] a little step forward for mankind.' I asked myself, is my child and grand children included in 'mankind'? By this time my parents-in-law were all dead, including my Father. I had to collect my [mother] to stay with me, and be with the house and children. Unfortunately my own children were never a success educationally. Instead my first born [...] had to attend to her children and mine as well as my mother who suffered from rheumatism for 21 years. But despite her pains, she was a pillar of my courage, she was never worried about my family but the other families.

So my trip was arranged for my first stop England, by sea. When I was in the ship already, [and] it had moved, it was returned to the harbour. [I was ...] hiding in the toilet with another [...] lady, Dora Tamana, from Cape Town. Our tickets were in European names. So we were arrested and got out of the ship. This was a moment of disappointment I shall never forget. When the ship pulled and sailed. As you know even Jesus had those among his disciples who betrayed him.

We tried other channels, this time it was an air passage which was an experience. I could hardly eat the lovely food in the other hotels, because of the showers of questions at each airport. 'Why have you no passport?' I had to think quickly of a lie to lead from one country to another. Before we flew from our airport, Jan Smuts, a white gentleman with a lovely white

---

55 Conference of the Women's International Democratic Federation.

shirt with a pile of documents came straight to me. As he stood before me, there was ice in my stomach. I thought, now I'm out again. Instead he gave a loving smile, and asked 'Are you Lilian Ngoyi?' 'Yes sir.' He stretched his hand and said 'Happy landing. In this plane there is no Apartheid, you use the same facilities.' I could not believe my ears. And off we went. We slept at Uganda. Black porters gave us a welcoming smile, but we could not understand each other, as they spoke Swahili and we English. Then we proceeded to Italy. My Dear, we were this time in hell. The Police the[re] were so aggressive and promised to send us back; they cannot let us go to England just because we were holding affidavits. When we got to the hotel, it was just the opposite, a wonderful welcome. But I could hardly go for Sightseeing as I was promised to be put in the next plane in the morning. We went straight to our lovely rooms. Meanwhile my brains are at work to find words to convince the customs [Immigration] the next day. Day break we went to the airport. Here this big Police. I said to him 'Sir, please let us go at least to England because we are supposed to be British subjects, but people of my colour in my country always have the difficulty of having their travelling documents.' 'Alright, alright. You take my word you shall never get to England.' Thanks God, we are getting to Amsterdam. A South African white who was also a passenger, came and set next to me and asked me why I do not give up as the whites in Amsterdam were most vicious. I started getting [an] icy feeling in my stomach. But to my greatest surprise, as soon as the plane doors were open, a tall handsome white man stretched his hand holding mine down the stairs, then went to fetch Dora. This time even our baggage was not searched, but just crossed with a white chalk. After our meals this gentleman asked what would you like for a drink? I said, 'orange and gin'. I hardly knew how it tasted like and we sipped a bit.

This time we got into a very big plane, no noise, and we took off for England. Within a short time there we were in England. 'Unbelievable,' I said to Dora. I told her never to answer any questions, as I will do all the answering. Customs officials demanded our travelling documents. Calmly I produced our affidavit. This gentle-man looked at me, 'I'm asking for your Passport.' I said 'I have none.' 'So you came up to here with this?' 'Yes Sir.' 'Why did you come here?' 'For Bible Studies.' 'Who is paying your boarding and lodging?' Lilian, 'My husband is an advocate in South Africa, and has arranged all that with a lawyer here.' Fortunately they did not ask me who the lawyer was. Whilst standing there, a white man who was sweeping just touched my hand privately [and] handed me a piece of paper. It read 'Helen and friends waiting outside.' Oh! Thanks. I was now really excited. 'Do you know where to go to from here?' Quickly, 'Yes, Sir.' 'Have you any cigarettes, gold in your luggage?' 'Oh! No, Sir we hardly smoke. As for gold it is being out of question, it is dug by our fellow Africans in the mines, we hardly know the colour of it.' 'How long are you intending to studying?' 'Six months, Sir.' Then we were let alone. As we went out, there [were] a lot of women in about 6 cars to welcome us. They hugged us, kissed us without looking around [in ...] fear of apartheid.

Well well, we preferred to be in a home than in a hotel. Part of this was now we were suffering from a complex, [because] during those days there were not so many black people as now, [so] as soon as we were in the streets the people would focus their attention to us, with broad smiles. We got to a Bathroom and refreshed ourselves and we had a most hearty welcome. No discrimination of colour, we were human beings. We sat there chatting with other women as women too. By the way our clothing was confiscated in Cape Town as we [were] taken into custody. Women are wonderful. In England they took us for shopping, we had even more than we had before. Warm hand gloves, boots with fur inside, warm coats. In fact, Dora actually was given by a certain lady a fur coat. When I left South Africa I was wearing size 36. But on my return, a size 48. The food we ate was all so nice and we had our baths morning and evening. For instance, the house I own here has not a bath room. We have to bath in the bed rooms. Shame, isn't it, in this modern century? We were for the first time taken to a theatre [and] we enjoyed every moment.

But my thoughts were cast on the Conference of the women of the world. I was very much worried by the little Education I have. It had not been difficult speaking my English in England, and I bluffed most of them [into] thinking I was an educated some body. I found out then that the language was not very important, but the knowledge of your country was the deciding factor. This time I had to have a visa to get to Berlin. Within a fortnight, all was arranged, and we flew out. Another change. I found out that the warmth of these people was above England. You could even feel it is as they grip your hand. At the air-port we were met by the young pioneers waving flags, some handing flowers to us. And the young ones were very much taken up by our colour. I remember one little boy rubbing my arm, and then asking, if I wash, do [I] not become as white as he is. Most fascinating. We were taken to a cottage, we were given a lady, a German of course, to cook, wash, and clean for us. We got on very well with this lady, as we were not used to sit back and have some one to do our work. At about 8 am there would be a car to collect us, to [meet], at their offices, all the women from different countries. So this time, South Africa had its representation. We were all the time with an interpreter, also in the evening we had a different one. Some times a male one [...].

One day we were going to see a woman giving painless Birth. As we left the [hospital] office with the Superintendent, [at] each ward by the door there was a Sister with their beautiful veils. As we passed, they would bow down their heads. I did not very much approve of this. 'Who am I to deserve such a welcome?' As we got into the other ward, the sister was standing with a girl about five years [old]. She bowed down so long and this touched me, and I could not keep quiet. Then I asked the Superintendent, 'What is this all about? Don't the staff of this Hospital mistake me to be some one with a high qualification of Education?' He stopped and said, 'You see, educational degrees do not worry us. But any one who respects his people and knows their suffering is most respected.' Oh! this was like a shower of relief. We then got to the ward, and a woman was lying in bed, and within half an hour as she was drinking her tea and talking to her Doctor, and she delivered a baby girl. And the man said her name was Lillian. Unbelievable. We went to another ward, and this time the doctor explained how they helped childless parents, and how they find which of the party is at fault by using a Hair as a guinea pig. Unlike here in this country, where some of our people are being used as guinea pigs. I have an example in my finger tips. My Daughter had given birth by caesarean forceps and I think one of their forceps tore her bladder. And was discharged from Hospital. When she got home, she would ask for a bed pan frequently, until I just had to fold a sheet under her and I took her back to hospital. Now listen to this. A professional Dr said to me in my face, 'I thought it was a small hole.' Could you believe it? It cost her three months in hospital there after. He answered me as he did, he knew I was powerless to get a lawyer and have this settled in court. The damage of my daughter bladder. I do not mind if this document is read, for I have records in their own hospitals.

And we were taken to health resorts of workers. We went to factories where mothers would be allowed to breast feed their children. The amount of crèches for the children whose parents work. Life was simply great. We were shown pictures of the destruction of Hiroshima. Most pathetic. What surprised me after the war, people in [East] Germany would make a remark that 'we were able to do this and that with the help from the Soviet Union'. I began to wonder, because in our country not a single good word is mentioned about the Soviet Union. I still remember one of my interpreters saying 'Yes, Hitler and his regime is gone, but the people of Germany are still there.' True, true. Those who oppress the children of God, all over the globe will disappear, but the people will remain to fight for humanity to be respected.

Now time had come for us to fly to Lausanne. My mind was always ahead of me. We packed. Women from all over the world had gathered here, at [the] Headquarters of the offices of Berlin. Cars took us to the airport. This time I had no complex, I was a woman and a mother. My colour was not a problem. All those concerned about Peace and Friendship got into a plane [which] flew above the Alps. (You will excuse my spelling, and please just piece it up.) [In] Switzerland [we met] more friends, mothers and Women, some highly educated, holding high degrees. And here am I without a profession, but armed tooth and nail with the sufferings of my people, problems confronting black and white. [There was] a large hall to accommodate women from 66 countries. The President then was a tall upright old lady, her name was Madam Cotton. She made the opening speech, and thereafter called a delegate to present her speech. This lady from Russia was polished and knew her facts. Then we went for tea. I was called to the office and asked to preside over the Conference [for] the second session. I nearly dropped down, but in a minute I said 'Why not?' I tell you I was close to collapse as those faces were looking up to me. I called upon a delegate from Madagascar, who appeared. [She was] a black woman with a baby strapped on her back. And a large flowers in her hand. Instead of me receiving the flowers, I embraced her and her baby. Oh! this was the Climax of the Conference. She gave her most touching report. When other women were talking about their progress, we were talking about being realised [recognised] in the family of human beings. My legs were now firm, including my voice.

After this we went for lunch, and what happened? Invitations were pouring from almost all the countries. Having listened attentively to the struggles and sufferings from other women, I choose to accept the Soviet invitation, also China. And on my way back, I touched Mongolia. Dear, Dear, life is great. I loved every moment of my stay abroad, and of course my mind was back home. This undone had to be done I said to myself.

I went to Peking. (I wish I was telling you my experiences verbally.) I went to four provinces as a human being. I joined some delegates from London. And [they] have been writing to me for the last 17 years, except one who passed away. A few have stopped writing but others are continuing. I was in China when they were celebrating their 5th Anniversary of Liberation. Oh! it was beautiful. I was staying in the Peking Hotel, the place was beautiful. Then I went to Shanghai. (You might wonder why I keep on saying I. Unfortunately Dora was taken ill and could not be with me all the time.) As we were sailing on one of the lakes, an old man said to me, Lilian: 'I wish I could be reborn so as to enjoy the freedom in our country.' He said, 'before liberation we, the people of China could not get in these lakes, but they were enjoyed by the imperialists from England. Through the Help of the Soviet Union, we are just what you see.'[…]

I was almost every evening to an Opera. At times I used to forget home […] The music, though I could not understand the words, was most beautiful. I mentioned nothing about music in Germany [where] the Conductors were sufficient to make you cry. You see I have no documents which could remind me of some things, as they were all confiscated at our arrival here. The Authorities here live in fear, fear of their cats passing from one room to another. For that they must place their security police, to raid & search, what for? They too do not know.

I'm now getting to the last one of my exciting journeys. I was to the Soviet Union, behind the Iron Curtain, as described by our country. I was restless, there we were flying from Mongolia to the Soviet Union. I was with mixed feelings about this most feared country. At the AirPort just as we were about to land, we saw the Young Pioneers in their red ties with flowers in their hands [and] women waving their handkerchiefs. The grip of their hands had a bang in one's heart, the warmth of their welcome was terrific. Inwardly I thought I would see a long Iron Curtain. Instead as the Volga River stretched before us, there was the Moscow University with a long star, a star which one could feel within. Then my new Interpreter said 'This is the University of Moscow.' I said, 'But when are we getting to the Iron Curtain?' She looked at me and paused. 'Very soon now.' Now every thing was most orderly, most clean, most welcome. I was at the Hotel opposite the Red square, about half a mile to the Kremlin. There were no questions of where are you from, why are you here. I mean at the Customs of all these places, the women had [made] arrange[ments] for us. […] We were given pens to write which places of interests we wanted to see. […] I first wanted to see the embalmed bodies of the leaders of the Soviet

Union. My Dear, this was a moment amongst other moments. There were thousands and thousands of people in a queue to see these bodies. I did not know whether to call them corpses. As my interpreter and I emerged [into …] the Red Square, in front of us was a soldier walking gracefully towards us. I thought he was just passing but when he was close to us, he gave such a salute, and turned to where he came from, to lead us still swinging his body as he moved, until we got to where these leaders of the workers were lying. Inside the place is so clean, and they were lying in their military clothes. I had a wreath which I placed at the other wreaths. In[side] me I said 'Here lies [the] great leader of the workers. Workers of the World Arise, you have nothing to lose but your chains.' Same day I went inside the Kremlin and I saw that Church Bell weighing tons and tons.

I had quite a lot of questions to ask them. I noticed that they believed very much in practising what they say. Me, as a Christian, I still criticise the churches for not practising what they preach, except a mighty few here in our country like Father Trevor Huddleston, Bishop Reeves, Rev Thompson, Rev Blaxall and a few like the Dean who is now waiting his appeal.[56] [He] might serve 5 years. No one can blame me for my convictions and ban me as having communistic Ideas. I personally feel in this case the Bible should be banned. As Christians our conscience [cannot be] at rest to see the sufferings of any human being. [But] if you protest and speak against injustice then you are named a Communist. I also wished to meet or be introduced to one, but never. I find myself, Lilian, amongst others being called a communist. I'm very much sure that if Moses, the leader of the Israelites, lived here with us he could be put in solitary confinement for 90 days, or sent to prison in Robben Island for life.

I went to see Lenin's place and the room where he died […] Now the Tsar was crushed. I also went to their Library. Books being trans[ported] from other departments by little wagons. Knowledge there is the order of the day. I also noted the fact that people are lovers of education and as they speak to you they try to teach you. They express to you the value of knowledge. I also paid a visit to the U.S.S.R. Agricultural Exhibition. You know Siberia was barren, but they showed us apples from there, remarkable beautiful fruits. I also attended a matinee for the children in the Hall of Columns of the Moscow Trade Union House. The children belonged to

---

56 Gonville ffrench-Beytagh was charged under the Terrorism Act and in 1972 was found guilty of 'receiving welfare funds from the Defence and Aid Fund in London, banned in South Africa, and of encouraging others to support acts of violence […] He won his appeal in a higher court on the grounds that the state had failed to prove its case against him' (Joseph 1986: 169).

the Young Pioneers Organization. I saw one woman milking cows with something attached to the breast of cows, and in Rostock, opposite Denmark, I was taken to a school were women only were building and designing ships. During the course of corresponding, I'll send you one of my pictures in Moscow. Finally I went to an Orthodox church. My dear the church choir is upstairs, and we were down stairs when the organ began music. I felt [like] running mad, I've never heard anything so beautiful. I also went below on a tube railway, they called it Matmoporitan.[57] (You can piece that up.) I have never seen such cleanness. What more would [one] want anywhere else. [...] I was so taken up by work done by women that I was now wanting to go home, and could not take any more invitations.

Back to Germany. I had to be busy telling them of my experiences. One wonderful experience to know I'm a human being, I can stay anywhere in other countries [...] Back to London. I was one day invited by Mrs. Ruth Seretse [Khama]. I had a lovely day, as during our talk Sir Seretse could speak our language. [...] From England I went to Kenya, from Kenya I came home straight knowing very well that trouble is awaiting me. As I landed already two security men were waiting, but from excitement I ignored them. I took off my coat, gave it to Mrs Helen Joseph who was waiting for my arrival. I touched the ground by stretching my legs. And the two men asked me what I was up to. I said I wanted to touch the soil of my country with my navel. I then gave the Salute of the banned African Congress and shouted 'Africa Mayibuye'. (That means let Africa be restored to its owners.)

My children and mother could not recognise me [...] Oh! what a reunion. And this was the end of the nice time and freedom of speech and movement. Next morning the Special Branch police were at my Door [and I was] asked to report at the Medical centre. To their disappointment I was vaccinated before I left.

I started being active, and organising the women against carrying a pass. Though they call it an identification card, with us Africans, I mean the blacks, it's an insult, this document. We [could] never [be] sure of our husbands coming back from work. In it there are ever so many loop holes [by which] to make sure one is behind the bars. We organised about 2000 women to see the Minister of Justice and he never met us. Then we organised another 20,000 women. He never met us. Then there was a nation-wide arrest for Treason. I was [...] among them. Then a State of

---

57 The Moscow Metro for which Lilian probably saw signs reading 'Moskovsky Metropolitan'.

Emergency [with more] arrests. Here was the first time I tasted to be in solitary confinement, for 19 days.

In summarising all, I was a machinist in a clothing factory; Member of the African National Congress 1952, National Executive 1954; Head of ANC Women's League and member of the National Executive of the Federation of South African Women 1954; National President 1956; on trial for Treason 1956–61; Acquitted 1961; detained without trial for 5 months 1960; banned from attending gatherings 1962; detained for 71 days without trial 1963; confined to Orlando for 5 years 1963; arrested 1964; banned and if all goes well, my ban will expire November 1972. If not, hard luck.

The main trouble is these whites seem to have in their mind that we are babies for ever [...] They divide us according to our tribes, mean while this is not the issue. We want franchise, the people must choose their own government, be he white, green or yellow. Instead much is said we are not ready. How can we be ready when we are being deprived knowledge, every thing given to us is inferior [...]

The people all over the world have been most wonderful, [so that] despite all these arrests and bannings, one could not point a finger at us and say this one has malnutrition because she or he is a political prisoner. At times we struggle to survive, but there is always help from somewhere [...] You see this solitary confinement is devilish. One is locked in a cell of about 10 by 10. You are given a bucket of water and a bucket to use for your stool, nothing to cover it. You are interrogated; your limbs are getting loose from sitting down. You count your fingers until you can count no more. One day I actually fainted, and when I complained to the Authorities, I was told that I asked for it.

The main thing is we do not want to discriminate. As mothers, a child is a child. For instance you take Mrs. Helen Suzman, the lonely voice of woman in our parliament.[58] Surely if we are given the chance, as white as she is, the people of South Africa would be obliged to have her as our prime minister [...] I just want to point out the evils of Apartheid. There was the death[s at] Coalbrook, the deepest grave in the world, where a white man was lying side by side with a black man. When it came to compensation,

---

58 Helen Suzman (1917–2009), a life-long anti-apartheid activist, was elected to parliament in 1953 and served as an MP without a break until 1989. She was part of the group of MPs who broke from the official opposition to form the Progressive Party in 1959. In the next elections (1961) she was the only 'Prog' to retain her seat and for the following 13 years she was the sole parliamentarian unequivocally opposed to apartheid.

the black women were promised £50, but the white woman would be taken care of by our Government, she and her family, until she dies. [...] We also have white women who have suffered for us, like Helen Joseph. House arrest was no child's play [...] Some of us cannot earn a living wage, because they actually intimidate customers when they try to come and support us. They get in my house, they find customers, they want their names, passes, where do they stay, what is their political affiliation. Meanwhile you are left to starve. Believe me or not, there was a time when I had to sell liquor against my will just to survive and be able to pay my rent, lights and water [...]

I hope this letter will reach you, and if so, let me know what your opinion is about my writing. I'm very much aware of my very wrong spelling. I sometimes cannot concentrate since after the '71 solitary detention.

Your wedding day is drawing near, may you have a husband who is understanding and loving. I have divided my letter into two lots, and this is the second. Thanks Dear, with greetings to all our friends. Lily

94. [first letter sent to Beirut]

9870 B Nkungu St,
Orlando West 2
P.O. Phirima
17 January 1973

My Dearest Brenda,

How wonderful to receive your letter, written on the 8th December 72, which was only handed to me on the 16th Jan, 73 and without hesitation I am answering it. Peter Roux was till Oct sending me my usual parcel but since November 72, not even a letter to say good bye. I have written three letters but no reply, even Professor does not write. Oh! My love on the 30th Nov 72 two special branch men came to my house to tell me that at midnight same day my ban is expiring and will not be renewed. I did not know whether to jump or cry, but at least I can now be with other women after 11 years. Do rejoice with me. I felt I could blow a horn to tell those of my friends who have went along with me. And Brinda I was just about to write to your mother in Britain. I still have the fear when I'm with other women, that I'm breaking some of the South African laws. No, No, I can be at a gathering. The pity is I cannot afford at least a two week [holiday] at a beach Hotel, go swimming, get to a Cinema, and relax financially empty. These are just wishes. I would please ask you to write to Peter from that end so that I may know my position, [rather] than to live in Anxiety. How wonderful to learn you are happy with Donald, and that he is happy with his job. That is the crack of Marriage Happiness. Study your <u>husband</u> and be flexible. I still repeat, never nag and be a good and understanding wife. Yes my Dear I did receive your gift enclosed in the letter, but I would prefer postal orders, because I can change them locally as long they are written 'pay Lilian Ngoyi'. Thanks a million it came exactly when it was very much needed. I miss your monthly correspondence, but I very much understand the reason. My American flowers had bloomed, and what a wonderful variety. I hardly get books from any body. It was beautiful to read you have been travelling with your husband [in] Iran and Kuwait, Jordan and Syria. Fancy you were just here in Egypt? I hope one day you will be in South Africa. I have the view of your house and would love to help gardening [and] be with you for a week or so. I hope you just drop a line to U.S.A, and find out what is gone wrong. Many, many tons of good wishes to you and your Husband, and also wish him good health.

Yr very fond Lilian

[*at the top*] PS. With friends to congratulate me, bringing prayers of thanks, my hands are very full.
Compliments of the Season

95.

9870B Nkungu St
Orlando West 2
P.O. Phirima
24 April 1973

My Dearest Belinda,
This is to thank you million in advance to what you intend for help. Gift arrived safely for which I had to be away for a few days for my Easter Holidays. I was in the Capital town Pretoria for five days. I received a gift from Peter Roux, but was less the [usual] Amount. Instead of the usual $25, he had sent $15, and said Amnesty said they would now only send me 15 dollars, as my ban was no longer renewed, still I'm grateful. Now Dear you wanted to know how far I was away from the Sea. Cape Town 1000 miles, and Durban 400 miles. These are the nearest seas. I feel so small. Dear you have been doing much for me, and I would not want you to take upon yourself heavy responsibility. You are only a new[ly]-wed. I will be happy to receive the Photos. My garden looks beautiful as small as it is I treasure it, it is my consolation to watch the blooms every morning. If there is any difficulty in sending the book, please do not over burden yourself. You have a husband, to look after. It is not difficult to change the Cheque, just the little distance. Here are many changes, in the History of our Country it was a new page to see the black play with whites.[59] Now cost of living is so high, and even the women are up on their feet to protest, I mean the black woman. I hope this will find you and Donald well and happy. Thanks once more.
Yours Sincerely
L. Ngoyi

---

59 This may have been a response to growing international pressure against segregated sport. In 1973 the South African Council on Sport (SACOS) was established locally and worked in concert with the international committee, SAN-ROC, to bring about a comprehensive boycott of apartheid sport.

96.

9870 B Nkungu St
Orlando West 2,
P.O. Phirima
29 May 1973

My Dearest Belinda,
This is to acknowledge your letter written on the 30th April and only received it on the 28th – 5 – 73. From the tone of your letter it seems as if you did not get my letter, in which I was informing you about the New York news that Peter wrote to me in March, enclosing 15 dollars and he added that instead of the $25 dollars, the Amnesty has decided on $15 dollars. But to my surprise nothing was sent in April, and May is also at its end. I would like you to ask Professor to check, as this really put me off. Your parcel comes as a blessing from God. At least I can keep the fire burning. For this I thank you a Million. I do not know whether it is the post. Re having your step-children, this is a wonderful step. I would wish you all the happiness. Try and understand them Dear. Love them as if they are from your own womb, and this will mean a happy home. Nothing to beat a happy home, and understanding I earnestly Pray for you. I was also happy to learn about your beautiful garden. How is Donald? Remember me to him. In the letter which I wrote to you I had already roughly indicated the mileage to Cape Town, also Durban, which are the spots [where] I would love to spend my holiday by the sea side. I would board a train. Mileage to Cape Town 1000. Train fare R34 second class return. Durban mileage 340, train fare R25 second Class return. I would not like to be a burden to you Dear. Seeing you have children and a new home I would also not stay in a Hotel but with friends so as to have a few coins for pocket Cash. I only hope this reaches you. Love to the family.
Sincerely yrs
Lilian

97.

[*posted in Durban; no address*]
24 July 1973

My Dearest Belinda and Donald

I immediately booked a second class coach to Durban, and within a day I was in a train bound for Durban. A wonderful coincidence when your parcel arrived also another from a friend in London. Yours amounted to R40 and the friend another. So I was alright for Durban, 430 miles from Johannesburg. As I write, I've been swimming in the Sea. Now as I'm having my lunch thought of writing to you and thanking you. May the love of God which is above all knowledge be with you, <u>now</u> and for ever. I never thought I would ever come here. I'm looking at the sea waves, the ships, the multitudes of people and I say yes 11 years [banning order], thanks, you were not renewed. I sat by the window noticing the wonderful changes, the guard of our train says 'Tickets, tickets Ladies', we were three black women. How nice to our ears to be addressed ladies. Then the next man comes in. 'Bedding, and Supper'. I proudly said yes, because of you, and your Family. As we were at a certain place called black rock, of course let me tell you Durban is full of Hills. At this place you notice the Hill is full of mud houses, and you notice a few women carrying water pots on their heads, you wonder where they do their shopping. Immediately you get to the next Hill you notice very nice white buildings, almost every house a garage. Then you get depressed. Is it because of the colour of our skins, Lord? Then as you enter Pietermaritzburg you notice a place called the Valley of a Thousand Hills. Oh! Nature can provide beauty. I felt now this is where I would suggest a University of our children should be erected, one without discrimination of colour, race or creed. I arrived at Durban to find no friends to meet me, as usual my telegram was delayed. Never the less I got to their place safely. Durban is noted for producing sugar, the place is marvellous. The Sunday the 21st July, I hired a taxi to take me to Groutville to the Grave of Chief Albert Luthuli. I'm sure you read about him, he was our [ANC] Leader. When he died I could not attend his funeral. According to our Custom, I do not need a wreath, and of course I could not afford one. Our car stalled for about 3 hours and it was getting dark. I was able to throw the sand [on the grave] on behalf of all those who did not have the privilege. And on behalf of those sentenced to life imprisonment. I will make a day to see his widow. Next week, I'll go back home to arrange for Cape Town. If allowed will try and see the

life sentenced Colleagues. You can answer to Johannesburg, you know my address. Here is too much activity. I'm rushing to go to the snake park. Much love to Donald and the children.
Lily

[*at the top of page*] P.S. Thanks a million.

98.

9870 B Nkungu St
Orlando West 2
P.O. Phirima
11 August 1973

Dearest Belinda and Donald

Your letter made me so happy, to learn of your latest condition, ending up in January. What made me happier is the fact that Doctors are satisfied. How lovely to learn the children are well and happy, so am I Dear, I think by now you received my letter which I wrote in Durban. I'm proceeding to Cape Town. I had made an application to see one of the Prisoner's sentenced to life Nelson Mandela.[60] You will be happy to learn the South African Authorities granted me to see him. So I'm entraining on the 16th – 8 – 73, a train bound to Cape Town. A very exciting scenery. I'll write as soon as I arrive. This wonderful happiness that I now enjoy, is through your wonderful efforts. May God Bless your home, and give you the happiness you deserve with your Husband. I'm happy you wrote to Professor. Since you left USA, the parcels were never regular. With the cost of living up, had it not been for your efforts I would be lost in the bush. I just received a letter from Peter Roux, no parcel, that he has left for [San] Francisco, where he got a job. So I do not know what next. Any how Dear expect one from me as soon as I get there. It has been so cold, these days my garden is not as nice as always, and it breaks my heart. But as I'm not settled down, I'll attend to it on my arrival back. I'll write again later and hope again to write whilst I'm on Table Mountain. I will be able to tell you more. At present am too excited Dear.

Greetings and love to the family.
Yours affectionately
Lilian

---

60 Nelson Mandela and Lilian Ngoyi were Treason Trialists together, and both served on the National Executive of the ANC. He was sentenced to life-imprisonment at the Rivonia Trial and had served nine years of his sentence on Robben Island when Lilian visited him.

99.

P.O. Box 16
Nyanga East
Cape Town
22 August 1973

My Dearest Belinda and Donald

I'm now in full swing holiday, as you will notice by the above address. The climate here is entirely different from my home town Joburg, that is the Transvaal Province. Now I'm in the Cape Western Province. Whilst in the train 152 miles towards Cape Town, when looking out the window you could see snow on the mountains, like a white sheet, and the sun also shining on it. What a beautiful sight and the train curving round the mountains like a snake. At times I could not believe its me, Lilian, amongst other human beings without restrictions. All the same the cold is really stinging. As it is, today I'm from the harbour, as I will be getting to Robben Island to see Nelson Mandela. I hope you have followed his trial politically. We were together in the Treason Trial but now he was sentenced to life. My heart bleeds when I think. I must thank God that my application was granted to come here and be able to see him. This will be on the 25th – 8 – 73. The eve of my arrival at the same address there were preparations of celebrating the 1st of its kind, an African man, I mean my colour, to be appointed as a Dean of all these churches.[61] Isn't it progress on our side? Not always Bantu Education. Other-wise I'm enjoying myself. I cannot swim out here yet, it's raining and bitterly cold. I also cannot get up Table Mountain, as it is raining and misty up there. But my Dear the scenery here is marvellous. You need not answer to the above address, but straight to my home, as next week I will have to go back. I wish to thank you and Donald for having been so fine, for all you have done for me. Now this is a most expensive Holiday, Train Fare alone has drained me. And one has to move around by buses and Taxis, also eat and look neat. I hope your health is on the good side. Remember me to the children. I shall write again, my hands are very much full at the moment.

 Greetings and Love

Lilian

---

[61] The council of St Mary's Cathedral, Johannesburg, appointed Desmond Tutu dean of the Anglican Church in March 1975 (Allan 2006: 144–5).

100.

9870B Nkungu Street
Orlando West 2
P.O. Phirima
14 November 1973

My Dearest Belinda and Donald,

I sighed when I saw the envelope written Lebanon. This war is wrecking our nerves. Geographically I'm lost, I just pray, and [give] thanks that you are well, I hope it will be over. I was thrilled to learn my letters were well written because I am bad in observing my punctuations. That is a compliment. I have enjoyed every inch of my Holiday and observed a lot of things left undone. In as much that I feel I should have a car to be able to meet groups of women to discuss the problems of our unruly children. No Dear, I have not yet heard from the Professor yet. I will really let you know. I'm so excited to learn you have sent books, I hope they do arrive. Yes my Dear I did get the double gift, and I immediately acknowledged even the Nov one. May I thank you a Million you are really making my life worth living. You are great my baby. I also hope they will interest me. How are the children? and is the unborn still kicking, hope so. A friend gave me a knitting machine, I hope I'll be able to operate it, so as to knit for the unborn. What a Granny. Allow me [to] stop. I shall write again.
tons of love to Donald and the family
greetings
yrs Lilian

101.

[*no address*]
10 December 1973

Dearest Belinda and Donald,

I wish to express my gratitude for the gift arrived safely. You both know I never hesitate to reply. Perhaps by now you have received a letter in which I was thanking you in advance for a book you referred to in your letter. True it may be [because] of bad post. But I think this one from you was posted on the 28th Nov, [I] received it on the 10th and am replying immediately. I'm most delighted to learn baby is Kicking. May god help you until its arrival. I'm anxiously waiting for its arrival. Please try to avoid fatigue at this stage. Work is less important. I wish I could be present to wash its Nappies while you and Donald pay all your love and attention to it. It was most pleasant to read how helpful your husband is. Then my child there is beauty in your home, may you please be an understanding wife to him. I envy your mother who will share your happiness. I have not yet heard from Professor. A few months back Peter asked me which month he had not sent the $15. So as to find out from his post office. Since then, he is punctual, but this month it has not arrived yet as I write. I received a telegram from London informing me of the Death of our friend in exile, Resha.[62] What a fine man. Fortunately his wife and children are also abroad. I earnestly hope the Ceasefire [in Lebanon] holds. I hate wars. As I was on Holiday, my garden was disappointing, but now it is beautiful Dear. As small as it is. Thanks for the card in advance. Wishing you all Happy Christmas and a very Happy New Year. Hello Donald Dear. Keep up the good spirit
Love Lily

---

62 Robert Resha had been a Treason Trialist with Lilian in the 1950s. He died in exile, a 'tragic, lonely and embittered man' because the ANC in exile rejected him for holding to his belief that the ANC should retain 'an exclusively African membership' (Joseph 1986: 173).

102.

[*no address*]
7 January 1974

'Compliments of the Season'

My Dearest Children,
I hope by now our expected guest has arrived. I was very much happy to learn your mother-in-law was there, and has prepared the room for <u>the</u> day. There has been this and that in England towards the end of '73 [and] I just wondered who was safe and who was not. To me it all seems a dream, I spent Christmas day with my friend Helen Joseph and it seemed a dream to be together unbanned, unrestricted.[63] Professor has not written, as you have put it, a busy-man. Peter is doing his best lately, writes and [is] punctual. I'm afraid the books you have sent have not yet arrived, I just hope they will, perhaps they are confiscated. I can be very sorry, because you always send material which interests me. We [are] having trouble with petrol.[64] Cars have to be filled on specific days except taxis and buses. I just hope by the time this letter arrives you will be too occupied to read a long letter, as there shall be some one to admire. Many thanks for parcel. I'm proud that despite all your days engagements, I have a space in your hearts. May God bless you Dear. Are the other children well? Hope so. With tons of love to the family
Sincerely
Lilian

---

63 Since the expiry of her banning order in 1971, Helen Joseph had made it a custom to celebrate Christmas Day at her home. At midday she and her friends would drink a toast to those who could not be present (Joseph 1986: 168).
64 Shortages were due to the growing oil embargo against South Africa.

103.

9870B Nkungu St
Orlando West 2
P.O. Phirima1848
6 December 1974

Dearest Belinda and Donald,

Many thanks for your letter and gift. I get very much concerned if I do not get any letters from you as I may say I feel I'm part of the family. We read about bombs, planes crashing, and one does not know if you are safe. Thanks God to learn of you being well and having your in-laws with you. Especially very beautiful to learn of the progress our Diana is making, perhaps she and the many young ones black and white will see a better world than ours. Dear for three months I had not a single letter from Peter, and suddenly during Nov I received a letter and parcel for Nov, and he complaining about my silence. Last year there was a break of correspondence about the same time. I was so stranded, when one banks on something, then get on making credits then sudden silence you imagine my embarrassment. Things seem changing fast I hope for the better though at a pace of a snail in our country. Any how we have hopes. I also received the separate parcel of printed material. I'm too happy, I just hope my books will reach me.

1. Aleksander Solzenisyn *The Gulag Archipelago*. Translated by Thomas P. Whitney.
(2) Aldous Huxley *The Genius and the Goddess*.
(3) Mark Twain *Letters from the Earth* Edited by Bernard Devoto.
(4) *Great Works of Leo Tolstoy* Edited by John Bayley.

I'm begging for pardon if I have asked too much. You have done so much [for] me that I feel very little [small] to ask for any thing. Your unselfish way of living is a torch to me. I hope some times in life, I'll be able to do likewise to others in my position.

Xmas Greetings to the family.

L. Ngoyi

[*at the top*] PS. I'll write again Dear.

104.

>9870 B Nkungu St
>Orlando West 2
>P.O. Phirima 1848
>28 January 1975

My Dearest Belinda and Donald,

I am surprised to learn you did not hear from me lately. During December I had written two letters in succession. I clearly remember 2nd letter was to acknowledge Professor's gift. The 1st was letting you know that at last Pete did write and the parcel of Dec and Jan received. Knowing you was God's send[ing] blessing. I would not have managed. Belinda Dear I have a big problem my Daughter who is the Bread Winner, at least, has taken up to drinks she is a real alcoholic. I wonder why should I really be punished so much my nerves are being wrecked. She was married and after divorce she choose to be at home. I envy your mother with daughter like you. We notice Smith is delaying matters.[65] Our hopes are scattered, we really live in a mad world. 1975 being the women's year, I think we should take over, perhaps we would undo the knots which men fail. I'm very anxious to see little Diana. She seems to be growing very well, my love to her. You surely read about Mr Vorster taking part in the affairs of Rhodesia, but home here it's just a mess. They cannot even release a dying man, Bram.[66] One of the life sentenced to Death. I some times wonder what Christianity means in our country. How is your garden, hey? We have so much rain and so much snails and worms, and hail storm. You then can imagine how our gardens look like. Other wise some parts of the country crops are beautiful including flowers. I have also marked the books which I want, looking forward to their Arrival

Greetings and love to the family

Lilian

---

[65] The Liberation War in Southern Rhodesia began in July 1964. In 1978 the white prime minister, Ian Smith, negotiated an internal settlement with Bishop Abel Muzorewa; in 1979 the Lancaster House Agreement was signed between Smith-Muzorewa, Robert Mugabe and Joshua Nkomo. This led to the elections of 1980 which were won by Mugabe's party, ZANU.

[66] After two years on the run, the distinguished lawyer for the defence in the Treason Trial, Bram Fischer, was caught and sentenced to solitary confinement for his membership of the banned South African Communist Party. Even when he was mortally ill with cancer the prison authorities refused to release him.

105.

>9870 B Nkungu St
>Orlando West 2
>P.O. Phirima (1848)
>3 March 1975

My Dearest Belinda,
I'm at present acknowledging the 20 dollars, and the separate parcels have not yet arrived, for which I thank you in advance. I'm so anxious to see the picture of our Diana, [if] she is keeping up with her months. I understood your letter very well, and just hope that time must not come when you shall be financially bad. If you only knew what a help you are to me. Yes Dear, I'm really on trial. Perhaps she might change, but it is not easy to get off the high liquor horse. I'm really on trial, but am trying to keep my chin up. Such things must not be a stumbling block in my fight for freedom. I once some years back read in the papers about Sarah Churchill being carried by Police in England being drunk in the busy streets of London. It is very sad experience my Dear. My Daughter has been wonderful all along. We have so much rain, houses at some areas were swept away by Flood. It is a great pity to listen over the air, that so many souls were lost [in the] train disaster in England. I sincerely mourn of such a mass loss of lives. My garden is not of the best, this year my love for it is being disturbed. I hope you and Donald will keep up the good work. We all hate war, and this settlement of Rhodesia (see letter 104) is a stumbling block. We live in a land of anxiety. Colour being a small issue. I believe if all is over we need not count on Human beings as Whites or black but as people. My Dear My love to Our Donald and Diana
Greetings Lily

106.

9870 B Nkungu St
Orlando West 2
P.O. Phirima (1848)
13 March 1975.

My Dearest Children,

Thanks very much for both letters, in which you both stated you have included our Diana's photo, and both were only the parcels. Any how I hope by now you have found your mistake. Also the other separate parcels have not arrived. Yes Dear Pete is out and for some time decides to keep quiet. I really understood your letters – re my gifts. I personally would be very much pleased if you would be looking after Diana. She must share that tender mother love and irrigated by the Father's when ever Donald is at home. It's beautiful to watch the young ones grow to our direction. It may be they will be in a better world. In which humanity will be respected. With Mr Ián Smith problems it puts us also back here, yet we were now having high hopes that there will be changes every where. But my Dear the disease of Capitalists and Imperialists is one, for once they have entrenched themselves in their wealths, it becomes difficult to reason. Your letter was a real comfort. Yes indeed I have trials. My beloved daughter, who has battled with me during my political troubles has suddenly just with a wink of an eye changed. I sincerely hope it will pass, but it is one of the most dreadful situations I have ever experienced. In as much that every body is asking why your garden such a flop? Inwardly my first garden which is peace and family love has deteriorated because of trials. Of course they will pass, but this time I have failed to keep my chin up.
greetings and love to the family
Lily

107. [*first letter sent to Switzerland*]

9870 B Nkungu St
Orlando West 2
P.O. Phirima
10 September 1975

My Dearest Belinda,

This is to acknowledge your letter and also to thank you very much for the gift. I wonder when shall you ever say thanks to me. Life is tough to some of us. I last [had] Pete's letter in May. I wrote two letters after that, but no reply. And the pity of it is I have misplaced Professor's address, so I have been in the wilderness until the arrival of your letter. I there[fore] hope you will tell Professor and also send me his address. It seems every year this time Pete does not write or send the parcel, it is not a new thing. I'm very much happy to learn about our Diana and the progress she is making. I can imagine you in a strange place. I just hope you get the home you are looking for. Could you imagine my ban only expiring 31st of May 1980. Every thing is tough with me. It is made worse by my daughter's drinking habits. I'm not happy about it and it worries me. I'm unable to get to gatherings. I can only speak to one person at a time, not even two. No church, no funerals, no cinemas. Could you imagine such punishment without any reason? My garden for a change was beautiful. The Daffodils though they bloom but once were beautiful. If you only knew what a comfort your letters are. May fortune, peace and a happy home be on your side. I personally did like Lausanne in Switzerland, though it seemed very expensive. Does Donald like the place? You will get used to it. It seems as if the world is not at ease, there is this and that especially in our African Continent. All the same we hope for the best. I wish to thank you a million, Dearest Belinda. I know how much busy you are but still you make it a point to fit in a space for me. That allowance is great my Dear. Also a consolation.

Do remember me to Donald and our Diana,
Greetings and love
Lilian

108.

9870B Nkungu St
Orlando West 2
P.O. Phirima
28 October 1975

My Dearest Belinda,

This is [to] acknowledge the gift and your beautiful letter of the 10th Oct. In it I was highly pleased to read one of your sentences which read:- Diana is flourishing. I'm very happy. I wish to thank you for the compliments re my writing. If you only knew. I only did my 1st session in form one, because of the low wages my Daddy earned. Could you believe that he earned £3 in 6 weeks, and we were ½ dozen in the family. We could never eat properly. Really I'm a woman of Sorrow. What a name. Up to now I'm unable to eat well, especially when Pete does not respond. No more cheese, no milk. Yet it is very funny. I'm very old, but do not look it, nor feel it. I have on the other end my alcoholic daughter but am strong and will face all without self pity. The bannings are in fact designed to see us perish. At times I have to say these words when my soul is descending. Christ Hold up my hands, the way before me is darkened. Then my strength somehow is revived. Yes love I was in Lausanne during 1955 as a delegate to the World Conference of Mothers. I even was asked to preside over the 2nd session. Could you imagine how embarrassed I was with such little Education. I realised it is not education that mattered, but facts. I enjoyed my stay abroad because I feel what I have to go through is less than the women who were in the Concentration Camps. I was actually in one of the worse ones in Germany, Buchenwald. Yes Dear, indeed Hitler is no longer there but the people of Germany are still there. I will be happy to get the books, also Professor's address. Up to now nothing from America. Had it not been [for] you I would have long perished. Do send my copy to Professor. Yes I only visited Lausanne, I saw Geneva Lake from far. Oh! Women were wonderful. There was no apartheid. We were all women fighting for the rights of our children. The theme of the conference was 'we want no more war'. But Peace and Friendship. China I went to 4 Provinces and Russia I was only in Moscow. Germany a few places and I stayed there for 2 months 2 weeks. Also the same period of time in London. My flowers have bloomed and they are the only [thing] that I can gather around. I hope Donald is well and that by now you will have regained him at home.

I envy your travelling. Kiss Diana for me.
Greetings and Love Dear
Lilian

109.

9870B Nkungu St
Orlando West 2
P.O. Phirima (1848)
28 November 1975

My Dearest Belinda and Donald,

I hardly know which word to use to express my gratitude towards the gift. It was a real relief. You know if you have noticed birds, the young ones open their mouths open whilst their mothers are gone out seeking food. Same applies to me. Thanks a million my Dear you have been most wonderful. I sincerely wish you all the luck. With my daughter in this unbearable position you fill the gap with your help also your loving letters. I also wish to thank you for the compliments of my writing. Only hope one day we shall meet, Diana in our midst, in a free world where there would be Peace and Friendship amongst Nations. I have also received the separate Printed Material. Without hesitation I will write out a few, and also if I'm not a problem.

<u>Religion Philosophy Issues of the times:</u>
    1. Ingrid Trobish. *The Joy of being a Woman*.
    2. J E Bruns. *The Forbidden Gospel*.

<u>Perennial Library:</u>
    1. Adelaide Bry. *Using Transactional Analysis in Your Life*
    2.   "   " *T.A for Families*
    3. Angela Barron McBridge. *The Growth and Development of Mothers*.

It is really embarrassing because of all you and husband are doing for me. I should not take advantage of your help. I hope Diana is fine and the family as a whole.

Greetings and love Lilian

[*next to the list of books*] P.S. Thanks for Professor's address I have written to him, and explained the whole problem. Perhaps Pete has a reason as a young man.

110.

[no address]
20 December 1975

My dearest Belinda and Donald.

Thank you very much for your charming letter. I was very happy to receive the gift from both your family also Professor's. I quickly got dressed and made myself pretty with my hand bag to the Supermarket. I'm very fond of my food. Once I have food, I'm able to think better. Also have to stand firm. I lead a quiet life because of the banning Orders, and go out so little. I haven't had the opportunity of meeting other women, and have tea round a table and discuss as women. The hard hand has a grip on the back of my neck. But how wonderful I'm not alone. So Pete has lost interest. He is young he should be writing love letters [rather] than reading depressing letters from me. Thanks very much for having written to Professor. I shall now bank on him. I hope Diana is fine. I'll also let you know as soon as the books arrive. Thanks in advance Dear.

With warmest Thoughts and Wishes to hope this Christmas will be especially nice for you.

Greetings and love

Lilian

111.

[*no address*]
12 January 1976

Dearest Belinda,

You always make me shy to write, as you comment on my writing. Any how thanks for the compliments. Oh! Yes indeed your [gift] covered a lot, I was just like any body who is not banned. I love good food. I know which Vitamins are good for my health and I did cover this because of your help and Professor. I will let you know as soon as I hear from him. I thank you in advance. Our Diana, I'm dying to see her picture. My fondest love to her. I shall also let you know if the books have arrived. I hope by now Donald's face has improved. A pity I'm of no help, but wish him speedy recovery. Our eyes are looking at Angola[67] and wonder what will be the out come. One fact is if you have a man pinned down by his throat, he will struggle by all means to free himself. Our South African Gov has called for National day of prayer to pray for our borders. So that the Communists must not invade our Country. To us 'Communism' is meaningless, for instance most of us are not Communists but because we were protesting against unjust laws in our country we are branded Communists. My prayer is for the unjust laws to be <u>abolished</u>. No change my daughter is one way an alcoholic. Thanks a million.

Love Lilian

---

67 By the end of 1975 Cuba had sent 25 000 troops to Angola in support of the MPLA, the left-wing liberation movement. The South African forces gave undeclared support to right-wing UNITA. Cuban involvement ended in 1991; the civil war ended in 2002.

112.

[*no address*]
14 February 1976

Dearest Belinda and D. Allan

Thanks for your kind letter also parcel. I owe my whole being to you really. Always I dig and rake my mind if I really deserve all these. A friend of mine did help me with Pete's problems, I also had written to him explaining my difficulties. I just hope it will not cause trouble of overdraft for I did not see the reason why suddenly this bank was so funny. He has not yet replied. Good God so you were in Cairo? Beautiful place hey? You are well travelled. One day you will find yourself face to face in this Country of segregation. We shall be happy to meet but cannot enjoy ourselves. I'm very happy to learn of Donald's face being better. Also the progress Diana is making. I'm also sorry to tell you the books have not arrived yet, its rather long. Also Dear the people in America, I mean the new group, has never written yet. I'm also sorry to learn our Professor is no longer with us. Oh! then I'll wait and see. I'm not very well these days, I'm having a Continuous head-ache. I have been to two Doctors already, they say its Sinusitis but I tell you help. I think my nerves have given in, because of the worry of my Daughter which does not improve. She is a real alcoholic, a blow on my face. I can hardly pray, such things break me down as a woman who is prepared to face life squarely but such silly things like being an alcoholic are what I did not expect in my family. But here am I broken hearted. Despite all Dear I keep my chin up. My pride as a citizen of this land will not dampen. I have written too long and have taken much of your time. Greetings to the family.
Love
Lilian

[*at the top of page*] PS I'll let you know if Pete has written.

113.

[*no address*]
5 March 1976

My Dearest Belinda,
Thanks very much for you informative letter. I'm feeling much better in health. And have also taken a resolution that my Daughters troubles are just but part of my domestic worries. I must say Dear after writing about them to you, then I feel very much relieved. I did get a letter from Peter Roux in which he was telling me that he is a Vice President of the Bank of America, and I showed that letter to the man of a bank this end, who did change his Cheque, but wrote Pete a letter asking him next time to send a Bank draft as personal cheques could not be changed. In his letter he said he was going away for 60 days but he will write. The other Prof's one who has relatives in Geneva wrote, asking me what help I needed and I wrote back to say financial, and he also promised to send me some seeds but this he has not yet done. Belinda you and Donald I shall never forget for you are practical. You know my Dear, my position and some of my colleagues in the struggle is difficult. In this manner, we are not a lazy lot, but the Government with bans of no gatherings [which results in] a problem of earning ones living, especially to people who were sewing, or knitting, like myself. I cannot demonstrate any thing or sewing for any body as three people are a gathering. We feel so small to say thanks all the time. But we are forced by circumstances beyond our control. I said your letter was informative because the news were rather good. I'm highly pleased to learn you might get a house of your own, and our Dear Diana will run around. No Dear she must get to parks to get a different breeze from her surroundings. How I envy you. With the little changes in this country we too are allowed to extend our houses. For instances I live in three rooms. The largest is 12 by 9. No bathroom. No bedroom for children or visitors. Some of us who are employed can afford to build or extend their Matchbox houses. But if I had R500 I would buy the removable houses so as to be able to have one side as a Bath room. We have been sponging in a dish for years. An unknown friend gave me a geyser for hot water, and this has really aroused my wish for a Bath-room. With all the changes of events you might come and see our Condition of housing. But [it is only] lately that people are allowed to extend. You notice here and there beautiful houses. I'm anxious to see Diana's picture. As I received your letter, two parcels of

books arrived. I did not open as I wanted this letter off. I very much love revolutionary books. I'll be very happy to read of your favourite Blessings. Thanks once more for the parcel, each time it arrives my kitchen smells good for a couple of days.
Peace and Friendship and Love to the family.
Lilian.

[*at the top of page*] PS. We do have libraries. But the stuff I want can never be in it.

114.

[*no address*]
24 March 1976

Dear Belinda,

Just a few lines before your Holiday. Firstly I received the Prayer Book, for which I thank you very much especially what you wrote out. My love you are surely God's sent to be along side with me. Also to let you know Mr Joy Bolfo, 32 East 64th Street, New York City 10021 has sent me $5, five Dollars. And has asked me to reply soon which I did. As for Peter, he only wrote last month. I'm sure you are busy packing up for your Holiday. Hope it will be a splendid one. It seems the whole of the Globe has no peace. London, you read of bombs here and there. And we fear for our friends and Human beings' lives. Do remember me to Diana and Donald. We've had plenty rain and [it] has caused Havoc in all the four Provinces.

Love
Lilian

115.

[*no address*]
7 April 1976

Dearest Belinda and Donald and Diana
I was delighted to have your letter also the beautiful picture of Diana. Isn't she beautiful, you see life in her. I must really congratulate you for having been such a wonderful mother. You are a mother even to me. Allan must agree with me that you have mastered mothership. How very kind of you to send me her picture. Thanks once more for every thing. I wonder what I would have been without your punctual gift. [The group in] America is a total failure, it seems even the other group will be like Pete. They do not seem to understand the position. We are like those who are buried alive. It was a pity you could not see your brother's family. You deserve being a lucky woman to move freely, to see your mother. She is a lucky woman to bear a Daughter like you. Unlike me, but despite all my troubles I've kept my chin up. There is nothing as bitter to watch helplessly ones child sinking. But I feel one day, she too will say, 'I'll rise and go to my mother and ask for forgiveness'. Which she will be received with both my hands open. I will also say, 'Bring her a ring' and if possible throw a bumper party. I hope in the Near future I shall ask you to stay with me in my Match box house. No Bath-room but we could be happy because there would be peace and love. Rain has stopped but much damage. I hope you will have a good time.
Love
Lilian.

116.

[*no address*]
24 May 1976

My Dearest Donald and Belinda,
How relieved I was to [... hear] once more from you since you had mentioned you were Holidaying to London. Also with the Earthquakes. One can never just know in which side of the Globe you are. Also a relief financially. May I thank you very much my Dears. Yes it [is] a friend in America by the name of Joy Bolfo who once sent $5. This time $10. It is very little but better than nothing. His friend had sent me Flower seeds. How very kind of them to remember me. I cannot grumble. I will be very happy to see a picture of your house, which is our home. Yes Dear then one could not be human if you could have no moods or with the husband cooking, children, at times one cannot help being a bit moody. That does not mean these things can make you a bad mother. You are most wonderful to care for your new marriage and still have an adopted me on the other side, believe me. Each month, I look upon your unfailing help, like a bird with its mouth wide open waiting for its mother to drop food in its mouth. May God Give you the Courage. I'm afraid the additional 5 yrs [of her banning] it's a bore to me, and who ever drops help I cannot blame. I know with a new house of your own, your hands are full. What colour curtains, and here and there finishing touches. Oh! I am grateful for you, wonderful. My Warmest love and greetings to the family. We are looking with hope for a change in our country. If I can be given a passport, I'll definitely visit you.
Greetings
Lilian

117.

[*no address*]
24 June 1976

Dearest Belinda and Donald.
Surely you are anxious to know what is happening. Students and just some children were on a protest March. They do not want Afrikaans, unless it is a subject [see letter 118]. Suddenly Tear gas was used and shootings of children. I'm telling you it sparked trouble. People were dying like flies. Buildings were burning. So you must still use the known address. Because our post office is burned down. You will forgive me for this short letter. I can still [hear] bullets ringing in my ears. Could you imagine the Army shooting dead children. How is Diana. [I] am still waiting anxiously for her Photo-graph. I will write when my nerves have cooled down.
Thanks Dear
Lilian

118. [*first use of Crassier, Switzerland address*]

9870B Nkungu St
Orlando West 2
P.O. Phirima
22 July 1976

Dearest Belinda, and Donald

Oh! What a relief to have received your note, plus the beautiful picture of you and Diana. Isn't she beautiful? You also appear to have a wonderful figure. I'm so delighted for I knew you must be concerned about my whereabouts. Thanks a million also for the gift. As I have mentioned, you notice ruins around us including our P.O. Phirima, and other buildings, vehicles, Beer Halls, but [worst] of all, our children were shot down like shooting birds, just because they protested against Afrikaans language being used as a medium of instruction but the students said it should be a subject.[68] Oh! Lord have mercy on us. I shall never, never, never forget or shall I ever care for racial discrimination. Even children of eight years are lying in the mortuaries. A simple talk would have saved an ugly situation. Police dogs were set on kids and in return just with stones the children killed the dogs and some police and whites who were in the area. But even then some whites were hidden in some black homes. But others died a painful death. Stoned mercilessly unto death. Why the white Police used guns, it's just a mess. Even now the whole of country is not at rest, isolated fires of Universities. This was no riot but war, because Soldiers had to be called. I envy your home. It will take time before some of us could own such beautiful homes. Some of our people do own them. But how many, just a drop in the Ocean. I also really need a good Holiday but it is just a wish, as I shall not afford one. I was so miserable before receiving your letter, we read of kidnappings, hijackings of planes, of Bombs, and always one ask herself if her friends are not involved. Any how, thanks God. How is our Donald? Warmest love to him. Let him carry on with his good work.
Greetings and love
Lilian.

[*at the top*] PS. I'm sure Diana will not see an ugly S. Africa when she grows up.

---

68 That is, to be studied like other languages.

119.

[*no address*]
14 August 1976

My Dearest Donald and Belinda,

I was surprised and grateful to receive your letter so promptly. Soweto, the area where I stay, is like a province on its own. And with Arson which has been the order of the day. Our post is very slow. I have just received letters from friends from as long [ago] as June. I must thank you for informing [me] about the death of our friend Professor Ivan Morris. We find us sad after Death. May we be comforted love. He died at an early age. You know, we here have never known what it is like to have war. During my visit abroad I saw ruins by bombs, in Germany especially and a few places in Italy. But Dear, our South Africa, the whole four Provinces, is burning. Students have set on fire schools, churches, clinics, libraries, cars, offices, Post Offices, administration offices, Police stations and shops. And the Police and Soldiers have shot down our children. Students are dissatisfied with Bantu Education amongst other grievances, such as discrimination in every sphere. So one notices ruins all over. We are not sure what will happen the next day or minutes. The situation is ugly, one does not know from which end the fire blows. No schools, children and students are idling around. I feel there will be some change after this. Our Government seems not to be moved. You see here we are looked upon as an inferior race, but the tide has turned. Not a single parent knows what is going on with her kid. The students, even if their colleague is shot, it does not worry them, they get to the police with stones, at times un-armed. The situation is tense, papers do not give the true picture at times. For instance it says students are gone back to school. Very untrue. As for [us], we parents do not know what is going to happen re education. How is my beautiful Diana? I am also thanking you for all, my love. I'm writing so many local letters, people want to know if we are safe. Thanks a million for all.
Greetings and love
Lilian

120.

[*no address*]
30 November 1976

My Dearest Donald and Belinda,

I hope by now our Donald is much better and up and down his duties. How lovely to see Diana's innocent picture. Thanks a million for every thing. Yes My Dear I was very happy your mother was at your home when my letter arrived. There is very much detentions under certain laws and many of them. So one does not know what next. The situation is still very tense though shootings are a bit less but Oh! Darling I just cannot understand a very stupid war if you are black and the other is white. What a wonderful place this would be had it not been our own stupidity. If only we all could respect humanity. The place is nice and has the beautiful sunshine. Necessary places of enjoyment reserved for those white skins, beautiful sceneries. But apartheid is the order of every moment. I still blame the women. As it is our sons are all over on the run, some are out of the country because they fear detention. Schools are at a stand still, especially in Soweto where the first protest started. When pupils get to school they are being surrounded and picked up by police. I have developed a serious heart trouble. Not because I'm a coward. I'm banned and have no saying, but watching bitterly at what is happening. I hardly can kneel and pray, as if God has neglected us blacks. How long will this oppression go on? We are segregated even at [not] being given Universal Education. When we protest and demonstrate our disapproval we [are] led by guns into the cells. I was praying the other day, I found myself walking in the house with hands on my head, asking God where he is, if he did help others, – what about South Africa? Otherwise it seems to be a sin to be black. My garden is so dwarfed, and it is at its best! Belinda I must say I owe you a big thanks for keeping in touch. I look forward to your letters always with keen interest. They are soothing to my soul and comfort to my difficulties. Thanks a [*continues in right-hand margin*] million. Reason for delay of post, I think one of the reasons is because several Post Offices are down during the burning of schools.
Greetings love
L. Ngoyi
Kiss Diana for me please.

121.

[*no address*]
26 January 1977

My Dearest Belinda and Donald,

I wish to thank you very much for your letter of the 18th Jan 77, am just surprised to learn you did not receive mine to you in which I was acknowledging the receipt of your Dec letters, also the gift. Also the January gift. Thanks a million my Dear. Very funny just before receiving your letter I was looking at your picture also Donald looking at each other peacefully. I went on further to read the invitation to your wedding, I was going through the hymns which were sung on that particular day. I also went on to know from what great families you come from, and I asked myself this question, 'Who am I that these great people are mind full of.' You will remember this question was asked by David the son of Jesse to God. Your letters are a great consolation. For we here are now at a steep hill. If you are a driver of a car you will exactly know which gear you use, or apply including brakes and your clutch. Other wise your car will [not] ascend. Your letters are a real help to some-days depression. When we look around we ask our self if it was a mistake or a curse to be black, the colour of our skin is the real issue. But we say no, it was no mistake, we all belong to the human-family, but the Capitalists and imperialists took advantage of our ignorance and kept us there. Forgetting that you cannot throttle a man without him struggling to gasp. The situation is tense. We do not know what is happening with the students in particular. Detentions without trials are the order of the day, including detainees dying in detention. 17 already since the riots. Lack of finance is the greatest problem. The heat is also extremely high, with showers of rain here and there. I have not yet received a letter from the late Professor's fiancée. Oh well she can never be him. I would have loved to hear from her. Also it's all quiet with all Americans. A lady called Barbara was supposed, according to her letter, to send me $10 a month and she only did this twice and all is quiet. As for Pete, I used to enjoy his letters. Also nothing doing from his side. My Daughter is sinking in alcohol a great Pity to my poor soul. How is Diana? Greetings and love, Lilian

122.

[no address]
9 February 1977

Dearest Donald and Belinda,

This is to thank you for your loving letter, and the beautiful picture of our Diana. She is making strides in beauty and also growth. I just hope by the time she grows, we will have paved for a better world. I'm surprised to[o] how this time the letters were quick to arrive. Since as I told you no letter from America, I would really want to know the reason. Whether they just lost interest or may be funny things happening. You will find my letter a bit cold. I'm disturbed by the killings of the 7 church priests in Rhodesia.[69] I cannot think properly but I had to acknowledge your letter. I must say Dollars are preferable my Dear. We have had a terrible time. Floods have been almost in all the Provinces [and] caused much havoc to lands and crops, animals, bridges, above all to human beings. Homes are swept by the floods. Thanks a million love I shall write again soon. The situation is still tense. I worry very much about my Dear Daughter. Liquor is terrible especially if it governs ones life.
Greetings and love to the family
Lilian

---

69 This was one of many attacks made on lonely mission stations in the late 1970s. The Roman Catholic missionaries who were killed included four nuns. Guerrilla fighters from ZANU were said at the time to be responsible.

123.

[*no address*]
4 May 1977

My Dearest Donald and Belinda,
I wish to thank you ever so much for coming to rescue my troubled feelings. I just received your letter dated the 24th April 77. I had quite a few letters, but when I noticed on the outside of the envelope Vaud, I tore it open quickly and was thrilled to learn you are alright. I had raked my mind of all sorts of flies were pictured. I was also at the point of writing to your mother in England to find out about my Diana. Bless me, let the Lord be praised. You people abroad have so many happenings, we read about Earthquakes then kidnapping of Aeroplanes, and all so forth. I could not think less than that. Also the Censorship of letters. Yes Dear, Barbara is right there is a little help from Germany and then I add up.[70] I'm also sorry to learn you [are] no longer working, for you have been a mother of orphans. All the same please even if you have nothing to send, your letters are a great consolation. Barbara's letters have been misplaced, because she wrote my address this way:- 9848 instead of 9870B. Also unfortunate, the wrong address belongs to people who never wrote to any body and do not check their letter boxes. Somehow, they have a school child.[71] You know there were slips upon slips as the Post Office was wondering why I do not collect my Registered letters. Also another thing our old Post Man had left, the new one does not know us. I'm getting $30 dollars every month, a great help. My spectacles fell and broke, now I will be able to deposit. Since my friend Pete Roux does not write from the blues, a friend [in] America is a regular writer, a Mrs O White. She says she read about me in books written by Helen Joseph. Last week she sent me a book. The story of a great woman in American history. Her *Name was Sojourner Truth* [,] Hertha Pauli,[72] and I have a few comments to make though not now. But I'm thrilled and also have mixed feelings as it also shows how the so called Nigger were treated. As for one to see how families were torn from each other, it makes me weep. I ask myself God why do you allow such? The

---

70 Lilian's regular household expenses are set out at the end of the report from Beyers Naudé, letter 127.
71 Lilian seems to be implying that a literate child could have seen the mistake and helped re-direct the letter.
72 The second name is that of the writer who published *Her Name was Sojourner Truth* in 1962. She was an Austrian-born journalist, author and actress who fled to France after the Anschluss and thence to the US.

situation here is tense, perhaps you saw recently about the students demo against High rents? It was good. I thought I did tell you about my son? I'll write about him in my next letter as here is no space.
My warmest love to the family.
Greetings and love
Lilian.

[*at the top of page*] P.S. Thanks a million for the gift

124.

9870B Nkungu St
Orlando West 2
P.O. Phirima (1848)
14 June 1977

My Dearest Mr and Mrs Allan

At least we are still not hurt, tension is mounting high, unnecessarily. Students had asked the public to observe June the 16th as a day in which we remembered the dead last year. Already so many students are locked up. My own observations are had the officials not intervened, this was going smoothly. Now Police have come in the picture, already as I write the situation is very ugly. Thus I felt I should write now as one never knows what next. The place is full of Police with their guns patrolling Soweto, there has been Stone throwing and Arson. Really how long does the South African whites think we shall be slaves, for ever? And be spoon fed, for instance with Education designed by them? The situation is very ugly. Before I forget my Dear I wish to thank you a million for the gift. I shall now be expecting Diana's Photographs. My feelings are so low that I lost interest in my little garden, it is so shabby. Oh! yes, wild flowers can be beautiful. As I write a friend shows me our English paper, *The Star*. There has been machine guns in the city, three Africans, according to the paper, have killed two whites. Just a situation we are trying to avoid. Now there will be hell, racial war. We are demanding our rights, not murdering each other. You just watch your T.V. Oh! God I wish I could get out of this ugly situation. South Africa could be a beautiful [country] with all colours of people living side by side. Now innocent people even innocent whites are cold blooded murdered. I do not speak about the blacks, they will be in hundreds. But why? When shall we be civilised and understand the scriptures, especially the Book of Revelation as it stands, by God. So many detentions, arrests, exiles, these are most primitive. <u>My son</u>. You will remember I said in one of my letters that my daughter was married, divorced, and married husband died. During the interval of divorce she gave Birth to a son, which I had to bring up.[73] Now he is a Form 1 student. I thought I had told you about this. It was one of those things in life. She still drinks, but a wee bit better. In this way she used to drink Monday to Monday, now at least some days she is sober. God will keep her. Some

---

73 His name was Neo.

people in life have trials just like me, I have to ask for courage. Please just name the lawyer. It is very chilly these days. Please do pass my love to your mother. Tell her I thank her for having given Birth to you, my friend in need and deed.
Greetings and love
Lilian.

125.

[*first line torn off*]
Orlando West 2
P.O. Phirima (1848)
13 July 1977

My Dearest Belinda, Diana and Donald,

At this time of tension it is really great to know some one some where has a soft spot for us. Accept my gratitude re the gift, also loving pictures, also Drawing from my Diana. I love her very much. I made a monkey from the back of card. Isn't she sweet, I hope by the time she grows the world will have changed for better, and peaceful. We really find consolation in your letters. Thus I worry so much about [Peter] Roux, if he could only write. All our friends' thoughts and prayers are a source of strength. Especially because my Daughter chose her own way of disgraceful life. I'm not against drinking, but to be an alcoholic? You are quite a big family. Keep it up my Dear. Life with you people is worth [it] while you can be able to get to the mountains. Here is a case which has adjourned. One of us, a white woman who is banned, was invited by a friend for lunch [and she] was arrested for accepting this simple lunch of two people. She has appealed against her suspended sentence of 9 months. For the magistrate said it was a social gathering. It means we no longer can speak to the 1st person. Life is unbearable. Now we, the older generation, are so conditioned to this kind of dirty life, and are doing absolutely nothing about it. Except praying and saying God must forgive our exploiters. Oh! no, the new generation say they are prepared to die if may be, or rather be jailed. I do not remember telling you about a friend who just came to my house and asked me about my conditions of living:- broken stoves, beds to pieces, no school uniforms, my spectacles were finished. This was noted. Next thing I got a cheque saying attend to your spectacles, also your fridge. I bought cheese, chicken, fruits all the kitchen necessaries, also a bottle of wine, there was a good smell. As the gifts I have to use for rent, coal, wood, and electricity. This has been very great my Dear. You started the ball rolling, and Barbara is now punctual. I also hope I'll be going for a Holiday in one of the Provinces, for a change be at the sea-side if all goes well. Though one never knows what next. Even the city is not safe. Any thing happens unexpectedly. It is icy chilly this month. We can no longer tolerate it any longer. What news do you get there from your end? About

South Africa? Have you papers like *The Star* or *Mail*? are they not biased? We, as parents, are not sure of our students. They lately asked the U.B.C to resign, this stands for Urban Bantu Council, which they did. Now they are demanding the School Boards, which represent Bantu Education. Can you imagine tear-gas being thrown at about 5,000 people at a funeral? Greetings and Love. I'll write soon.
[Lilian]

PS. Another letter to follow soon, lovey.

126.

[*no address*]
24 August 1977

My Dearest Mrs and Mr Allan,
This is to thank you, for your letter of the 15ᵗʰ August which I received promptly. Lately [your] letters to me takes a month or a little less than a month. It always pleases me very much to read the family was together and that this pleases you in particular. You are a wife to be kept. I admire your sincerity to the children. May courage and peace throne you my love. Your expressions of saying you people are in Heaven makes me wonder if one day I shall speak the same language. God Bless you my love. Yes, chickens, cheese, mutton etc are lately the order in my fridge after years of severe starvation. You and my other friends have kept the fire burning, and [are] all the time asking me this question:- Is there any thing else we could help? I always felt embarrassed, because my needs were rather too much to mention. Until one day, just after spring cleaning this Match box house of mine – as I have already told you that it is cement on the roof, cement on the walls, cement on the floor. Now the house is a fridge in Winter and an oven in summer. This is my story, that very day a tall gentleman knocked at my door. Unlike the special-branch men, he smiled and I in turn smiled. He said 'I would like to see Mrs Ngoyi'. I said, 'Come in my Dear', and I said, 'You are talking to Ngoyi now'. He then introduced himself and said he was sent to ask me my needs. I was ashamed to say. He took a notebook and went to the kitchen. Yes, you need a stove, bedroom a bed, and asked me what kind. Shyly, I explained. I think blankets as well. I said yes but the most burning issue is my boy's school uniform. Then I got a wonderful stove it is only four days old and my Dear, the Warmth! I have forgotten about the surroundings of cement. [I] am a changed woman. I now can in my budget include milk, fruits, and vegetables. Then I got a note. The rest of my needs will be attended to by Barbara, so she has written to them to give her an address of where she must send them. Is this not marvellous? I'm happy it happened this way. Not forgetting that you kept the fire burning in all fields, books etc. A friend in England had asked me to ask my friends in America to try and get me Miss Jane Pitman's Biography.[74] This I did, it was sent early July but it is not received yet. I'm so worried about all this.

---

74 The *Autobiography of Miss Jane Pittman* is a novel by the African-American author Ernest J Gaines published in 1971.

The latest in our country is, the position is ugly. It is simmering, let me put it this way, it is like a Volcano which can erupt any minute. As it is now I'm just a pack of nerves, I was in bed for two solid weeks. My Blood Pressure is very high. This is what happened, one morning I was picking up papers in my garden, when I suddenly heard screams. When I lifted my head up I saw Women at the corner. As a banned somebody I stood aloof when I looked towards the school opposite, our Mzimhlope this is the name of my area. 4 Police trucks and each truck had two Police dogs, chasing children from the lower Primary and biting them. I screamed to the top of my voice, helpless, and suddenly I lost conscious[ness]. I was carried to my bedroom and a Doctor summoned. After examining me he said you better try and be Calm. I got more angry. I said how on earth can I be calm when my children are bitten by Dogs? Oh! Belinda my Dear, we are in an age between ages. Hell is loose here. I would not like [to] see the brutality of Hitler happening in any Country. You must Pray for Southern Africa. Pupils are shot dead almost every day, dogs set on them in school rooms, right up to the grave yard. School are empty, students are determined to oppose Bantu Education even if it cost their lives. Jails are full of our students, detentions without trail. Some die in detention. Oh! Donald my Dear can you imagine war fought by students and their parents standing and watching? Students with stones against guns, tear gas, and dogs. This is so simply [solved], our Government to meet the students and scrap Bantu Education. This will go on, and the scars on our children will create ever lasting hatred between white and black. An unfortunate position, when our children will hate each other because of Colour. When there is a variety of colours, it is beautiful and, in other words, apartheid seems to challenge God for having created a black man. Any how do not worry much about my health, I have really improved. Also I wish to thank you a million as always for the gift. You have always been a mother to this family. How is my Diana? I said so much.
Love, Lilian.

127.
This report by Beyers Naudé is on headed notepaper. He was the first national director of the ecumenical Christian Institute, which was founded in 1963 and declared an unlawful organisation in 1977. Beyers Naudé was personally banned in October 1977.

DIE CHRISTELIKE INSTITUUT VAN SUIDER-AFRIKA
THE CHRISTIAN INSTITUTE OF SOUTHERN AFRICA

DIAKONIA HOUSE,
P O BOX 31134,
BRAAMFONTEIN,
TRANSVAAL
2017.

80 JORISSON STREET.
BRAAMFONTEIN.
JOHANNESBURG.
2001

TEL.: 724-0346

May 12, 1977.

Mrs. Hedi Meinhold-Vielhaber,
23 Kiel-Schulensee,
Dorfstede 15,
West Germany.

Dear Mrs. Meinhold-Vielhaber,
Re: Mrs. Lilian Ngoyi
Following my letter of April 14 I wish to state that I have had the opportunity of personally meeting Mrs. Ngoyi and discussing at length with her her personal domestic and financial position as well as the possibility of her banning order being lifted.

Regarding her domestic and financial position I wish to report as follows:

1. Mrs. Ngoyi is in urgent need of a pair of glasses (spectacles) for her eyes which have been giving her very serious trouble for some time. I have arranged with her to have her eyes tested and to obtain a pair of glasses, the price of which will be R53, 35. Through a contribution made by two or three sympathetic persons in Johannesburg this amount has been obtained and Mrs. Ngoyi would hopefully receive her spectacles within the next two or three days.

2. I have furthermore ascertained that the existing furniture in Mrs. Ngoyi's house is not only scant but also out-worn and partly broken with an urgent need for a new bed (divan) with headboard and mattress, plus a wardrobe for her clothes. In addition to this the coal stove which she is presently using is in a hopeless condition and with the coming winter it is most urgent that a proper stove should be installed in her home. We have obtained a quote for the above materials from a firm in Johannesburg which we regard to be very reasonable for a sum of R741, 75. I shall suggest to Mrs. Ngoyi that we buy the bed, headboard and mattress as well as the robe from a good second-hand dealer at a total cost of not more than R200 but I wish strongly to recommend that we accept the quotation of R373, 95 for the installation of the stove.

3. <u>Monthly expenditure</u>: You are undoubtedly aware that Mrs. Ngoyi has to pay R12, 13 per month as rent for her house plus an additional approximately R4, 00 per month for electricity. In addition to that she has had to erect a fence around her house (for reasons of personal safety) at a cost of R200 of which she has already paid four monthly instalments of R10 p.m. I think therefore, with R160 still outstanding. Mrs. Ngoyi calculates that her monthly expenditure on food, clothing, medicines, etc. would amount to ± R100 p. m. of which <u>R50 p.m.</u> is being contributed by <u>your group</u> – for which contribution she is deeply grateful.

4. <u>Education of grandson</u>: As you know Mrs. Ngoyi has undertaken the responsibility of the care and education of her

grandson, Neo (aged 16) of whom the mother is an alcoholic. With the student unrest in Soweto last year he was unable to write his exams and he only went back to school last Monday. He had to enter a new school where the school uniform (which is obligatory) amount to R56, 00 plus school fees for R10, 00 which she has to pay before the end of the month.

5. <u>Illness of brother</u>: Mrs. Ngoyi has an aged brother, George, 68 years old, who tried to obtain a livelihood during the Second World War by being employed as a manual labourer for the army. His jaw was fractured so seriously that his face was never properly restored with the result that this has affected him psychologically very deeply. He has no war pension and at the present moment he is seriously ill in the Pietersburg district of Northern Transvaal. He is regarded as a mental case with hospitalisation urgently required, but without Mrs. Ngoyi having any means to support him and with nobody else being able to give any support in view of the fact that he is unmarried and that she is the only relative who could possibly give any financial support.

I am enclosing for your information, a photostat copy of the invoice for the glasses (Bifocals) as well as the quotation for the furniture and the stove. I shall be grateful if you could please let me know as soon as possible whether the group supporting Mrs. Ngoyi or any other group is able to make a contribution to the above costs, with the exclusion of her glasses, for which we have raised the necessary funds in Johannesburg.

Regarding the possibility of the lifting of the banning order I wish to state that this is being discussed in order to see whether anything could be done in this regard. We hope to convey to you any suggestion which may be forthcoming in the future about possible steps which could be taken in this direction, although we are not very hopeful that anything positive or concrete could come out of such an effort at the present moment.

Yours sincerely,

[*written signature*: Beyers Naudé]
<u>C. F. B. Naudé</u>

P. S. May I remind you that, in view of the fact that the Christian Institute has been declared an affected organisation in May 1975, our organisation is not allowed to receive any funds from overseas into the Christian Institute account. A financial contribution to Mrs. Ngoyi would therefore have to be made to her personally or to another individual or organisation which is entitled to receive such financial support on her behalf.

[*Statement of expenses submitted by Beyers Naude*]
5/ 5/ 77
Mrs Lilian Ngoyi
VR
Refraction Bifocals
I Christel Pinky Mauve
52. 20

	53 - 35
Deposit	<u>20 - 00</u>
	33 - 35

Readers on Loan

12/ 5/ 77

3'6" ROSA HEA BOARD.	99-95
3'6" D. Q MATTRESS.	75- 95
3'6" DIVAN	29. 95
LAURA ROSE	161- 95
950 H/ MASTER STOVE.	<u>373- 95</u>
	<u>741- 75</u>

128.

[*no address*]
30 September 1977

My Dearest Diana, Belinda and Donald,
This is to acknowledge receipt of your long expected letter. As always the words sprang from paper to my ears. Very funny I did not realise it was a pumpkin but thought it was just a letter box until you said it was a pumpkin. Beautiful picture of Diana. Belinda your efforts to help me have so expanded to the extent that it draws tears of joy to my eyes. I have a wonderful stove, and a bed with inner spring mattress. My boy and I just pick up our basket to a super market. Our skins of our faces too have changed to beautiful. May God bless you. I also thank you for the gift therein. A friend has sent me Mrs Jane Rettermans Biography.[75] Oh! Yes this black skin has always been subjected to misery. My health has very much changed because I'm abiding with the prescribed food and medicines by my Doctor, a white man, and he is very pleased to see me complying with his orders. I was already ready for my coffin. I'm happy you are able to read about our country Oh!! 'Lord where are you? why forsake us in the hands of this evil regime.' Something interesting. Teachers were all the time doing down the struggle, [now] to our surprise, they have sacrificed their livelihood [rather] than to be part and parcel of this evil Bantu Education. But the detentions without trials, the shootings of the students, setting Police dogs on Human beings. Then this reminds me of the gas chambers. Never, never should this happen, but the Capitalist will go any length to keep their Identity. In passing my Daughter is just the same. Re the Christmas book I'll think of one very soon and shall let you know. My boy no schools these days, all at a complete Boycott. We have never experienced such before. Diana must be full of life, a child must be show[ing] health by its movements. My match box garden is in bloom, it is the centre of admiration. One woman just said, 'one must just turn and look'. I am happy about such remarks. We also just had good rain for the 2nd time. I'm also replying [to] Barbara's letter. She says she just came back from Germany. How I envy her. I will now try and accumulate so as to be able to get to Durban by the seaside. It will not be soon as I have too many things to mend, also the situation does not call one to part [from] her or his place of residence. I wish to thank you very much for your kind

---

75 See letter 126. Lilian Nyogi may be mis-remembering the name Jane Pittman.

wishes. The atmosphere is stinking, it's simmering for the worse. We never just know what is next.
Greetings and love.
Lilian

129.

Soweto
7 November 1977.

My Dearest Mr and Mrs Allan,
May I thank you once more for the always expected letter. Also for the gift enclosed therein. It also makes me feel happy, because my financial position is much better, whilst you really kept the ball rolling. I must say, with banning orders, especially if one is unemployed, it is only Hell. But wonders always occur. I always want [to] know very much about Diana's progress, and my album is full of her. Yes my Dear you are justified to worry. We are now in a frying pan, from here we do not know where we shall land. It is heart breaking to see one self being unable to rescue yourself. No schools and now no examinations, though pupils are roaming around and will be mischievous. It's a position we cannot avoid. We are stretching our arms for help and it may take us time but there will be help some-how. I notice U.S.A. is firm this time, as we here use[d] to despise it because of its investments. Yes Dear spiritual agony, at least I can warm my house, and have my ribs to rest on some inner-spring mattress. I thought I would have some-one to take my flowers, a snap. But people take it for granted that Oh! she will not be able to pay. Ah! they are making a great mistake. So our Diana will be a musician, that is really great. It is sounding funny you talk about winter, when we are sweating, heat being so much. Re the question of a book, I think I'm able to save you the trouble, as Mrs White seems to have her fingers on the books. She is in U.S.A. and if next time she fails me, then I'll turn to you for help. You have shouldered me Darling. Now we are sharing the burden. How is Donald? You will be happy my health is improving a great deal. Greetings and love
Lilian.

130.

>9870B Nkungu St
>Orlando West 2
>P.O. Phirima
>9 December 1977

My Dearest Mr and Mrs D Allan and Diana,
This is to acknowledge your beautiful letter as always. The news springing from your letter to my ears, [is] as [if] we are sitting round a beautiful table without discrimination of any description. I thank you a million. I was only not too happy when I read about Donald being strained. I just hope it will not affect his heath, as a strain usually racks one's health. I mean nerves. He must just be calm. I'm writing being very much upset by the condition in my country. The look of things seems there will be no peaceful settlement, also racial hatred is getting worse. Yes I say worse. We have been following Steve Biko's inquest, it is stinking.[76] For our Leader, I say a South African young leader, who had the most following of the peace loving people of this country black and white to be treated in the manner he died whilst in the Hands of the supposed Christian Government of South Africa. Darling, the horrors within have been exposed. Those who love and enjoy the gold, the riches of this Country. Picture a man being stripped naked, chains on his hands and feet; had already foam in his mouth. Could not move his limbs, being incontinent. Still placed in a Land Rover on a mat, no facilities of Urine, thus he was wet and smelling, no face cloth no wash. I feel like scratching my hair off my head. Beloved Son of Africa. The verdict was by a magistrate, 'I find no body responsible for his death'. Oh Belinda my Dear if this is the way white Doctors plus white Policemen, and white Prosecutors plus their magistrate behave, then we can close our chapter. I never felt someone's death from my veins as I

---

76 Steven Bantu Biko was the founder of the Black People's Convention which brought together many Black Consciousness groupings. His ideas are published in *I Write What I Like* (1979). The inquest was held two months after his death in police custody on 12 September 1977. In a judgment that provoked a national and international outcry, the chief magistrate of Pretoria, Mr Martin Prins, found that '... the available evidence does not prove the death was brought about by an act or omission involving any offence by any person'. Some 20 years later, the Truth and Reconciliation Commission concluded, after its hearing in 1997, that Biko's death was 'a gross human rights violation ... The magistrate's finding contributed to a culture of impunity in the SAP [South African Police]. Despite the inquest finding no person responsible for his death, the Commission finds that, in view of the fact that Biko died in the custody of law enforcement officials, the probabilities are that he died as a result of injuries sustained during his detention'. The doctors who failed to care adequately for Biko in prison were ultimately found guilty of 'improper or disgraceful' professional conduct by the South African Medical Council.

did with Biko's. Naked death, could you imagine being interrogated facing other men being naked? I mean I would never support such torture, even [of] the same Policemen I would never allow it. This are Human. God breathed the breath of life, and they became alive with the image of God. You will excuse me for this letter but once I start, I cry my tears dry, which helps nothing. We are banned so we have no platform to show our people what is coming, and only peace, love and Friendship can over come all these. Cost of living [rises], people are jobless and have nothing to enjoy. The other day I was in a shop in the City of Joburg. A white man with his two children spending over R50 for toys. Mean while the average black worker hardly gets that amount [per month] to feed his little dear ones. I'm sorry I did not mean to depress you. But me, through you am able to stock my fridge. But when I look back where I come from I feel like screaming. My boy is alright in a way, no schools, pupils are roaming around and much mischief. Detentions without trials are the order of the day. The situation is like a volcano, which may erupt any moment. 'God save Africa.' Ah! let me see, my garden is beautiful, my Blood pressure is under control, I have a most wonderful white Doctor. Had he not come to my rescue I would be paralysed, as my fingers had already being Dead. Have a Wonderful Christmas and a Happy New Year

Greetings to the family
Lilian

131.

[*No address*]
20 December 1977

My Dearest Donald, Belinda and Diana,
I acknowledge with thanks the beautiful gift, wonderful colour. You just don't know how they envy me. It is just a pity I received a letter from the women in West Germany who wanted to give me and my boy a Holiday, but the letter which they wrote on the 2nd Dec, I only received it on the 19th Dec, so they too might get my letter after 19 days. A wonderful feeling I have to know we are not alone. Our Whites have voted him back again.[77] Just for white supremacy. What the out come of discrimination would be to the future of our children do[es] not count, as long there be a kaffir in the kitchen to do their dirty work. Could you imagine that? Here have been bombs here and there. Just God's luck no one was killed. Why? the devil alone knows. There is no sign of schools, and the young ones are roaming in the streets. We are asked not to be joyful, but to wear black as a sign of sympathy with the dead, detained, banned, imprisoned. I must say there is a little change amongst some whites, if one gets behind the counter. If an African shopper approaches the white woman or man before serving. Firstly says 'Good morning, Can I help you?' This never happened before. My health is very much better, also my standard of living financially is much better. I owe it all to you my Dear. Thanks a million. I hope me too, with my Grand son will be able to send you a gift. My hands are full, I shall write soon. My Warmest love to Donald and Diana not forgetting your Dear Self.
Best wishes
Lilian

---

77 PW Botha succeeded BJ Vorster as the prime minister in 1978, see letter 136.

132.

9870B Nkungu St
Orlando West 2
P.O. Phirima
S.A.
21 March 1978

My Dearest Belinda,

I'm replying to your letter of the 13 March 78. According to it you had written one before, which I never received. May be it is still coming. Can you imagine my excite-ment? I was only surprised you mentioned nothing about our Diana. How is she? The parcel was very much welcomed, thanks a million, My Dear. I was very happy to learn about Donald, and yes indeed he has seen for himself West Africa. This world is full of confusion, we all belong to human family, but our conditions of living are poles apart. Some luxurious, and the others very sad. I just read a book entitled *My Life* by Golda Meir. In it, I'm strengthened to note that, we blacks are not the only ones to under-go such miseries. This woman tirelessly worked for the Jews, her fortunate part of her courageous struggle is her education. Schools are still not normal, the atmosphere still stinks. I some times stretch out my hands trying to feel God, but never do I feel him. Your efforts to see me live a normal financial life has touched my feelings, as Barbara unlike Peter is regular. And the other women bought me a stove and one has promised me a car. My only problem is getting a license which means hard study, practically and orally to know what the road signs mean. Then a garage which only will need R400 for erecting it including the Building Materials. Is this not wonderful? Can you imagine me without any income but owning a Car? Women are Wonderful. They made it possible for me to fly abroad from no where. I mean who am I to deserve such grace? Detentions are still the order of the day, especially the youth. Mine was also picked up for interrogation, [but] for only 2 hours. Yes Belinda, I have the strength and courage because I'm not alone, those who admire freedom are with us. I shall write again. We had so much flood, which swept away our gardens even people, farmers are more hard hit, and caused the loss of people.

My love to the family.

Lilian.

133.

> 9870B Nkungu St
> Orlando West 2
> P.O. Phirima
> 28 July 1978

My Dearest, Belinda, Diana and Donald,
I was looking through my diary, trying to confirm if I did reply your letter of the 4th July, the answer was Nil. You will pardon me my love, my hands have been very full and my mind also un-settled. I wonder if I did write and explain the gift given me by a friend this end. A car. Now it is not yet with me, because I did not have a driving licence. Now you will rejoice with me, after failing three times on the fourth time I got through. You can imagine an occasion which need you and your family to celebrate. I wonder if you do get our post from this end, some friends are complaining bitterly about my silence, mean-while I reply each and every note, as soon as it arrives. I have nothing much to tell you about us this end, except the fact that most of the detainees, specially in our province are being released, but the unfortunate ones being re- detained. Can you feel the agony felt, when you sigh, saying, 'I'm meeting my family' [and then being sent] back to the cells. Schools are not really in good swing but at least June the [16th] was a mourning day, and this went without riots, though here and there, clashes with Police was reported with a few students. As we pray, and ask for peaceful changes. There is a sentence in the Bible which reads:- knock it shall be opened, ask you shall be given. It goes further to say, if a child asks for bread, the father will not give the child a stone. In our prayers God will listen to us knowing very well that most Revolutions in other countries were bloody. If only the ruling powers could come down [from] the High horse they are climbing [and] get round the table, it would without doubt save any ugly situation. Now it's black against white, and white against black. Very silly, these two parties are human difference of colour only. Another factor is Capitalism. Most of us blacks live below the bread line, as it is it was reported that unemployment is 1.3 million, cost of living very high, now the Sales Tax is worse than all. A Rand is not a Rand but far more less. My boy is well thanks, at school doing Form 2, though it did take him time to decide going to school. One time I was just pulling his leg by saying I was going to send him to a boarding school. He reacted by saying if I send him then must I also send all the students in Soweto.

I had to keep quiet. I knew I would not afford a boarding school. He is now 18. His interests are engineering, foot ball, and gardening. I did love the post-card, though I really preferred one of Diana's photographs. Yes Dear I did love Diana's drawings. May she grow in a better world with less wars. I hope Donald and the rest of you are well, pass my greetings to your mother if you do write.
With tons of Love
Lilian

134.

[no address]
25 October 1978

My Dearest Belinda,
Thanks a million for your letter written on the 4th Oct, and I received it today. Because you wrote you were going on holiday I decided to reply immediately so as to catch up with you. Oh yes Belinda, instead of us seeing progress towards peace in the world, things seems to be getting bad every day, it is just like a riddle. Here we are no better off, instead of Bantu Education being scrapped, we only notice the change of names being changed, and we are not interested. You see Dear in every Nation there is bad and good, but the South African Whites have so entrenched them selves to be the Bosses, the Superiors, the Slave drivers in the name of Christ. If you were to come here one day and for an hour be a black man, you would never, never try it again. How we really survive is a problem. Years after years we cannot afford a single Holiday. No security of any description. Yes, I'm in wander land with my Datsun it makes all the world difference. Living in a three roomed Match box house, my neighbours around me have to sacrifice a great deal to extend their houses, make them spacious and lovable. Here amongst others this woman who lives by thanks. At least with the Datsun I enjoy having driven a sick woman to Hospital, or any Human being, then [their] saying, 'Thanks Lily'. I feel great. I also hope one day I'll be able to extend just one more room, so that my boy will also have privacy. You know detentions are at their highest height, we thought there could be change with the New Prime Minister. It is just a mess, also crime has stepped up. Here are also gangsters who knocks at ones door, when opening you are shot cold blooded. If ones car is left outside it is stolen and some valuable parts stripped. Some small children are also stolen, the age of Diana, and found murdered, by the ritual murders. This means it's a primitive thinking of witchdoctors mixing their medicine with human flesh. Oh! Dear I just do not know what is not happening. I must be boring you with all this, but my pen goes on and on. I just finished a novel, *Mother of Earth*, Agnes Smedley.[78] Yo, Belinda I love such books of revolutionary women. Like *My Life* by Golda Meir.[79]

---

78 Smedley (1892–1950) published an autobiographical novel, *Daughter of Earth* (1929), and several books on China which were sympathetic to the revolutionary cause there.
79 Meir (1898–1978) was the fourth prime minister of Israel (1969–1974). Her autobiography was published in 1975.

These are really inspiring, and many others, some which you had sent me. God bless you my friend. I was very much pleased to learn Donald is well and busy.

Dearest Diana,
Your Photos I always treasure much and I have kept them in my old display Cabinet. I enjoyed your scribbling my love. May you grow to be a fighter for peace.
Greetings
Lilian

135.

> 9870B Nkungu St
> Orlando West 2
> P.O. Phirima(1848)
> 30 March 1979

Dearest Mr and Mrs Allan and Diana,

Belinda love you are rather too quiet. I have been thinking of your family and then wonder how is Diana and whether she is still in a Creche, or have started schooling? but no one to answer me. Also there are so many misunderstanding in our Globe I some times wonder where you are. Where is your mother? is every body safe? Well Dear I'm alright, living better than before. Also a local friend gave me Ford Cortina, a four cylinder. It is not new but real fun to see me driving, from a wheel barrow into a Car. If you answer, I'll send you its picture including me, and the boy. I'm sure you are aware of all the funny happenings here, but there is much better in behaviour towards a black man but what is surprising is instead of free compulsory international education, only the name Bantu is changed to Black Education. The unrest is not much except here and there. But I have never seen such turn-up to schools, it is really progress. Not until the Education is changed will I, as others, see the beginning of understanding. I was very ill, you nearly read that I was late. Any how I am much better. So much unemployment, and also very little rain so you can image hunger from all sides. Farmers as well. We listen with much fright the happenings in Rhodesia, South W. Africa. The loss of life also in Iran, people seem to have gone Amok. Also Kampala.[80] What is happening Dear? And those who are in power seem to have entrenched themselves, even if people die it does not matter. I just hope there will [be] no blood shed in South W. Africa. I'm still weak, cannot sit too long. Kiss Diana and her Dad for my part.

Love Lilian

---

80 Idi Amin was the president of Uganda (1971–1979) and at the time was becoming increasingly tyrannical. In 1978 Uganda was at war with Tanzania. When defeated, Amin fled first to Libya and then to Saudi Arabia where he died in 2003.

136.

9870B Nkungu St
Orlando West 2
P.O. Phirima(1848)
1 May 1979

Dearest Belinda,

'May Day greetings'

I hope you are back by now. Am herein acknowledging the most wonderful gift. Very funny, it always arrives when most needed. Thanks a million. There was one only missing news about Diana. We have attentively [been] watching the Rhodesian Elections, with a great hope of change, but there Sithole having a lot to say, but personally am not surprised.[81] There has been so much about the South African scandal.[82] While it was a topic, suddenly the spy plane of America took over the news and scandal dead. Big news about the peaceful and fair elections. Oh my Dear wait and see. One thing which will happen is the will of the masses shall prevail. Just have little patience. I'll send you the pictures. I made a big mistake by paying a young man for them in advance to reproduce [them and] others, as I had sent some to Robben Island. Any how you will get them. I no longer get reading material, I do not know if they are being confiscated. Also some of your letters I never just receive. We live in this suspicious world, some people fear big events but those in power fear movements of rats. The weather this end has not been in favour of plants or even to farmers as such. I'm sure they too will suffer a great deal. I have no longer any space in my garden, as I had to erect a sort of a garage in one of the spaces of my garden. I really cannot say much about changes in our favour yet, as signs like 'Whites Only' still are, and this is not exactly what we are looking for. For instance this is the year of children, look back to our children. No.1, free and compulsory Education, Nil. I personally think this is most important. This will lead to great understanding, not only lip

---

81 Rev Ndabaningi Sithole founded Zimbabwe African National Union (ZANU) in 1963 with Robert Mugabe as its secretary. ZANU was banned by the government of Ian Smith in 1964 and Sithole imprisoned on charges of planning his assassination. In 1975 ZANU split along ethnic lines: one wing under Mugabe (ZANU-PF) and one under Joshua Nkomo (ZAPU). In July 1979 Sithole, having formed his own party, joined the transitional government and attended the talks at Lancaster House which led to the 1980 elections. Sithole's moderate party, however, did not win a seat.

82 In 1973 Prime Minister Voster agreed to the transfer of R64m from the defence budget to the Department of Information under Dr Connie Mulder. The money was to fight a propaganda war. An inquiry followed and Voster, after having lied to parliament about the matter, resigned in disgrace in 1979.

stick propaganda to impress the out side world.
Greetings and love to the family
Lilian

137.

>9870B Nkungu St
>Orlando West,
>P.O. Phirima(1848)
>27 February 1980

My Dearest Belinda,
May I right away thank you for the timely gift, $30. God is most gracious, when I think now I'm stranded he says no, no. It is just that God has been with me, every body trying to help. Even my daughter, though alcoholic, my position of life was so delicate that she had no alternative, had to leave work to come and be with me on my bed side. So last week she bundled me up, took me to some faith healers which I must praise the Lord, though not very cured, there is some change. I had an attack of Asthma every night, but now there is a breathing space. Thus after Hospital my Doctors said little writing, less reading, especially news-papers. Also I had tremour in my hands. I shall write again when I can sit up a little longer. The boy is back to school after the '76 riots. It was just a mixture of feelings, and not yet quite normal. I envy Donald travelling, but me with Cardiac on the other side must be nursed like a baby. I think by now Diana is attending school. Thanks a Million for the gift.
God bless
Yours Sincerely
Lilian

Afterword

The pleasure of reading personal, intimate letters like those that have been published here proves to be complex and intriguing. Their appeal comes both from how the letter-writer presents people, events, feelings – to which our response is largely emotional and psychological – and from their evident relation to their historical context – to which our response is largely intellectual. Letters reveal their charm at first glance but then, as we register their mystery, gradually make us aware of what they might conceal as well as reveal.

As secondary readers, not the person to whom the letters were written, we might feel that we are eavesdropping or intruding on the writer's private world, and some uneasy guilt or embarrassment might form part of our response. On the other hand, once published letters enter the public realm, they take on an historical as well as a personal interest so that they can be read with a certain detachment that includes respect (a deferential standing back) and empathy (an imaginative coming forward to engage, but not identify, with what is being recorded). In a parallel dynamic, we are drawn in two directions at once. When this double valency is present, private letters such as these afford a particularly satisfying glimpse into the personalities of their writers and the sense they tried to make of their lives in context.

When they speak to us from their lives in the past, what Lilian, Dora and Bessie reveal may seem both strange and familiar. Those matters that we recognise can carry us further into the daily details of the past as 'another country' which we have either never known or might be in danger of forgetting. At the same time, glimpses of what is familiar in the lives of the women who write remind us how much and how little is revealed in even the most intimate form of communication. We understand why Dora Taylor says that she would much rather see her family face-to-face than write letters to them. Letters such as these require a particularly sustained imaginative response if the words of Lilian, Bessie and Dora are to allow each of them to gather into what we feel is a knowable presence.

An active but critical empathy is also required because the experience of reading letters is unlike that offered by other personal narrative forms such as an autobiography, novel or a travelogue. It is different even from diaries which also record a person's ordinary, daily life. One of the differences is that a letter, as part of a dialogue, requires us to read over the shoulder of the other participant, the primary reader. As a result, we are constantly aware that a letter may draw on mutual knowledge in which we do not share and that it simultaneously invokes and creates the sensibility of another person. In these letters, such connections are being invoked and created when, for example, Bessie tells Paddy how angry she gets with white instructors at the Farmers' Brigade who automatically assume that they are superior to those they are teaching, and then suddenly realises that she must reassure Paddy that she is not including her in this anger (letter 21). There are other contrasting moments when this sharing or creation of knowledge seems to be not quite complete, as in Lilian's long silence about Neo, the grandson who lives with her (news of him begins only in letter 124). It is a silence which is puzzling in view of her own delight in news of Belinda's child, Diana. What might be a modest reticence in her silence is offset by Lilian's readiness to advise Belinda on how to be a good wife (letters 92 and 94). Already established, mutual knowledge is drawn on and constantly supplemented by Dora when she gives Sheila loving advice about her children, about the plays she might choose for her reading group, about the next country to which they might consider moving. We can infer a good deal directly from what is articulated in these exchanges, but the process of reading also requires us to ponder what may remain unspoken. We are in the presence of two interacting minds, two sets of emotion and attitudes, two histories, none of which we automatically share but which we must take into account. In this book too, the absence of the recipient's replies places special obligations on us to imagine, to speculate, to be tolerant, to allow for seen and unforeseen possibilities; in short, to enjoy a measure of uncertainty.

Uncertainty can be heightened by the fact that to an outsider personal letters to an intimate family member or friend may seem rambling, disorganised or even inchoate in comparison, for example, with an essay or a short story. Private letters do not require the same sustained focus and organised presentation of a topic, in fact they may tend in the opposite direction as myriad thoughts are put down at a speed that does not allow for connections to be articulated. The primary reader would probably have understood each passing reference, followed each connection, anticipated each change of subject matter, but as secondary readers we do not have the prior knowledge to be so immediately adroit. (Dora's way of referring to friends by their initials as she advises Sheila about disposing of the household goods remains, for example, an impenetrable, coded reminder of what we cannot know.)

Although private letters do not demand that we call on the orderly conventions of other forms of writing, the dialogue they set up does, however, follow certain customs (such as salutations, the use of a date and address) so that variations on them, such as Lilian's different modes of greeting Belinda and Donald or of signing her name, function, like repetitions with a difference, as invitations to interpretation. Thus, letters usually enact thinking and remembering aloud more directly than other forms of written discourse. On the other hand, if we are prepared to earn a familiarity with what they convey, then their informal, cumulative charm will envelop us.

If we allow it, insights into the past offered by the letters can stimulate in us related (similar or different) insights into our present but here too the tension between ourselves in the public realm and the writers in the private is strong. We might indeed be inquisitive intruders in a private communication as we read, but we may at the same time be learning something about ourselves and our context through the considered words of the woman whose lines we are reading. The rhetoric of the writers in this book is carefully chosen to impact on their primary readers and as a rule conveys little intention to affect us, or anyone but the original recipient – the primary reader, or the family unit to which Lilian's letters, for example, are often addressed. Each woman writes with a direct focus on one person; there is no posturing and seldom is there an eye on a larger public or on posterity. So the letters' bearing on our world will be one of our making rather than of the writers themselves.

But these intensely private documents may occasionally be inflected by public forces in their rhetoric too. Bessie did expound ideas to Paddy that were integral to the fiction she was writing at the time, so we could say that indirectly she had an eye on the wider future in some of her letters. And Lilian brings echoes of her past political oratory into some of her letters, but even these passages are now intended for Belinda and sometimes her husband, Donald, rather than for public consumption. All three women did of course know that the surveillance arm of the state might be taking an interest in their letters, but this knowledge served to make them more circumspect, and probably curbed any desire that they might have had to play to the public.

Because these letters are so private in their focus, we also have to ask ourselves whether they might reveal a self or aspects of a self that each woman would rather have sheilded from the gaze of strangers. As readers, we might relish having access to the secrets of other lives, but as persons our pleasure might well also carry a certain dread of the same exposure happening to us. Hence our ambivalence and our desire not to be positioned as unwelcome intruders.

In the instances of Bessie Head and Lilian Ngoyi, the answer to the question of unwanted disclosure is relatively straight forward. They were writing to women that they had never met and whom they could get to know only through their letters. Thus they had a clean slate and could actively choose what to say, what to originate; their letters gave them the free space to present, to create, their selfhood in all its complexity as they wished their correspondents to meet it. The only constraint on their communication, and at the same time its strength, was that each could know of the other only what was put down on the page. For Dora Taylor the matter was more complex, and so is our response. She and Sheila had known each other intimately in daily life (although Dora often says that she wishes that she made more effort to know her daughters better) and their long mutual knowledge had to be sustained in their correspondence if their letters were to be effective. In other words, sincerity was required of Dora as she wrote to her daughter. Sincerity in writing is not always easy for an outsider to test or to judge, but in Dora's case her capacity for self-criticism, what we might sometimes feel is an anxious self-consciousness, is likely to persuade us that Dora was as honest and sincere a letter-writer as she could be. The same is true of her expressions of anguish when the loss of her home and its cherished objects afflicts her, especially as her words are followed by her regret at having burdened her daughter with, perhaps, too much emotion.

The question of honesty and sincerity extends not only to the writer's revelations of self, but also to her creation of her reader. Any communication implies the response it desires; in this way a letter shapes the person reading it and consequently the possibility of manipulation is always present – as the epistolary novelists of the eighteenth century in Europe knew so well. Samuel Richardson's *Clarissa*, Choderlos de Laclos' *Les Liaisons Dangereuses* and even Jane Austen's *Pride and Prejudice* are all testimony to their author's interest in letter-writing as an exercise of power. In the twentieth century, in his *Letters to Milena*, Kafka called the act of letter-writing a 'traffic between ghosts' for he too felt the extent to which he and Milena might actively be (mis)shaping themselves and each other in their communication. (His word 'ghosts' recognised that in one sense the created selves remained unreal, with only words for substance.) So we can say that in her letters Dora is reciprocating and to some extent using her daughter's affection, good sense and dutifulness; Bessie is creating, reciprocating and using Paddy's delight in good, humorous stories; Lilian is creating, reciprocating and using Belinda's sympathy for her as a silenced, displaced political figure who is struggling with financial and other difficulties.

Although biographers and historians find personal letters most useful for the information about people that they provide, the complex psychological interactions that happen in letters mean that they cannot be read as a straightforward source of information, let alone as historical fact. Even if, as many statesmen and literary figures have done, personal letters are originally written or later revised for publication, they do not carry an automatic stamp of truth or authenticity but convey a subjective point of view which, like any other, has to be assessed against outside evidence. Put in more positive terms, in letters we find all the individuality, drama, variability and excitement of moment-to-moment encounters which are not predictably experienced or told.

The encounters in these letters were usually recorded in the heat of the moment in all its complexity of feeling. Now, when we read that Dora felt anguish in her loss of home but simultaneously delighted in her grandchildren, that Bessie relished her work in the garden but worried about Howard's future, that Lilian despaired over her daughter but knew joy when the gift of a car enabled her to visit friends and help her neighbours, we feel afresh the emotions that might otherwise have been eroded by time. Their letters bring back all the intense feelings that were mixed into the moment.

While these letters appeal as documents from the past that can open our eyes to the present, and while they elicit a psychologically complex response from us as readers, they have another historical charm. As handwritten letters that were transported by air by state-run postal services, they are now relics of an age that is disappearing. We are reading letters in a moment when this form of communication has all but disappeared so that the pleasure they offer is a rare one. There are references in all of these letters to the vagaries of the postal system – entrusting a letter to a system of international carriage was often an act of faith which produced its own anxieties. Dora kept diary entries in which she tracked her receiving and replying to letters; Bessie could do the same because she kept carbon copies of all of her letters which she filed in date order with the letters she had received from each of her correspondents; Lilian's letters usually begin by noting the letter from Belinda to which she is replying, and she often comments if she has not had an expected, regular letter from another of her Amnesty correspondents.

Afterword

* * *

Intimacy with another person, the relationship into which letters place us, is something that the wise South African critic and novelist, Njabulo S Ndebele, has pointed out is usually what family life teaches us to value and to conduct with respect. In place of a stable home and family where such lessons could be learned, the majority of South Africans have known only dislocation or exile and rootlessness, a condition of not belonging and of lacking anchored memories. In Ndebele's view, the apartheid state's sustained destruction of family life helps to explain why in the last two decades South Africans have shown themselves to be both 'charmingly kind and hospitable at the same time as being capable of the most horrifying brutality and cruelty' to each other (Ndebele 2003: 70). Having been denied the opportunity to learn, as children, to cherish and respect those with whom they live in the intimacy of family life, people now lack the capacity to live in close proximity with others whom they should want to learn to know and respect. We need, Ndebele suggests, to cultivate a fresh understanding of the value of personal, one-to-one relationships and of intimate spaces like the home, for this might equip us to conduct public life in a less harsh and intolerant way.

Ndebele is responding to the rise and frequent eruption of animosities between black people under apartheid and particularly during the years around 1994, and he is perceptive about an underlying psychological reason for the brutality of many incidents. But inter-group animosities (between all of the official population groups) were also deliberately developed over decades of separatist policies which encouraged ignorance and fear, and it was not only black South Africans in whom an understanding of intimacy with the other was inhibited or overtly proscribed. Apartheid was the great example of the worldwide practice of 'othering' (of classifying people in order to separate and denigrate them) that came with colonialism and continued beyond the two world wars. Under apartheid no one was officially allowed, let alone encouraged, to want to imagine the experiences and inner lives of those who had been made the 'other'. All South Africans, white even more than black, were probably crippled in the process.

Against such damaging official policies, the letters of Dora and Lilian are a triumphant indication that even at its height apartheid's prohibition on imaginative intimacy was not always successful. Bessie, having moved to Botswana and having felt herself denigrated as a 'coloured' woman, had to confront barriers to the imagination which did not arise from the same ideology of race, but which were still cruelly exclusionary in their intent. In coping with imaginative exclusions, all three writers showed themselves to be remarkable women. Lilian and Bessie, each designated 'other' by state or community, were exchanging warm and affectionate letters with white women; similarly, Dora's letters constantly indicate her imaginative empathy with and active participation in black lives that were officially off-limits to her.

Finally, a further note of hope in these letters is that all three women had to grapple with dislocation or relocation, and they did so successfully at least once in their lives. When allowed the small freedoms that creating a home requires, even if it has to happen within a larger unfreedom, many migrants do manage to create new lives for themselves. Therefore, reading these letters about creating a home life (both viable and difficult) and about the suffering brought by the loss or denial of a home should be instructive for us as secondary readers. And delighting in the honesty, sincerity, joy and pain with which these women write could bring about some of the re-education that Ndebele envisages. It could serve as a step towards recreating a capacity for empathy among South Africans.

Margaret Daymond
Durban
December 2014

Bibliography

Allan, John. 2006. *Rabble Rouser for Peace: The Authorised Biography of Desmond Tutu.* London, Sydney, Auckland, Johannesburg: Rider Books (Random House).

Baldwin, James. 1963. 'Down at the Cross: Letter from a Region in My Mind.' In James Baldwin. *The Fire Next Time.* London: Michael Joseph.

Belshaw, Sheila. 2009. 'My Mother's Gift to Me.' *Baobab: South African Journal of New Writing* 2; 46–49.

Bernstein, Hilda. 1989. *The World that was Ours: The Story of the Rivonia Trial.* London: S A Writers.

Biko, Steve. 1979. *I Write What I Like.* Oxford: Heinemann.

Birch, Kenneth. 1995. 'The Birch Family: An Introduction to the White Antecedents of the Late Bessie Amelia Head.' *English in Africa* 22(1); 1–18.

Blythe, Ronald. 1972. *Akenfield.* Harmondsworth: Penguin Books.

Brown, Duncan. 2013. *Are Trout South African?* Cape Town: Picador Africa.

Cullinan, Patrick (ed). 2005. *Imaginative Tresspasser: Letters Between Bessie Head, Patrick and Wendy Cullinan, 1963–1977.* Johannesburg: Wits University Press; Asmara, Eritrea: Africa World Press.

Currey, James. 2008. *Africa Writes Back: The African Writers Series & The Launch of African Literature.* Oxford: James Currey; Johannesburg: Wits University Press; Athens: Ohio University Press.

Driver, Dorothy. 2008. 'Afterword.' In Taylor, Dora. *Don't Tread on My Dreams*, 282–291, Johannesburg: Penguin Group.

Eilersen, Gillian Stead. 2007. *Bessie Head: Thunder Behind Her Ears*. Johannesburg: Wits University Press. (Cape Town: David Phillip; London: James Currey, 1995).

Eilersen, Gillian Stead. 1990. 'Serowe, Bessie Head's "Bits of Ancient Africa".' *Lekgapho: The Khama III Memorial Museum Review 1988–89* 1: 61–66.

Gardner, Susan, Michelle Adler, Tobeka Mda and Patricia Sandler. 1989. 'Interview with Bessie Head'. In Mackenzie, Craig and Cherry Clayton (eds). *Between the Lines: Interviews with Bessie Head, Sheila Roberts, Ellen Kuzwayo and Miriam Tlali*. Grahamstown: National English Literary Museum.

Greene, Felix. 1962. *The Wall has Two Sides: Portrait of China Today*. London: Jonathan Cape.

Guardian, 2005. 'Paddy Kitchen: Novelist at the Heart of a Bohemian World of Art and Letters'. Monday, 12 December.

Head, Bessie. 1963. 'Letter from South Africa: For a Friend, "D B".' *Transition* 3(11): 40.

Head, Bessie. 1968. *When Rain Clouds Gather*. New York: Simon & Schuster, (London: Gollancz, 1969).

Head, Bessie. 1971. *Maru*. London: Gollancz; New York: McCall.

Head, Bessie. 1973. *A Question of Power*. London: Davis-Poynter; New York: Pantheon. (London: Heinemann, 1974).

Head, Bessie. 1975. 'Dear Tim, Will You Please Come to My Birthday Party …' In Barber, Dulan (ed). *One Parent Familes*. London: Davis-Poynter.

Head, Bessie. 1977. *The Collector of Treasures and Other Botswana Village Tales*. London: Heinemann; Cape Town: David Phillip.

Head, Bessie. 1981. *Serowe: Village of the Rain Wind*. Cape Town: David Phillip; London: Heinemann.

Head, Bessie. 1984a. *A Bewitched Crossroad: An African Saga*. Johannesburg: Donker.

Head, Bessie. 1984b. 'A Search for Historical Continuity and Roots'. In Daymond, M J, J U Jacobs and Margaret Lenta (eds). *Momentum: On Recent South Africa Writing*. Pietermartizburg: University of Natal Press.

Head, Bessie. 1993. *The Cardinals, with Meditations and Short*

Stories. M J Daymond (ed). Cape Town: David Philip, London: Heinemann.

Joseph, Helen. 1963. *If This Be Treason*. London: Andre Deutsch.

Joseph, Helen. 1986. *Side by Side: The Autobiography of Helen Joseph*. Johannesburg: Ad Donker.

Kitchen, Paddy. 1970. 'Interview [with Bessie Head] by Post.' *Times Educational Supplement*, 11 September, 36.

Kitchen, Paddy. 1985. *Barnwell*. London: Hamish Hamilton.

Lewis, Desiree. 2007. *Living on a Horizon: Bessie Head and the Politics of Imagining*. Trenton, NJ; Asmara, Eritrea: Africa World Press.

Mphahlele, Eskia. 1989. 'Guts and Granite: Lilian Ngoyi.' In Michael Chapman (ed). *The Drum Decade*. Pietermaritzburg: University of Natal Press.

Ndebele, Njabulo S. 2003. *The Cry of Winnie Mandela*. Cape Town: David Phillip.

Ngcobo, Lauretta (ed). 2012. *Prodigal Daughters*. Pietermaritzburg: University of KwaZulu-Natal Press.

Rassool, Ciraj. 2004. 'The Individual, Auto/biography and History in South Africa.' Unpublished PhD dissertation, University of the Western Cape.

Readers Digest. 1992. *Reader's Digest Illustrated History of South Africa*. Reader's Digest Association Ltd: Cape Town, London, New York, Sydney, Montreal.

Rose, Jacqueline. 1994. 'On the "Universality" of Madness: Bessie Head's *A Question of Power*.' *Critical Inquiry* 20(3): 401–418.

Rosenthal, Jane. 1995. *Dora Tamana*. Cape Town: Maskew Miller Longman.

Rytter, Maria. 2008. 'Origins of the Bessie Head Archive.' In Lederer, Mary S, Seatholo M Tumedi, Leloba S Molema and M J Daymond (eds). *The Life and Work of Bessie Head: A Celebration of the Seventieth Anniversary of her Birth*. Botswana: Pentagon Publishers.

Sandwith, Corinne. 2002a. 'Dora Taylor: South African Marxist.' *English in Africa* 29(2): 5–27.

Sandwith, Corinne. 2002b. 'Dora Taylor: A Bibliography.' *English in Africa* 29(2): 81–84.

Sandwith, Corinne. 2014. *World of Letters: Reading Communities and Cultural Debates in Early Apartheid South Africa*. Pietermaritzburg: University of KwaZulu-Natal Press.

Slovo, Gillian. 1997. *Every Secret Thing: My Family, My Country*. London: Little, Brown & Co.

Stanley, Liz. 2002. 'The Epistolarium: On Theorising Letters and Correspondences.' *Auto/Biography* 19(1/2): 201–35.

Stewart, Jean. 1996. *Lilian Ngoyi*. Cape Town: Maskew Miller Longman.

Tabata, I B. 1950. *The All Africa Convention: The Awakening of a People*. Johannesburg: Peoples Press.

Taylor, Dora (as Nosipho Majeke). 1952. *The Role of the Missonaries in Conquest*. Johannesburg: Society of Young Africa. (Republished in 1986 by APDUSA).

Taylor, Dora. 2008a. *Don't Tread on My Dreams*. Johannesburg: Penguin Group.

Taylor, Dora. 2008b. *Kathie*. Johannesburg: Penguin Group.

Taylor, Dora. 2009. *Rage of Life*. Johannesburg: Penguin Group.

Vigne, Randolph (ed). 1991. *A Gesture of Belonging: Letters from Bessie Head 1965–1979*. London: SA Writers; Portsmouth: Heinemann Educational Books.

Index of names

A
Abrahams, Kenny 33
Abrahams, Peter 6
Achebe, Chinua 96, 163, 194
Alexander, Neville 33, 34, 73, 74, 75
Allan, Belinda (née Keown) xii, xv, 248–345
Allan, Diana 254, 259
Allan, Donald 259

B
Baez, Joan 112
Banda, Hastings 163
Barber, Dulan 83, 90, 96
Belafonte, Harry 163
Belshaw, Andrew 13
Belshaw, Colin (Jr) 13
Belshaw, Colin (Sr) 12
Belshaw, Peter 13
Belshaw, Sheila (née Taylor) xii, xv, 1–77
Biko, Steve 256, 334, 335
Blaxall, Arthur William 281
Blythe, Ronald 90
Bolfo, Joy 309, 311
Bowling, Dan 90, 95
Bowling, Frank 90
Bruns, J E 303
Brutus, Dennis 86
Bry, Adelaide 303
Bryce, Jane 214, 216, 220, 221, 222
Burns, Robert 209
Busia, Dr Kofi Abrefa 164

C
Cadmore, Margaret 84
Campbell, Roy 6

Carter, Gwendolen 25, 29, 69, 74, 76
Chou-En-Lai (Zhou Enlai) 195
Churchill, Sarah 298
Clutten, John 12
Clutten, Muriel (née Taylor) 8, 16
Cole, Nat King 113
Craig, Mary-Anne 2, 3, 54
Crompton, Richmal 131, 156
Cullinan, Patrick 86
Cullinan, Wendy 86
Currey, James 188, 206, 235

D
Darwin, Charles 153, 176
Darwin, Robin 90
Dostoyevsky, Fyodor 95, 108, 109, 198
Driver, Dorothy 7
Duffy, Maureen 209

E
Eilersen, Gillian Stead 83
Ellington, Duke 133
Ellsworth, Whitney 258

F
Finley, Terence 114
Fischer, Anne 40
Fischer, Bram 297
Fleming, Ian 178
Forchhammer, Ruth 83
ffrench-Beytach, Gonville 281

G
Ghosh, Mrs 130
Gibberd, Vernon 87
Godwin, Mary 209

Gollancz, Victor 241, 242
Gool, Jane 16, 33, 41, 47, 55, 65, 69, 71
Gordimer, Nadine 24
Gorky, Maxim 7, 46, 189
Gordon, Giles 93, 125, 134, 136, 142, 186, 206
Gottlieb, Bob 181
Greene, Felix 19
Grigson, Jane 237
Gummidge, Worzel 137

H
Hall, Chinisa 159–161
Hall, Nouannah 157, 158, 159–161
Hall, Peter 159
Hall, Tony 157, 158
Han Suyin (Rosalie Matilda Kuanghu Chou) 195
Hansberry, Lorraine 119
Harrell-Bond, Barbara 260
Hawes, Christine 95, 140, 191
Hawes, Peter 95, 140, 191
Head, Aaron 100
Head, Bessie vii–viii, xi–xxi, 81–244, 248, 257, 347–354
Head, Harold xxi, 85, 218
Head, Howard xiv, 84, 86, 88, 89, 94–100
Heathcote, Nellie 83, 85
Highland, Jean 88
Hitchcock. Alfred 238
Holliday, Billy 177
Honono, N 33, 65
Huddleston, Trevor 281
Huxley, Aldous 296

J

Jack, James 2
Jacques, Eileen 191, 193
Jacques, Richard 191, 193
Jagan, Cheddy 107
Joseph, Helen 247, 251, 252, 261, 274, 277, 295, 318

K

Kennedy, J F 61, 114
King, Martin Luther 112
Kitchen, Paddy vii, viii, xiii, xv, xviii, 81–244
Kromberg, Marit 98

L

Lawrence, D H 95, 101, 103, 108–110, 112, 209
Lenin, (Vladimir Ilyich Ulyanov) 3, 4, 59, 65, 281
Lessing, Doris 192
Letele, Alfred 252
Lewis, Desiree 91
Luthuli, Albert 256, 289

M

Mailer, Norman, 190
Majeke, Nosipho (pseudonym for Dora Taylor) 5
Makeba, Miriam 95, 112, 157, 163, 166
Malan, D F 250, 273
Mandela, Nelson 256, 291, 292
Mao Tse-Tung 195
Marx, Karl 165, 176
McBridge, Angela Barron 303
Meinhold-Vielhaber, Hedi 326
Meir, Golda 337, 340
Mitchison, Naomi 88, 127, 129, 137, 147, 151
Moore, Margaret 134, 137
Moore, Stan 134
Moosa, Rahima 247, 252
Morris, Ivan 258, 314

Morris, Nabuko 258, 265
Muskett, Doreen (née Taylor) 12, 21, 22
Muskett, Michael 12, 21, 22

N

Naudé, Beyers 249, 253, 326–329
Ndebele, Njabulo S 353–354
Ngoyi, Lilian vii–viii, xi–xxi, 86, 247–345, 347–354
Nilson, Bee 237
Nixon, Richard 164

O

Odetta 95, 112, 167

P

Pasternak, Boris 47, 95, 108, 109, 168
Pauli, Hertha 318
Peterson, Oscar 95, 113
Pitman, Jane 324, 331
Porter, Cole 133

R

Rand, Ayn 114
Rassool, Ciraj 4, 13
Reeves, William 281
Rodgers, Joan 211
Roux, Peter 319
Rubinstein, Hilary 97, 178, 180, 187
Rutterford, Ron 233
Rytter, Maria 82

S

Sachs, Solly 250, 274
Salter, Bill 113, 163, 166
Schreiner, Olive 6
Serote, Mongane 235
Shelley, Percy Bysshe 209
Sianana, Bosele (Kenosi) 94
Silone, Ignazio 5, 28, 29, 58
Smedley, Agnes 340
Smith, Ian 299

Smuts, Jan 275
Snow, Edgar 195
Sobukwe, Robert 85
Solzhenisktyn, Aleksandr 296
Stanwood, Susan 189
Stern, Irma, 46, 51
Strydom, J G 252, 260
Suzman, Helen 283

T

Tabata, Isaac Bangani xii, 3, 4, 5, 10, 18, 33, 38, 64, 65, 69, 71, 74, 75, 76
Tamana, Dora 251, 275, 276, 277, 280
Tambo, Oliver 238
Taylor, Dora vii–viii, xi–xxi, 1–77, 86, 91, 248, 257, 347–354
Taylor, James Garden (Jim / JG) 3, 4, 6, 10, 11, 14, 16, 21
Thatcher, Margaret 227
Thomas, George 219
Thompson, Paul 281
Tolstoy, Leo 296
Trobish, Ingrid 303
Trostsky, Leon 264
Twain, Mark 246, 296

V

Van Rensburg, Patrick 87, 88, 102, 124, 130, 141, 153
Verwoed, H F 22, 32
Vigne, Gillian 118
Vigne, Randolph 82, 85, 114, 118, 188
Vorster, B J 165, 297

W

Welensky, Roy 21, 22
Williams de Bruyn, Sophia 247, 252
Wilson, Nancy 95, 167, 177
Wright, Frank Lloyd 114